Vegetable Gardening

Anstace Esmonde-White

McGraw-Hill Ryerson Limited

Toronto   Montreal   New York   St. Louis   San Francisco
Auckland   Bogotá   Guatemala   Hamburg   Johannesburg
Lisbon   London   Madrid   Mexico   New Delhi   Panama
Paris   San Juan   São Paulo   Singapore   Sydney   Tokyo

Vegetable Gardening in Canada

1 2 3 4 5 6 7 8 9 10 D 0 9 8 7 6 5 4 3 2 1

Printed and bound in Canada

Canadian Cataloguing in Publication Data

Esmonde-White, Anstace.
  Vegetable gardening in Canada

Includes index.
ISBN 0-07-548059-X

1. Vegetable gardening — Canada.
2. Fruit-culture — Canada.   I. Title.

SUB320.8.C2E85   635′.0971   C81-094156-2

Contents

Acknowledgements

Gardening encompasses so many different sciences that it would be virtually impossible for any single person to be a master of them all. With each passing year old theories are discarded and new ones take their place, so to put this book together I have asked the advice of many people. However, the final decisions regarding the text rested with me.

There are a great many people who have unknowingly contributed to the book. My first words of gratitude are to those TV viewers who suggested I put my gardening experiences into print; others who gave me ideas and tips; and friends whose gardens I visited.

"You can't teach an old dog new tricks." I learned this quickly when attempting to type my own manuscript. Therefore, my next expressions of appreciation are to my neighbour Father Royden Thoms who volunteered to type the first submission that I sent to my editor. Without Father T. I might never have proceeded.

When the book was seriously underway and Father Thoms no longer had time to spare, Wendy Earl came to the rescue. She patiently deciphered my writing, corrected my spelling and grammar, and would quietly ask such questions as, "Do you want the seed or the container to be sown?" We had many laughs together. Also, it was helpful that Wendy had only recently started vegetable gardening and would question me when things were not clearly explained.

Many hours of discussion took place with Roger and Anne Gunthorpe. Roger, a horticultural consultant with the federal government, is well-known to Ontario residents for his phone-in radio programs. Anne was my advisor regarding the nutrient values of vegetables and fruit.

Wendy Dion gave me invaluable scientific assistance answering the many questions I asked, and I pestered Barbara Clark when I wasn't sure I was getting my technical material clear.

I am most grateful to Cecilia Powell, whose herb garden was the source of many of my plants, and to my neighbour, Siglinda Matura, whose large market garden provided a wealth of information.

I must also give credit to Ruth Elliott and Donna Gilchrist for maintaining the garden while I wrote during the hectic garden season. Their abundant energy and cheerful attitude made working a pleasure for us all.

Drawings and photographs are essential in a practical gardening book. I am lucky in having my husband as my artist, photographer and gardening partner. Without him this book would not have been possible. Thank you, Larry.

Agriculture Canada and Guelph University provided a few photographs illustrating diseases and pests, and the photograph on page 9 was taken by Robin Brass.

My sincere appreciation also goes to my editors, Robin Brass and Colleen Darragh, for their patience and advice, and to the "behind the scenes" crew that have combined to transform my rough work into this finished book—a book that I hope will encourage more folks to enjoy gardening as I do.

Introduction

Until I actually began to write down how I garden, I had no idea how difficult it would be to explain the "hows," "whys" and "whens" of growing things. My childhood was spent in a home where gardening was a way of life. My mother and her friends gardened for the sheer joy of it, and most of the gardening knowledge I acquired I was never conscious of being taught.

My home, Broomfield, was in the country in southern Ireland, about ten miles north of Dublin. The countryside I knew and loved is now an urban development, with Dublin airport only a few miles away: another example of rich land giving way to progress and paving. Our main garden comprised about two acres and was surrounded by a 12-foot stone wall, within which grew luscious peaches, plums, pears and, in a warm corner, a huge old fig tree. In another area there was a small orchard, and a bay tree to supply the flavour for "souced herrings" fresh from the harbour of Malahide and for the seasoning of soups and stews. Horseradish and mint had their permanent locations, as had the globe and Jerusalem artichokes, sea-kale and asparagus.

There were potting sheds, greenhouses and all sorts of nooks and crannies which made fascinating play areas for children. But much of the time I was without young playmates, and then I helped in the garden — running errands, seeding, potting up and planting out, and generally absorbing garden know-how.

One autumn, when I was in quarantine for chicken pox and not permitted to return to school, this unscheduled holiday gave me three months at home during the fall season. I spent most of the days helping with the perennial borders, from which plants were being dug, divided and replanted. Before replanting, the soil was prepared by double-digging and manuring. The depth of topsoil in those old, established gardens was considerable, no doubt through many years of good management. These old-fashioned methods certainly produced good results, and ever since I have remained a firm believer in digging and manuring. In a home garden where crops are planted every year, it is essential to build and maintain a rich, fertile soil. With careful crop rotation a bountiful harvest can be gathered year after year.

Throughout my childhood only home-grown vegetables and fruits were on the daily menu. Oranges and bananas were considered a luxury and only purchased for special occasions. Although I drank my first glass of orange juice as an adult in the Middle East during World War II, I did not lack vitamin C. In Ireland many other fruits and vegetables supplied it in plenty: black currants, raspberries, strawberries and broccoli, to name just a few.

There were few freezers in domestic use before the war. Bottling and preserving provided our household with a well-stocked larder for winter use. An apple loft and potato and onion houses were maintained, and in our moderate climate green vegetables, leeks, parsnips and carrots were available from the garden all winter. We have found it just as easy in Canada to provide the household with a year-round supply, but a freezer and a cold storage room are needed to ensure satisfactory winter-keeping.

It is a long step from the Irish to the Canadian countryside, and the route I took was by no means direct. Soon after World War II broke out, my father died and mother converted Broomfield into a market garden. I left Dublin University Veterinary College to help her with this project. Fields were ploughed and crops such as spinach, cauliflower, Brussels sprouts, lettuce, onions and beets were grown. We supplied certain Dublin hotels and restaurants which demanded only high-quality produce. As the war dragged on I became restless, and in 1941 I found myself in various wartime occupations, including working for the Air Ministry in London and in service canteens and hostels in the Middle East. During this period I married a childhood friend from Ireland and, as he was in the Indian army, we returned to India after the war. While overseas I was introduced to many new vegetables and fruits which we had not grown in Ireland. It has been a continuing interest to me to try growing some of these here in Canada.

Paradoxically, wartime was less of a disruption to my husband, a regular soldier, than peacetime. In 1947 India gained its independence, and the British officers of the Indian army had to start a new life elsewhere. We moved to Canada and for several years farmed in Alberta. In adapting my gardening methods to the rigours of the Alberta climate, I was surprised to find that I could grow more exotic vegetables in the short, hot season there than we had been able to grow in the temperate climes of Ireland.

With the outbreak of the Korean War, Larry joined the Canadian army. When posted to Montreal, we acquired a cottage in the Laurentians and there developed a lovely and prolific garden in a beautiful natural setting. Unfortunately, the season was very short. It was always heartbreaking when the early frost came, killing the flowers still in bloom; but in compensation the sight of the spring growth was an annual miracle that we enjoyed as the new season approached.

Our enforced travels are now behind us, and we have settled into a corner of the Ottawa Valley where we can indulge in gardening as a more serious hobby. After we moved to Evergreen Farm, our youngest son was still attending college. When he came home for holidays he often brought friends with him. Practically all these young people had been brought up in cities or suburban areas, and it came as a shock

to me to realize that few of our young generation could even recognize a potato or a carrot growing in the ground.

It was at this time that I started to take an interest in encouraging young people, especially school children, to grow vegetable gardens. I know myself that what I learned as a child growing up in a gardening family and starting my own garden I have never forgotten. As the years have passed, I have been able to build upon and increase my knowledge, and the more I learn about gardening, the more I realize how little I know. For the past six years I have had the good fortune to be able to bring my experience in gardening to TV viewers on the CJOH Morning Show from Ottawa.

There is no doubt in my mind that the flavour and nutritive qualities of home-grown vegetables and fruits cannot be overestimated. To collect a salad from the garden and serve it within minutes; to pick vine-ripened tomatoes and melons; to munch a crisp carrot freshly pulled from the ground; to eat freshly picked corn, dropped straight into boiling water — these are the fruits of one's labour in a very real sense. Once you've tasted vegetables like these you will not want to return to the wilted, tired, well-travelled produce offered by supermarkets.

I often hear people complaining about the flavour of vegetables and how the children refuse to eat them. I am convinced that the reason in most cases is in the cooking, or rather the overcooking. Do not overcook vegetables; steam whenever possible, and serve when tender but still crisp. Vegetables have a much sweeter flavour when freshly harvested. This applies to potatoes too. When the early potato crop comes in, we dig only enough for one meal.

Often I am asked whether I am an organic gardener. The answer is yes and no. Yes, because I firmly believe that all organic materials available should be returned to the soil. No, because I supplement manure and compost with chemical fertilizer when I think that this would benefit a particular crop. Where chemical pest controls are concerned, we use these sparingly after all other methods have proved ineffective. I am hopeful that new developments in insecticidal soaps will provide me with another organic alternative. I have used these soaps successfully in the greenhouse and the garden but my experiments are not of a truly scientific nature. I have not made many specific recommendations concerning the chemical control of diseases and pests. Instead, I suggest readers keep up-to-date by obtaining the appropriate government pamphlets. These are always well-researched and provide much valuable information on control methods.

When people ask me, "Why do you do all that work?" my answer is that hobbies are for pleasure and for me gardening is a hobby. I like gardening. I get tremendous satisfaction seeing crops and flowers grow. The fact that my hobby happens to supply us with all the vegetables and fruit we need is just an added benefit.

So much for my background and general approach to the land. I hope that you will find the gardening tips I give you of interest and value.

Part One

The Well-Kept Garden

About Your Garden

The circumstances of each family have a direct bearing on the size and nature of its garden. For example, one family may be renting an allotment on a year-to-year basis, while another may own property and be able to plan years ahead. Suburban or country gardens will usually have space for a large sunny plot, while city gardeners may have to settle for a smaller, partially shaded one. Because each case will be different, the suggestions contained in this book may not apply in every respect to your particular gardening activities.

The art of vegetable gardening is to aid nature in the production of healthy crops. If the environment is hostile, it makes your job that much harder. Our gardening practices have, by and large, proven to be successful, and I hope that those who are able to follow them through this book will have equal success.

It is certainly true of gardening that "the best laid schemes o' mice and men gang aft a-gley." While general timing can be planned ahead, nature has a way of throwing timetables off schedule. The very weekend you plan to transplant seedlings a heat wave may arrive, or a snow storm, or failing this, a family crisis is sure to arise. You must therefore be very flexible, attending first to the most important jobs that time and weather permit.

When faced with spring work, it will seem to the novice gardener that he cannot possibly get around to doing all the necessary jobs. It may be better for that reason not to be too ambitious the first year. Start small, and allow the size of your cultivated area to increase along with your skills. Practical experience makes for lighter work.

Gardens require attention throughout the growing season, not just in the spring and fall. If you are planning a vacation during the summer, try to select crops that will not mature during your absence. Bear in mind that when a vegetable is at its prime, it should be harvested. A good neighbour on these occasions is invaluable, and often you can return the favour.

The list of jobs is never ending, and no gardener ever completes them, nor does he expect to. This is one of the "joys of gardening"; we are working with nature and every living thing in the garden changes with each passing day. A row of seeds may emerge; the first tomato may set fruit; and white butterflies may be fluttering among the cabbages.

I am never sure what jobs I am going to do on any given day until that day has dawned and I have some idea what the weather will be like. Spring and summer rain does not stop work outdoors. On the contrary, it provides ideal conditions for such jobs as transplanting. A warm light rain is nature's way of helping young transplants to suffer as mild a set-back as possible. A soft rain is far more beneficial than any watering that man can do. Not only is the rain's temperature warm, but it also contains valuable nutrients which aid the growth of the young plants. So on a rainy day I may transplant or, if the seedlings are emerging in the rows, I may weed down the rows.

Another rainy-day job is maintenance of equipment and tools. Blades constantly need sharpening and oiling, and there are always flower pots and flats to be washed and disinfected.

Hot, dry sunny days are for lawn mowing and hoeing. Hoeing has a very high priority in our garden, and my aim is to never let the weeds grow more than an inch or two in height.

Larry and I have made a practice of wandering through the garden and grounds after we have finished work in the evening. This is a leisurely stroll, a pleasurable one, when we take time to enjoy the surroundings we have helped to create. We also observe more closely the different plants, and if we notice anything amiss, like caterpillars or a wilt, we know we will have time to remedy the ailment before it gets out of hand. Sometimes all that is required is to remove and burn the offending material. Tent caterpillars are one example.

A garden is never dull, nor is it truly quiet. Although to city folk it would seem that I am alone most days, I am never lonely. Apart from my dogs who are wonderful companions and excellent at controlling groundhogs, the whole garden is constantly alive. We encourage birds and have quite a wide variety including a number of hummingbirds; insects are always numerous, "good guys" as well as bad. Birds and insects are fascinating to watch, and I sometimes find myself diverted from my job as I watch a bumble bee pollinate a squash or a hummingbird gather nectar. There are many occasions when it is well into the afternoon before I realize it is long past lunch time. With a hobby like mine I am never bored, and find there are never enough hours in the day to complete all I want to do. The hard work of the garden does not bring mental strain — instead it supplies a rather pleasant form of physical fatigue.

As you read further, you'll also notice that although we do work long hours in the garden, we ease our labour by organizing the sequence of our tasks carefully; this is the secret to maintaining a garden as large as ours.

Zone

Having lived in a wide range of climates, from Ireland to India to Alberta, I have learned to adapt my gardening to the prevailing conditions. English gardening books are fine for an English-type climate, and most American books are usually written for a considerably more moderate temperature and a longer growing season than we have in the Ottawa Valley.

Some garden catalogues carry zone maps which list the average annual minimum temperatures of the different zones, show the zones in different colours and number them. Because temperatures vary with altitude, the mountainous areas all across the continent make the accurate mapping of zones almost impossible.

Unfortunately, zone maps are not standardized and the zone numbers will vary from one catalogue to another. When ordering stock, always use the zone map in that particular catalogue. The plant material offered in the catalogues is listed showing the zone or zones in which it is hardy. This does not apply to annual vegetables, only to rooted stock such as fruit trees and some small fruits.

This book is written in a zone which, under average conditions, is frost-free after May 24 and where frost can be expected after September 5. If the dates in your area are different, adjust your planting out and seedling times accordingly, but remember, there will always be seasons that are exceptions to the rule. Newcomers to an area will have to determine the frost-free dates for their garden. The most reliable source for this information is often the neighbour with the best garden.

Some readers will have a far longer frost-free season than others, enabling them to harvest such crops as tomatoes, peppers, and eggplant for possibly six to eight additional weeks. When this is the case, fewer plants need be grown to produce the equivalent crop. Where the season is shorter, the opposite would be the case.

An example of how the length of the frost-free season can vary throughout a small area is well known to Toronto gardeners. Those living close to the lake have several more frost-free weeks than those in the north part of the city.

For vegetable gardening we are not concerned with the official zone in which our property lies. For certain fruit trees it would be advisable to inquire from the provincial government or state department of agriculture which varieties are recommended for specific locations.

We have lived at Evergreen Farm for eight years. During this time we have found that the squash grown behind the garage always survives the early fall frost, whereas the cucumber and beans growing in the main garden, only a matter of a hundred feet away, are blackened. These light early frosts are very localized, and after working in a garden for a number of years, you will learn where the warm and cold areas lie. Many vegetables are improved by light fall frosts, and it is sometimes possible to grow these crops in the cold, lower areas.

In our area early fall frosts are often followed by a long frost-free Indian summer. By protecting the frost-tender crops during the chilly nights, we frequently extend the growing and maturing period by several weeks. Protect tender crops against these early frosts by covering them with sacking, paper, plastic or old sheets. A special misting attachment for the garden hose can be used with great success. This must be switched on before the temperature drops below the freezing point, usually sometime around midnight.

Sunshine

In determining the area to be allotted to a vegetable garden, the most important factor is sunshine. In our short growing season, vegetables require all the sunshine possible. A limited few will tolerate partial shade, but most need at least six hours of sunshine a day, longer if possible. The shady areas of the garden can be allotted to certain flowering plants, lawns or ground covers that thrive only in shade.

Because a garden lacks the perfect amount of sun does not necessarily mean that vegetables cannot be grown. The leafy crops, such as lettuce and spinach, will do well in partial shade, and it is well worth experimenting with others to find out which can be grown successfully in your particular area. If you must decide between morning and evening sun, choose the area with morning sun; it is more beneficial to the crops. Try to avoid locating the plot too close to large trees or hedgerows which would shade the area and sap valuable moisture and nutrients from the soil. Generally speaking, the roots of trees grow below ground to the same extent as the branches above; you can tell, therefore, whether the roots are likely to interfere with cultivation, or deprive the crops of nourishment.

In a small property several areas can be allotted to vegetables. There may be corners with plenty of sunshine suitable for tomatoes or peppers; a fence for beans, peas or squash to climb upon; a more shady area for lettuce and other leafy vegetables; and sunny flower beds which can be interplanted with several crops. As an example, beets and burgundy or rhubarb chard have very colourful foliage and can be used as a contrast in a flower bed. Parsley and other herbs can be used to edge borders, and scarlet runner-beans are a colourful climber that produces very tasty beans for "frenching." However, when space permits it is more convenient to have all the vegetables in one area.

Drainage

Good drainage is essential. If the proposed site remains water-logged late into the spring, or if the water does not seep away rapidly after a heavy rain, drainage conditions are poor.

Vegetable crops will not succeed in water-logged ground. The roots will be deprived of oxygen and, although the plants may survive, their growth pattern will be permanently damaged, and the resulting crops will be poor. In the majority of gardens this condition can be remedied.

Often a simple ditch is all that is required to drain water away. In our garden the drainage was very poor during the first couple of years of cultivation due to the hardpan, and in some places sheet rock, about 3 feet below the topsoil. Hardpan is a cement-like layer of subsoil through which water penetrates very slowly. To remedy this, we hand dug the entire area very deeply, breaking up the subsoil, and at the same time taking care not to incorporate it with the topsoil. Fortunately, our area of sheet rock is not extensive, and we have learned to live with it, though occasionally it prevents us from driving stakes deeply into the ground.

After the initial digging we used the rotary cultivator to work in plenty of compost, well-rotted manure and other organic material that was available. This has permitted the spring "run-off" to soak in more rapidly, allowing us to work the garden much earlier than in previous years. The ground also warms up faster, and drainage after a heavy rain is no longer a problem.

In a limited space where the gardener has been unable to overcome the drainage problem, raised beds may be the only way to have a vegetable garden. This requires considerable work, as well as expense. Railway ties are the easiest material to use for making the enclosure, but if stones are available locally, and are free, they do the job equally well; stone walls, however, take far longer to complete.

The major expense is the purchase of the best-quality topsoil available. Time spent in checking just what type of soil is delivered is time well spent. I have seen a load dumped at a friend's house that was little better than fill, and contained clods of quack grass and weeds. Be sure you are at home when the load arrives; check it before it is dumped; and make sure it is dumped in the most convenient spot — you are going to have the job of carting it to the bed in a wheelbarrow. Garden areas are rarely accessible to trucks.

No vegetable garden can be truly successful without good drainage. Time spent correcting this condition will amply reward the gardener.

Water Supply

Access to water is another factor to be considered. Most homes nowadays have one or more outdoor taps. With sufficient length of hose, watering the garden should not present a problem. But moving the hoses around the garden is time-consuming, especially in hot, dry weather. After several years of dragging the hose around, we decided to install outlets in

Throughout these pages you will find references to keeping the soil moist. We frequently experience hot drying winds in the early summer and the soil has a tendency to bake and dry out. Make sure that there is no place in the vegetable garden that you cannot reach with the hose. Hoses should be stored neatly when not in use.

more convenient locations. This proved to be remarkably simple and surprisingly inexpensive. We did the job ourselves, and the main work was in digging a trench approximately 18 inches deep. In it we laid a plastic pipe leading to various outlets in the garden.

Heavy plastic hose is available at hardware or plumbing supply stores. It is easy to install and will not be damaged by frost in winter if the water supply is turned off inside the house and the outdoor taps opened and drained. We now have several taps in the garden which saves many hours previously wasted in shifting hoses around.

Another very important source of water is salvaged rain water. We collect it in 45-gallon drums, located beneath all the downpipes from the house. In households with small children it

Rain water collected in 45-gallon drums wherever we have a drain pipe provides water at atmospheric temperature to give young plants an emergency supply in time of water shortage.

is advisable to put some form of lid over the top of the drum to avoid accidents. The lid must be detachable to permit the gardener to collect water in a watering can.

I always keep a plastic garbage can filled with water from the tap in the vegetable garden. Left standing overnight, it allows the ice-cold well water to warm up. I use this to give individual plants a good soaking or maybe some liquid fertilizer which I have added to it. This is especially good for newly bedded plants. Being plastic and light, the garbage can is easy to move from one place to another. During dry hot spells, when there is a possibility of water scarcity, keep the drums filled from the tap and water plants individually.

The use of sprinklers during a water shortage is often banned and water barrels are a tremendous asset during these periods.

Always remember that when watering plants it is best to water a few thoroughly, that is, making sure the moisture goes beneath the root system, than giving a large number of plants a light sprinkling. In dry conditions roots will search for water, and if only the top of the soil is wet, the roots will reach upwards to obtain it. When this occurs, the root systems of plants are weakened and permanent damage is done. Although the plants may live, the size and quality of the crop will be poor.

When watering a garden, whether it is the lawn or the vegetable plot, always make sure that sufficient water has been applied, and that the water has indeed gone deeper than the root systems of plants or grass. I use a fork to check the depth of moisture. Remember — it is far better to water thoroughly once a week, rather than giving a daily light sprinkling.

Placing the sprinkler on top of a step ladder increases the range of the spray. The higher the spray, the more evenly and rain-like the water will fall on the garden.

Access to the Garden

The lack of a convenient access to the vegetable garden is most frustrating. Whether the garden is large or small, there is frequently a need to bring in equipment, manure, fertilizer or lime. In a large garden the access should permit a truck or tractor to enter; in small gardens the gate and path should be wide enough to accommodate a wheelbarrow or garden cart. When landscaping the property, this is an important feature to bear in mind.

Hedges, Fences and Intruders

Wind can cause severe damage in the garden, especially to newly set-out transplants. Many city gardens are protected by tree and shrub plantings or by fences which divide one property from another. They give privacy, muffle the sound of traffic, and help to protect the family from highway fumes. Rural vegetable gardens are sometimes very exposed and farm gardens often form part of a ploughed field, convenient for the farmer to do the spring cultivation, but inconvenient for the family to maintain.

When properties are situated very close to roads that are salted freely in winter, there is sometimes a problem growing any plant material near the road. The owner can do little except either dig a ditch to carry the spring thaw away, build a wooden fence, or erect a plastic barrier for the winter to try to protect the plants.

I prefer to give the vegetable garden a permanent location, convenient to the house and protected from prevailing winds. Far more rewarding results will be achieved if the garden "climate" is conducive to the vigorous growth of crops.

We have planted cedar hedges around our vegetable garden, giving the area a "walled-in" look. A wide grass patch divides the plot from the hedges, allowing plenty of space for the roots of the cedars to feed without robbing the crops of valuable nutrients. The mown grass

The accesses to our garden are wide enough to permit the entry of a small trailer. Each entry can be closed with a wooden gate, and the hedge provides protection against the wind.

space is also sufficiently wide for the garden tractor to operate and the hedge does not shade the garden plot. A hedge also acts as a barrier against air-borne weed seeds and harmful insects that lurk in weeds growing in nearby uncultivated areas.

Many city gardeners use fences to grow climbing vegetables such as pole beans, cucumber or squash. This practice not only provides space for a useful crop, but the fence acts as a wind break.

Fences, gates and hedges can also be a good aesthetic addition to the landscape. The gates can be rustic, formal, or whatever fits the landscaping scheme, and should be wide enough to allow equipment to enter.

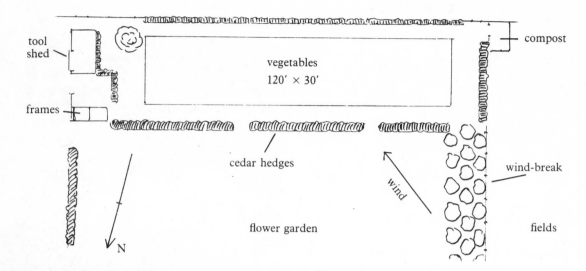

The vegetable garden at Evergreen Farms. Cedar hedges separate the vegetable from the ornamental garden and provide a windbreak. Grass paths and wide gates provide easy access. The tool shed, frames and compost heap are within easy reach. The exposure allows for full sun throughout the growing season. We have piped a water supply to the garden.

Fences also protect the garden from assorted strays. In rural areas cattle, sheep or goats can be the offending animals, but for city dwellers it is usually dogs, cats — and children. Nothing is more annoying than to find your garden a neighbourhood shortcut. The only way to prevent this is with some form of barrier.

We have trained our dogs not to run through the garden beds, not too difficult a task if you train the dogs when they are young. Rabbits and groundhogs can be a serious problem, and they must be prevented from entering the garden. The best method is to run a narrow strip of poultry netting along the base of the fence, hedge and gate. Alternatively, you may prefer to keep a dog or two, as we do, to help to keep the rabbits and groundhogs away.

Birds are sometimes a nuisance. They may eat the heart out of newly planted Brassicas, damage growing crops such as peas and corn, or eat fruit just as it is ripening. Scarecrows are often effective in deterring the birds and are fun for children to make. Glitterbangs can be purchased at garden centres, or homemade streamers can be flown over the crops being damaged. Anything that will flap in the wind will frighten birds away.

Raccoons can devastate the corn just as it is ripening. Uncannily, they *know* when it has reached its peak. A friend of ours has overcome this problem by setting a radio in the corn patch and playing music all night. If you try this method, protect the radio from the elements and make sure the cable is suitable for outdoor use.

Garden Tools and Equipment

The really necessary tools for a small home vegetable garden are few in number. As the result of good advertising, I have several tools that are seldom used. So for the sake of one's pocketbook, buy only good quality tools that will last a lifetime, know which tools are essential, and learn how to use them for the least expenditure of energy. As with any hobby there are always plenty of gimmicky tools and machines ready to tempt the unwary. The enthusiastic gardener is especially vulnerable early in the season.

Most garden tools are a combination of hardwood and steel, both of which suffer when exposed to the elements. To get the best value out of them, they need proper care and maintenance. This means keeping them under cover when not in use, cleaning and oiling both the wood and the metal and, where appropriate, sharpening the cutting edge.

There is nothing more annoying than a splinter in your hand from a badly maintained tool. In my garden, I keep the tools in a shed adjacent to the plot, and always try to put them under cover after work. If they are very dirty, they should be washed off with the hose or, as I often do, rinsed in a convenient rain-water barrel.

All good quality garden tools come in different sizes and weights. Do not be intimidated by the salesman who tells you otherwise. Get the one that suits you. I cannot dig with a fork or spade built for a man, so I have my own. I can do all the work I need to with lighter equipment and save my energy.

For someone starting to garden, my advice is to purchase only the essential hardware. First in this list would be a garden spade (not to be confused with a shovel), followed by a digging fork, a rake, one or more hoes (garden, draw, dutch, or stirrup), a trowel, a sharpening file or stone, a watering can (plastic), a garden line (cord), and finally a garden hose and sprinkler. With these tools you can get your first garden under way and by that time will have become acquainted with other gardeners and their tools and be able to judge better what else you need — later on!

The tool shed.

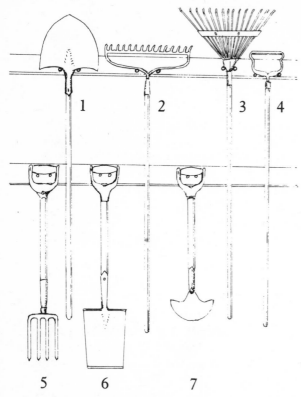

1: shovel; 2: garden rake; 3: grass rake; 4: stirrup hoe;
5: garden fork; 6: spade; 7: grass edger.

Spade

The garden spade has straight sides and a straight, sharp cutting edge for easy penetration of the soil. There is a "tread" on the upper edge which the shovel does not have, thus making the spade the digging tool. A spade is short-handled with a grip at the end of the handle.

Before the advent of rotary tillers, the primary use of the spade was to dig the garden, turning the soil. As we can now rent equipment to do the heavy digging for us, we use the spade to straighten and tidy the edges and work areas where larger equipment cannot be used. You can use it to dig trenches for such crops as leeks and celery, its width and square lower edge being perfect for this job. Also, spades are used to cut and divide plants such as rhubarb.

Digging Fork

The digging fork is straight with four round or flat tines. The tread is wide as with all tools intended for digging; the handle is short with a grip at the end. The fork can often be used instead of the spade, particularly when digging clay or other heavy ground or breaking up surface clods after digging. It is also handy for spreading compost or manure and picking up garden refuse, in addition to harvesting many crops.

Forks come in a very wide range of sizes and weights.

One standard-size fork is all that is needed to start working a garden plot, but most gardeners find as their gardening interest grows, so does their interest in acquiring the garden implements that will save time and energy for specific jobs.

We have three different forks: my small, light digging fork with rounded prongs; a medium-sized flat pronged fork for general use such as spreading compost and stacking the bonfire; and a large, flat pronged fork which we use for digging potatoes, parsnips and other root crops — the wide, flat prongs are less likely to damage the tubers. Forks do not need sharpening, but the prongs must be kept clean and smooth in order to penetrate the soil with the least expenditure of energy on the part of the gardener.

Garden tools should be washed down and wooden handles treated with linseed oil during and at the end of the season.

Garden Rake

A metal-headed garden rake with a long handle is in constant use. After the ground has been worked in the spring, the rake is used to pulverize the soil, level the surface and make it suitable for the "seed bed."

I often use the end of the handle to make a furrow in which to sow seed. After seeding I rake soil over the seed and, finally, tamp or press the seed row with the prongs flat on the ground. A garden rake is essential to make a good seed bed.

Another use is to rake up weeds and garden refuse before removing them to the compost heap. Rakes come in different widths, the small ones being suitable to clean up hoed weeds between narrow rows. One standard-size rake is all the average gardener requires and is the only one I use. Make sure you do not leave your rake in a position where it can cause injury.

A selection of hoes used in our garden.
(Left to right): Narrow Dutch hoe, wide Dutch hoe, three-pronged draw hoe, stirrup hoe, flat draw hoe.

Hoes

The garden hoe comes in a variety of types and should be one of the hardest worked of all tools in a garden. Its purpose is to annihilate weeds which rob soil of food, harbour insects, and compete with crops for space, light, air and nutrients.

Hoeing loosens the surface soil and permits air, warmth, rain and sunshine to enter. If the hoe is used correctly and at the right time, many hours of unnecessary weeding labour are eliminated. A hot, dry, sunny day is ideal for hoeing; as soon as the hoe disturbs the weed, the sun shrivels it up. It is a waste of time to hoe when warm, humid conditions prevail, which permit the weeds to re-establish themselves. Constant light hoeing is the best, killing the weeds as they emerge through the soil. Never permit weeds to grow to any size and never, never let them go to seed.

Although I say this, I know that even in the best kept gardens there are weeds that escape the eagle eye of the gardener, especially those weeds that germinate in the rows of vegetable seedlings and have to be pulled by hand. When I am wandering around my garden just looking things over, I often take a hoe with me and hoe down any odd weeds that have previously escaped my notice. The hoe is a constant com-

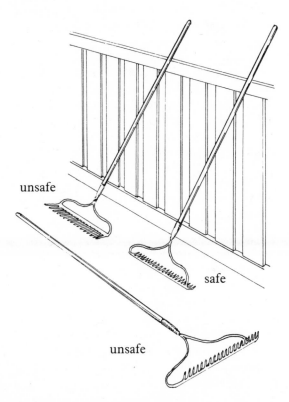

unsafe

safe

unsafe

panion and if used continually when the weeds are just emerging, very little expenditure of energy is required to control them.

You need a little general information before purchasing your first hoe. Consult with friends who have garden hoes, and maybe watch a demonstration as to how to use them. Note that with some hoes you walk forward over the ground you have just worked. With others, you walk backwards, hoeing the ground in front of you. Some hoes can be used both ways.

Garden or draw hoe.   Work walking forward and "chopping" at the ground. This hoe is often effective where the "Dutch hoe" fails. The garden or draw hoe is useful in making furrows in conjunction with the garden line before seeding. It is also used for hilling up potatoes.

Dutch hoe or scuffle.   This hoe is a great favourite of mine. Work walking backwards and cutting or disturbing the weeds just under the soil surface. Care must be taken not to scuffle too close to rows, thereby damaging the roots or stems of crops. The blade should be kept sharpened to make work lighter. I have two sizes: a wide one for use between rows and a narrow one for work between and around certain plants — for example, onions, cabbage and beans.

Using a stirrup hoe between rows of emerging seedlings. The hot sun will shrivel up the weeds.

Stirrup hoe.   An excellent all-purpose type of hoe also in constant use in my garden. It has a cutting blade on either side of the "stirrup" and is easy to use. It can be worked in any direction, but is particularly useful for hoeing weeds close to crops. Use a "pulling" action towards you, thereby running no risk of damaging the plants, always a possibility with the Dutch hoe. Keep the blades sharpened for easier work.

Sharpening File or Stone

This is an extremely important item of garden equipment; no serious gardener is without one. The time and energy saved by keeping equipment sharp cannot be overestimated. Many old-time gardeners always carry a stone in their pocket to keep cutting edges sharp.

I keep referring to timing. Ten minutes spent maintaining the edges of garden tools before starting a job can not only save the gardener time to complete his project, but allows him to do the job with far less expenditure of energy. You will find that most well-maintained gardens will also have well-maintained garden equipment.

As our garden increased in size we found it necessary to purchase an electric sharpener, enabling us to keep not only the garden tools sharp, but also the blades of the lawn mower. Blunt lawn mower blades put extra strain on the motor, damage the grass and leave the lawn an ugly, untidy mess.

A hand-sharpening file or stone is still essential, even when the gardener has an electric sharpener.

Trowel

A small garden trowel should not be confused with the flat-bladed type used by plasterers. The garden trowel is scoop-shaped and is used to dig small holes in the soil. It is in constant use in the spring when bedding out transplants. Purchase a good-quality stainless steel trowel; cheap ones are likely to rust and soon need replacing.

I use chemicals as sparingly as possible. However, it is absolutely essential to use certain sprays at certain times. Because we often have enthusiastic assistants at weekends, one precaution we have taken is to spray weed killers and driveway sterilants from a watering can kept especially for this job.

Watering Can

I prefer plastic watering cans to metal ones because they are so much lighter to carry. A watering can is especially important during seeding and transplanting times. They come in several shapes, and the better-quality ones have different sizes of "roses" which deliver various intensities of spray depending on the direction in which they are turned. The cheaper one is perfectly suitable for most gardening needs. Never use the garden watering can for weed-killer or sterilant for gravel paths. My personal experience has taught me a severe lesson. Although I thought I had washed the can thoroughly, subsequent use killed a bed of precious seedlings. The "poison" watering can is now marked clearly with a skull and crossbones and is used for nothing else!

Spray Equipment

If you intend to use liquid spray to control pests and diseases, you will need some form of equipment. A trombone spray is handy for small gardens, but a pressure tank is more convenient when there is a large area to be covered.

We have a small (3-gallon) pressure tank that is designed to be carried over the shoulder. I find it rather heavy and cumbersome, so I have devised a more convenient homemade method. We have replaced the short hose with a much longer one, so that when I climb a ladder into a tree, I do not have the problem of carrying the tank with me.

Always carefully wash spray equipment after use; good maintenance is essential. We also find the washers frequently need replacing. Otherwise leaks occur, and if you are using chemicals this could be dangerous.

The average pressure tank carries only a short length of hose (see black hose in foreground). If you wish to spray the top of a tree, this means taking the tank with you. A good plan is to attach a longer hose, say twenty feet, which allows you to leave the tank on the ground.

Hose and Sprinkler

These items are essential for all gardens. Since coming to North America in 1949, we have not known a season when we did not need them. It is false economy to purchase poor-quality garden hoses and sprinklers. Both these items should last for many years if well-maintained and stored under cover when not in use. Quality hose will not deteriorate when exposed to sunlight as will the cheap plastic ones. The same applies to sprinklers.

All garden hoses should be a standard size, so that when replacements are needed there is no problem fitting new hoses onto old.

Standard screw-on couplings are fitted on all garden hoses and attachments. I find it very tedious and time-consuming connecting and disconnecting these couplings when moving the hose around the garden. The answer to this problem is simple: attach "spring-couplings," which are available through certain seed catalogues and at some garden centres, to all the connections. They screw into the standard coupling and when you wish to change the attachment, you have only to pull the spring back to release the coupling. They provide a quick, easy, nonleaking connection and are made of strong-quality metal which will not break if accidentally dropped on a concrete surface.

Sprinklers are sold in a wide range of styles. Study them carefully and find the one best suited to your individual needs. You may end up with both a sprinkler and a seepage hose. There are two types of seepage hose, plastic

and canvas, which have tiny holes along their surface and closed ends. They allow varying intensity of spray, controlled by water pressure, and are excellent for soaking a row of vegetables individually and conserve water in time of drought or shortage.

Garden Line or Row Marker

Any strong string, cord, or twine can be used to keep rows straight when planting, or to maintain well-defined edges around the various beds. When not in use keep it wound around marker-sticks and store it under cover. We use binder twine not only for a line, but also for innumerable jobs when things have to be tied to prevent wind damage. Binder twine, being treated, seems to last longer in exposed locations than do other forms of string. However, nylon, which is virtually indestructable, makes a very suitable garden line. In England, garden lines are sold in garden supply stores. They are marketed like fishing reels, but have metal spikes attached to insert in the ground. With the increase in popularity of home vegetable gardening it is likely they will soon appear in our garden centres.

Wheelbarrow or Garden Cart

As the garden develops, the need soon arises for taking all kinds of things from place to place. Each time I set out to work in my garden, I go first to the tool shed and load up my garden cart with all the equipment I may need. This may include garden tools, a basket with stakes, twine, scissors, a knife, some rotenone powder, and other extras such as garden labels and markers. You soon learn what you need, and save time and energy by loading the cart before you begin your gardening.

I do not like the wheelbarrow with a single wheel in front. I used to have one, but always found it heavy to manoeuver and tippy to use. In the last few years I have had a well-balanced garden cart and find it a joy to work with — well worth the extra initial cost. Wheelbarrows and garden carts are available in several sizes, materials and weights. Do not rush into this purchase. The initial expenditure can be quite considerable and you want to be quite sure you are buying the right model. A good-quality wheelbarrow or garden cart should last many years.

Shovel

The shovel is a long-handled tool without a tread, usually used for scooping up and moving soil or compost from place to place. Technically, it is not a digging tool but we find it essential for many jobs that the spade cannot cope with.

One example is in digging large holes for fruit trees. The shovel will scoop out the soil after the sod has been removed with the spade.

Grass Rake

The grass rake may be metal or bamboo. As the name implies, it does a much more efficient job than the garden rake in cleaning lawns. It is used to rake leaves in the autumn, to clean and aerate the lawn in the spring, and to tidy up the grass after work has been done in the beds. Unlike the garden rake, the grass rake, being flexible, is used in a light "sweeping" motion which "flicks" rather than drags. Therefore, it can be used effectively in the spring on perennial crops to remove leaves or mulch.

We use the grass rake constantly throughout the gardening season. When working in the garden I have a habit of throwing weeds and garden refuse onto the mown grass surrounding the vegetable plot, then raking them up and carting them away to the compost (or incinerator). The grass rake is light in handling and leaves the grass clean and tidy. We have found it false economy to purchase any but the best-quality metal grass rake. The cheap metal or bamboo models will not last even one season.

The garden cart.

Grass Edger

Many vegetable gardens are surrounded by lawn and may be close to the flower garden. It is visually much more attractive if these lawns are kept well-manicured by cutting and edging. It also prevents the grass from encroaching into the vegetable plot. The grass edger is the tool for keeping edges neat and straight. It consists of a short, wooden handle with a hand grip at one end and a metal banana-shaped blade at the other. This blade should be kept sharp. Although mechanical edgers are a time and labour saver when there is a great quantity of edging to be done, they are seldom needed in the average home garden; and they are expensive.

Shears

The garden shears have innumerable uses in keeping a garden in shape. Their main job is to clip hedges and trim around trees and shrubs, so they are always among the tools loaded into my garden cart. Because their use requires considerable expenditure of energy, often under difficult circumstances, great care should be taken to select good-quality light shears. They should be kept well-sharpened and oiled.

Pruners or Secateurs

Pruners, or secateurs, are a small scissor-like tool used for pruning. Fruit trees must be kept shaped and under control, allowing light to enter and air to circulate. Raspberries must be thinned and dead canes removed. Good quality pruners make a clean cut, reducing the likelihood of disease entering the plant's wound. Keep them well oiled and under cover when not in use. Being small, they can be lost in high grass and rust in no time. Tie a brightly coloured ribbon to the handle to make them conspicuous.

Rotary Tillers

A rotary tiller is a major garden expenditure, and the need to own one will depend on the size of your garden.

If the garden is small, it is more practical to rent one for the few hours a job may take in the spring and fall. Between times, digging can be done by hand. For larger gardens it is more convenient to own your own. You can use it on and off throughout the season cultivating between rows, after early crops have been harvested, and before late crops are planted. The rotary tiller works up the ground in preparation for planting.

Most models have the prongs in front of the engine, others behind (it might appear at first glance that having the prongs so close to the operator would involve some risk, but this is not the case.) I am told by friends who have used both types that the latter are the easier to use. Depth of tilling can be adjusted, and the action of the rotating prongs pulverizes and aerates the soil. This leaves an excellent seed bed, but in a dry season care should be taken not to overwork the soil, thereby permitting it to dry out too rapidly.

When tilling in the fall, the ground should be left "rough," that is, no raking or levelling should be done. This subject is discussed in more detail in the section on "Putting the Garden to Bed."

Spring cultivation using a 3½ hp Bolens rotary tiller with prongs in front.

A Troy-built Pony Rototiller with prongs behind engine.

A word of caution: as with all power tools, care must be taken, particularly when children are around. If the motor is left running, the rotary tiller can very easily be put into gear and started up when least expected. Observe all the warnings given on the machines.

Lawnmower

The lawnmower is another major garden expenditure, and therefore a good deal of research should be done before purchasing it. Power or hand operated? Rotary? Spool? Electric or gas powered? The choice depends on the individual garden, its size and whether there are trees, shrubs and hedges that might be inconvenient for an electric cable. Whether you intend to leave the grass clippings where they fall on the lawn or whether you wish to collect them for mulch or compost is another factor to consider.

As I have a comparatively large garden, over the years I have acquired three machines — one large riding tractor type; one gas-driven model with a bag to collect grass clippings; and one rotary electric. The latter was my first purchase and can only be used in areas close to the house where an outlet is handy.

On weekends when my family is home all three machines are at work, and the grass cutting can thus be completed in a very short space of time. The trimming of edges and clipping around trees is by far the most tedious job, but makes all the difference to the overall appearance of a property.

Grass cutting can be hazardous and emphasis on safety must be observed. Not only should leather shoes be worn for protection when using any mower, but the risk of stones being picked up by the mower and thrown at high speed at a bystander is also a real possibility.

Pocket Knife

This is an indispensible part of the gardener's equipment, and everyone has their favourite type of knife. I have found it necessary to attach a long piece of string and/or a brightly coloured ribbon to the knife. Knives had a habit of getting lost in my garden, and this trick has helped enormously in avoiding this problem.

Scissors

Scissors are often very useful, but not essential if you have a knife. Tie a ribbon to the scissors too.

Finding Your Tools

A friend of ours has solved the problem of tools being left out in the garden overnight by grandchildren and other enthusiastic "helpers." She paints a bright red band around each tool, which makes them conspicuous when she is packing up for the night.

Garden Clothing

The photographs in this book will reveal that while gardening I am not one of the ten best-dressed women in the world. Garden clothing should be functional, comfortable, have plenty of pockets for putting things into and easily washed. Consequently, I wear cotton or denim coveralls. They are loose at the waist and comfortable when stooping and stretching.

The hot weather brings out my white painter's overalls and the cool weather, heavy blue denim, preferably with a zip up the front and elastic straps over the shoulders. If the weather gets chilly, there is plenty of room for a sweater underneath.

I always find I can work far better in clothes that are meant for the job and "don't matter." When the knees wear out, I just cut off the legs.

When working around power tools, such as a lawn mower or rotary tiller, I wear leather shoes. An added safety precaution is to avoid clothing which could get caught up in machinery. Jackets should always be fastened and neck ties and scarves avoided.

The clothing I wear when out in the rain varies. When the temperature is cool, I don a plastic suit, pants and jacket like the fishermen wear. When it is warm, I just allow my clothes to get soaked. Once the work is finished, I relax in a nice warm bath.

Soils

Often in my reading I have become confused over the complexity of soil, what with micro-organisms, carbon/nitrogen ratios and other such terms. With time and experience I have come to understand that this wonderful material need not be an imponderable mystery. "Soil-building" is a necessary part of garden soil management, and in the next few pages I will "build" the picture of soil and explain how an appreciation of the way it works clarifies so many other mysteries and makes an understanding of plants and how they grow so much clearer.

Soil Formation

Soil has developed and continues to develop from the breaking down of solid materials, primarily rock, during various physical processes, such as expansion and contraction, that occur continuously. This action gradually forms smaller particles of varying sizes. Depending on the type of rock, these particles contain a variety of chemical minerals which can be described as chemical properties. Physical weathering of this now superficial material is followed by the natural invasion of living organisms; soil formation has begun. With time and weathering the chemical minerals in the soil change form, usually very slowly. Depending on the amount and activity of the soil organisms, the soil begins to "build." An environment that is now capable of supporting plant growth is developing, and the subsequent cycles of growing, then dying and regrowing of plants over the seasons build the *physical characteristics* of the soil. Organic materials or *humus* increase as the soil activity develops. This is an extremely variable process, explaining why soils differ so greatly from one area to another.

Soils that have formed from rock formations with adequate minerals and enriched with an abundance of organic life will naturally develop into the best growing environment. As the acids produced by the breakdown of the organic matter in turn break down the mineral particles, nutrients are released.

I have mentioned both *physical* and *chemical* properties which I will elaborate upon.

Physical Properties of Soil

Such characteristics refer to the consistency of the soil that can be seen and felt. This soil will be a combination of particles from very fine grade clay to coarse sand and decaying organic matter or humus.

Texture refers to the actual particle size, the smaller the particle, the tighter the soil and the less space for oxygen and water. This explains why clay-type soils are often poor drainers, crack during the summer and present quite a challenge in growing some plants, particularly root crops. Silt and sand are the progressively larger particle sizes; the latter is coarse and well-drained but with the disadvantage of drying out quickly and retaining nutrients poorly.

When describing a soil, an equal amount of these major ingredients listed above is called *loam*. As these ingredients are rarely found in equal proportions, the terms sandy loam, clay loam, etc., are often used, indicating which particle size predominates.

A typical soil sample will, when put in a glass jar, mixed with water and shaken, settle out to show the various layers of different particle sizes. Although not very scientific, this method does serve as a basic way for the home gardener to evaluate the type of soil in his garden. Any humus will, of course, float on the surface and the sand will sink.

Humus is produced from the decomposition of animal and vegetable matter. Aside from its nutrient value, it helps to retain moisture and air and also to bind smaller particles together in developing the "crumb-structure" that is often talked about.

Virtually any soil type can be made productive with modification to its texture. The addition of coarse sand and organic matter to a clay loam will improve drainage and aeration. Similarly, the incorporation of organic matter to coarse, sandy soil will increase moisture retention and its ability to retain nutrients. Very few people are fortunate enough to begin with an ideal soil, but much can be done with the most hopeless looking land.

In addition to the soil modifications, soil texture can be improved by using nature and its methods. Clay soils, deeply and roughly dug in the fall and allowed to weather, will have developed a noticeably improved tilth, or working quality, in the spring. The incorporation of materials such as leaf mold, compost, ashes and manure will quickly result in an improvement.

You can check the texture of the soil by taking a handful of moist soil and squeezing it tightly in one hand. If it can be compressed into a thin thread without breaking, you have a very heavy clay soil. On the other hand, if the soil falls apart as soon as you release your grip, it is very high in coarse particles. A loam soil will retain its form but break up when touched lightly.

The other extreme would be a soil from almost purely organic origin such as peat (also called "muck" soil) which is primarily organic matter. Its moisture retention is very high and it is frequently acidic. Although when altered with some "substantial" ingredients it may produce an excellent medium for growing vegetables, in its raw state it is unlikely to be highly productive.

Chemical Properties of Soil

As I mentioned previously, chemical minerals are released as the solid particles break down.

This is usually a slow process, and although often adequate in nature to support annual growth, in the home garden some nutrient management becomes necessary. First, it is advisable to identify what the soil contains in the form of minerals. These are usually referred to as the *major*, or macronutrients, and the *minor*, or micronutrients. All are essential, but the plant relies more heavily on the three elements of *nitrogen* (N), *phosphorus* (P) and *potassium* (K) than they do on the others. These elements are present in varying amounts in most organic manures and form the basis for commercial-type fertilizers.

Nitrogen (N) is important for the healthy growth of leaves and stems. All leafy vegetables require nitrogen, but too much will cause excessive growth and delay flowering and setting of fruit in fruiting crops.

Phosphorus (P) is essential for the formation of flowers, fruit and seed. It is also necessary for the development of a strong root system. Watering with a cupful of high phosphorus transplant solution is beneficial when setting out young plants.

Potassium (K) is necessary in the development of strong roots and stems. It also aids cell formation. All root crops require an adequate supply of potassium. Wood ash is a source of potash.

When present in an organic or natural form, the minerals are released slowly; their availability depends to a great extent on the rate of organic matter decomposition. The formulation of commercial fertilizers and particularly their solubility will dictate the rate at which they break down and become available to plants. Remember, plants can only absorb nutrients when they have become soluble in the soil water.

We can now see that soil is quite simply a combination of solid particles, organic matter, air spaces and moisture containing minerals which dissolve as they are released. Most important in maintaining the smooth operation of this mechanism is the pH or acidity of the soil.

The Importance of pH

The availability of nutrients and the activity of small soil organisms is dependent upon correct acidity. This in turn, when adjusted, influences the release of certain minerals for specific crops.

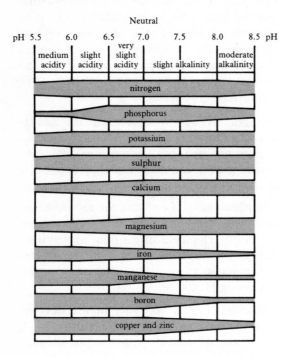

The chart shows how all the major elements are made available when the pH is neutral, that is at 7. Extreme variation on either the acidic or alkaline side reduces their availability.

The pH level can be checked with a simple test kit which should be a part of every home gardeners' equipment. This will also enable a check to be made of the elements N, P and K, and fertilizer applications adjusted accordingly.

Adjusting the pH

Most vegetables prefer a pH of around 6.5, except for the Brassicas that do best in a pH level of 6.8 to 7.5. The following table shows the pH preferences for the vegetables and fruits that are of concern to us.

pH 6.8-7.5	pH 6.0-6.8	pH 5.0-6.0
Asparagus	Beans	Apples
Beets	Carrots	Blueberries
Broccoli	Celery	Eggplant
Brussels sprouts	Corn	Peppers
Cabbage	Cucumbers	Potatoes
Cauliflower	Leeks	Raspberries
Plums	Lettuce	Squash
	Onions	Strawberries
	Parsley	Tomatoes
	Parsnips	Turnips
	Peas	Watermelon
	Radishes	
	Rhubarb	
	Spinach	

When the pH is out of balance, various methods of correction may be tried. The acidity may be increased (the pH lowered) by the addition of organic matter such as natural peat moss, which is usually quite acidic. Large quantities are necessary to change the pH even a small amount, so for larger adjustments the addition of sulphur or iron sulphate will help.

> To lower the pH ¾ of a point:
> add sulphur or iron sulphate at the rate of 1½ lb per 100 square feet
> or 600 lb per acre

Where large adjustments are required, it is best to spread the applications over two or more years so as not to disturb the careful balance of other soil ingredients.

The pH may be raised (alkalinity increased) by the application of lime, usually in the form of ground limestone.

> To raise the pH (sweeten the soil) ¾ of a point:
> add finely ground limestone at the rate of 5 lb per 100 square feet
> or 1 ton per acre

It will take several months for the effect to become apparent. Although many gardeners still practise "liming" as an annual routine, it is best to check the pH level first. Do not use lime in conjunction with manure or commercial fertilizers.

The soil structure and texture will, when suitable, assure good aeration, drainage and root development. Good roots mean that the plant can make the most use of the nutrition that surrounds it. Now for supplying that nutrition, there are various methods.

Chemical Fertilizers

Fertilizers fall into two groups, *inorganic* (chemical) fertilizers and *organic* (natural) fertilizers.

Chemical fertilizers are either mined or produced chemically, sometimes as a by-product from industrial processes. Both the organic and inorganic forms of fertilizer supply plants with the essential elements needed for good growth: nitrogen, phosphorous, potassium, and trace elements. Many organic gardeners believe chemical fertilizers cause disease in humans and animals and refuse to use them. So far, there is no scientific data to support this claim.

When the novice gardener visits a garden centre to purchase fertilizer, he finds a large selection of bags, bottles and tins to choose from. The price tags will vary considerably. I have heard people claim that fertilizers were far cheaper at certain stores. When I investigated, I discovered they did not understand that the fertilizer contents of the containers varied greatly too.

For example, a 100-pound bag of 10:10:10 has only half as much fertilizer as a 100-pound bag of 20:20:20. The rest is fill. The three numbers on the bag denote nitrogen (N), phosphorus (P), potash (K), always in that order. The number gives the percentage of each element contained in the bag. Therefore it will require two bags of 10:10:10 to do the same job as one of 20:20:20. A bag of 20:0:0 contains only nitrogen, and one with 0:15:10 contains only phosphorus and potash.

A complete fertilizer contains all three elements. Experienced gardeners often take soil tests to ascertain what ratio of N:P:K their garden requires. A soil test is the only way to be certain of your garden's nutrient deficiencies.

In spring, we apply a correctly balanced "slow release" fertilizer in granular form to the whole vegetable garden. This is tilled into the soil at the same time as the manure and compost.

Slow release fertilizers have been manufactured to release their contents over a period of time rather than all at once. Although more convenient in that they may be applied just once for the season, a soil analysis must be made before adding the nutrients. Some slow release types may have just their nitrogen content in a form that dissolves gradually. This type of fertilizer is beneficial with crops such as tomatoes and peppers which need nitrogen throughout the season.

I prefer to feed the crops individually with liquid fertilizer. I use "Bounty" 6:2:2 (which is a fish-based organic type) for leafy vegetables, and "Sturdy" 0:15:14 (partly organic) for tomatoes, peppers and eggplant after the fruit has set. When plants require a balanced fertilizer, I use a combination of the two. I mix the solution in a plastic garbage can which is easily moved around the garden, and add water to it from the garden hose.

Nutrients in *liquid* fertilizers are immediately available to plants. They can be applied to the soil around the plants and some are suitable for foliar feeding. The directions given with each product should be followed carefully to prevent fertilizer burn. Overfertilizing is a common error and will damage plants.

There are many brands of liquid fertilizers on the market, and many are suitable for foliar as well as root feeding. The purpose of foliar feeding is to bring nutrients quickly and directly to the plants through their leaves rather than through the roots. It cannot replace root feeding and should only be treated as a supplement to it. Foliar feeding is a quick way of correcting minor nutrient disorders such as a boron deficiency. I have never considered it necessary to foliar feed my vegetable garden, but I have friends who consider it a good practice. Dispensers, which can be attached to the garden hose, are available at garden centres for applying either water soluble or liquid fertilizers.

On the other hand, some gardeners prefer to apply a light application of granular "*quick release*" fertilizer by hand along each side of the rows or where plants (cauliflower, cabbage, tomato, squash, etc.) are widely spaced in a circle around each plant and about three to five inches from each stem. The fertilizer can be worked into the soil using a hand cultivator and then watered in with a garden hose. Do not allow the granules to fall on the foliage of the plants as this will damage the tissues.

Overapplication of any fertilizer could cause root damage and kill the plant or severely set it back. Always make certain that the soil is moist and that fertilizer is not applied to plants that are wilted. (Probably all they need is a good drink.)

Often the directions on the manufacturers' package may be reduced; it is better to apply a weaker solution and then follow up later with another similar quantity. Dry fertilizers are best applied just before rainfall or watering, and great care must always be taken to spread them evenly.

Because home gardeners grow a wide range of vegetables in their garden plot, one ratio of fertilizer is unlikely to suit them all. With an ample quantity of humus in the soil, and the advantage of being able to fertilize each vegetable according to its *specific* needs, the home vegetable garden can produce many types of crops, all of superlative quality.

Organic Fertilizers and Animal Manures

It is common practice for people to buy all their plant food in the form of chemical (inorganic) fertilizers. I have nothing against these fertilizers, but feel that they should only be used *in addition* to manures, compost and humus, and not *instead* of them. For our garden we consider both organic and inorganic fertil-

izers to be essential in maintaining a constant supply of nutrients in the soil. A combination of the two is far better than either one alone. Inorganic fertilizers become rapidly available to the plants, but can be leached, or washed, out of the soil during heavy rains, particularly in light soils. Organic fertilizers are more slowly available to plants, contain trace elements (micronutrients) and add humus to the soil.

Animal manures are often scarce and expensive, but whenever obtainable are the best form of humus. Next on the list as a source of organic nutrients is compost, which every gardener can make at home and has the great advantage of being cost-free. Many organic materials that are commonly discarded can be recycled in the compost heap. (See page 34 for instructions on composting.)

Other forms of humus such as peat moss and sawdust improve the texture of the soil but have practically no food value — though in combination with manures they are very beneficial.

NUTRIENT VALUES OF SOME ORGANIC FERTILIZERS
(% on dry weight basis)

Fertilizer	Nitrogen (N)	Phosphorus (P)	Potassium (K)
Blood	13	1.5	0
Fish Scrap	9	7	0
Seaweed	1	0.5	9
Bone Meal (raw)	4	22	0
Bone Meal (steamed)	2	27	0

The foregoing organic fertilizers may be purchased at garden centres, and applied to the garden in the amount required by that particular garden soil.

Wood Ash: N:P:K 0:2:6 (this may vary depending on the type of wood burned). Keep the ashes dry until needed, then work sparingly into the surface of the soil before sowing or planting. Wood ash is a free source of potash. Avoid using it where you plan to plant potatoes; it could cause scab. Too heavy an application will raise the soil acidity.

APPROXIMATE NUTRIENT VALUES OF SOME MANURES

Fertilizer	Nitrogen (N)	Phosphorus (P)	Potassium (K)
Cattle	0.5	0.3	0.5
Chicken	0.9	0.5	0.8
Horse	0.6	0.3	0.6
Sheep	0.9	0.5	0.8
Pig	0.6	0.5	0.4
Mushroom compost (spent)	1	.5	1

Liquid manure made by filling a small sack with manure and immersing it in a garbage can of water.

The readings are only given as guidelines. The nutrient value of all manures and composts will vary considerably depending upon the amount, quality and type of feed given to the animals. (You will note from the chart that sheep and chicken manures are particularaly high in nutrient value. Care should be taken in their application and the directions on the bag followed carefully.)

Unless you have your own livestock, manure may be purchased from local farmers or mushroom growers. Most manures are low in fertilizer value and can be used in relatively large amounts to improve soil structure. Damage may occur if the manure is too fresh; also weed seed will be brought into the garden. We prefer to "compost" our manure before incorporating it into the soil. The heat generated destroys most of the weed seeds. Manures also provide micronutrients which may be lacking in chemical fertilizers. For city gardeners, obtaining fresh manure is often impractical and a satisfactory solution is to purchase bags of dried manure at garden centres.

All manures are beneficial in maintaining and improving the fertility and tilth of garden soil. However, too much manure will cause rank growth and may contribute to other problems such as delayed flowering, fruiting and poor flavour, plus a greater occurrence of disease problems.

Liquid Manure

All animal manures can be given to plants in liquid form in spring and summer, but not to plants still in the seedling stage. Healthy plants benefit from a boost every two or three weeks, but never apply liquid manure when the soil and roots are dry. Wait until after a rain or watering before fertilizing, but remember not to overfertilize.

Put the animal manure in a sack or an old cloth bag and suspend it in a barrel of water. Allow it to soak for several days, poking the bag occasionally with a stick — the solution should be the colour of weak tea. If it is too strong, dilute it with water before soaking the ground alongside the rows of vegetables. As the liquid is removed from the barrel, replace it with water until the richness is exhausted; the barrel contents will become increasingly clear.

The manure left in the bag can be emptied alongside any vigorously growing crop, such as rhubarb or asparagus.

Compost

Compost is another source of nutrients and organic matter which should be used and understood by all home gardeners. The materials you can put in your compost heap are listed on page 35. The N:P:K ratio of compost varies according to the materials composted. It represents an excellent source of free humus and

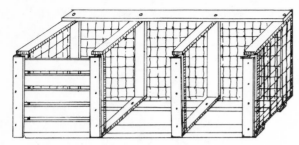

Homemade bins for making compost.

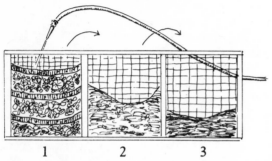

1   2   3

Bin 1: Freshly collected organic debris
Bin 2: Contains materials from previous year
turned from bin 1
Bin 3: Contains ready-to-use compost turned from
bin 2

micronutrients when worked into the ground in spring or fall. The value of a compost heap in every garden large or small cannot be over-estimated. It is simply a matter of collecting and subsequently returning to the soil much of the "goodness" that previous crops depleted.

All healthy garden and organic household waste should be composted. Even if it is not scientifically perfect compost, it will so improve the texture of the soil that this alone will produce better crops. Cooked vegetables are of little value as compost as they lose much of their structure during the cooking process, but may be used in small quantities. Do not use any meat-type materials — they will certainly attract vermin.

In our garden, we try to make composting as simple as possible. The actual "making" of the compost does not have to be a high priority, but collecting all the refuse does. The care which the compost heap gets during the season depends on a variety of factors. If the season is extremely hot, there is no more exhausting job than turning compost. This is one of the tasks which we usually put off until the cooler fall weather. Some seasons the compost heap gets far more attention than others. I prefer to compost leaves separately because I like to have leaf mold on hand to use when re-potting plants or adding to the soil mix for potting some transplants.

In every garden there should be an area allotted for compost. In a large garden like ours, this is relatively easy. The compost heap is contained in a temporary enclosure of wire and boards out of sight behind a hedge. Ours does not have to look neat and tidy all the time, but in a city garden this aspect may have to be considered.

For a city garden lot a "compost bin" can be purchased at a garden centre. It takes up very little space, has a neat appearance and, in addition, will not attract flies, dogs or rodents. My friends who have plastic compost bins tell me that it is surprising how much these bins hold.

Our compost heap is usually enclosed in old wire netting or snow fencing. Throughout the season we throw in all the refuse, adding soil between the layers. It is most important that air can circulate through the heap to keep the beneficial bacteria active and prevent the "anaerobic" bacteria from forming and caus-ing the often objectionable odour. Each heap contains one season's refuse. The following season we use the freshest heap of compost on which to grow our cantaloupe and squash. After two years the compost is well-rotted and returned to the garden.

The "pit" method can be used in large or small gardens. You simply dig a hole or pit in the ground into which you dump all compost-able materials. The depth of the pit depends to a certain extent on the depth of the top soil in your garden. An area of about 3 feet by 3 feet is sufficient for most city gardens. Do not dig out too much subsoil — this will later be incorpo-rated in your compost. The soil you remove

CONTENTS OF THE COMPOST HEAP

Leaves	Manure
Garden waste — weeds	Wood chips
Grass clippings	Hay — spoiled
Household vegetable and	Straw
fruit scraps	Earth
Coffee grounds	Newspaper —
Tea leaves	crumpled
Sawdust	Rags — shredded
Egg shells	

WHAT TO AVOID IN THE COMPOST HEAP

Diseased garden waste	Glass
Plastics	Meat
Synthetic materials	Fat
Metal	

will become the walls around your pit and will be added in layers to the refuse as the pit is filled up. Eventually, all the soil from the walls is added to the refuse and the height of the compost will be two or three feet above soil level. Try to keep the centre of the compost heap lower than the sides to retain all moisture possible. Apply a sprinkling of ammonium sulphate, a high nitrogen fertilizer or soot to each layer, together with a little ground limestone. These assist the rotting-down process and increase the nutrient value of the mass.

To allow for better seepage, try to punch a few holes with a pointed stick throughout the heap. Also, it may be necessary to water the compost heap if there is not sufficient rainfall. Do not saturate because this slows down the decomposition process and leaches away valuable nutrients. This mass of compost will take a couple of years to rot, but once the pit is dug there is relatively little work until the compost is ready to be dug in to the garden. This organic matter is of such value for enriching the soil that it more than repays the time and trouble taken.

The "bin" system makes excellent quality compost but requires some labour. The technique for making the compost is identical to the pit method, but first the bins must be very strongly built. Old lumber can be used and the size will depend on whatever space is needed to accommodate the amount of refuse your garden will produce. The bins will look like three small stalls and the partitions between them should be of such a height that it is easy to move or turn the contents of one bin into the bin beside it. To accelerate the breakdown of the materials, you should always move compost; the micro-organisms in the fertile soil need both moisture and air. There are a number of commercial compost activators on the market, but as I have never used any of them I cannot give a personal opinion. (I consider them an unnecessary expense.)

You can speed up the breakdown of organic wastes by using a specially designed rotating drum made of galvanized steel which revolves on a cradle and is turned manually once a day by the use of a crank handle. It is filled and emptied through a detachable door and is designed to allow oxygen-consuming bacteria to

Emptying the contents of the compost drum.

The temporary enclosure has been removed from a two-year-old compost heap to allow easy access.

hasten the decomposition process. It is our experience that during warm weather drum composting takes two to three weeks, but in cold weather considerably longer.

The economic value of a drum composter will depend largely on the length of the warm season in your particular area. Composter drums are available in several sizes, the small ones being suitable for use indoors. They are odourless and do not attract flies or vermin, and are ideally suited to city and suburban gardens.

Green Manure

Another method of putting humus and nutrients into the soil is called "green manuring," a term describing the practice of growing certain grasses and legumes especially for turning into the soil to improve the tilth and fertility. This method of improving the soil has been practised for centuries, but fell into disuse when chemical fertilizers became cheap and easily obtainable.

In colder, northern areas green manure crops are usually seeded in the spring or summer and dug in before going to seed. In warmer areas green manure crops may be seeded in the summer or fall and turned under in the spring.

I would suggest to anyone planning to improve their garden soil with green manure that

they inquire from the local agricultural representative as to which crops are recommended for their location and soil condition. The legumes or clovers are generally considered the best because of their ability to add nitrogen to the soil. A mixture is often recommended.

I would like to add that legumes seed that has been inoculated with nitrogen-fixing bacteria can be of particular benefit. These legumes take nitrogen from the air and when used as green manure crops will incorporate this valuable element into the soil at the same time. This practice is excellent for gardeners with sufficient space to permit them to rotate their plot, placing one-quarter or one-third in green manure each season. Green manure is a time-honoured method of improving the soil.

The Importance of Micronutrients

We have now discussed common methods of applying nutrients to the soil and particularly organic nutrient replacement. The object of manuring or composting the ground is to replace some of the plant food, especially the micronutrients, that all crops need in very

Spreading well-rotted compost in the fall on areas of the garden after crops have been harvested.

minute amounts and extract from the soil. If they are not available, the plants may be stunted or starved, whereas an excess of some can be toxic.

Micronutrients are not generally a problem to the average home gardener who regularly uses manure, compost and/or green manure crops. However, constant crop production without such additions will eventually cause micronutrient deficiencies. It is next to impossible for any gardener, especially a home gardener, to know whether micronutrients are lacking in the soil unless he were to have a complete soil analysis.

If the vegetables in the garden are not growing healthily, and the reason not readily apparent, a nutrient deficiency in the soil may well be the cause. Many of the symptoms of these deficiencies are very similar, and it is *only* through a professional soil analysis that the situation can be remedied. As this is an area so often overlooked, I have listed the symptoms of *specific* micronutrient deficiencies. If these occur, they can be corrected by the application of sprays or by soil treatment.

Boron This is perhaps the micronutrient most commonly deficient among garden vegetables. Boron deficiency causes cracked stalks of celery and discoloured patches on cauliflower heads. It is also important to apples (Cork disease), broccoli (Brown rot), cabbage, beets (Heart rot), tomatoes and turnips (Brown heart), though boron deficiency may occur in many plants and often is confused with other problems. (Our garden had a boron deficiency, which we have remedied. We are now able to produce excellent celery.)

Borax, available in supermarkets, drug stores or garden centres, can be applied to the soil at the rate of one tablespoon per 100 feet of row. Only a small excess of boron is toxic to several plants, especially beans and cucumbers, so the borax must be applied very evenly. It may be thoroughly mixed with fertilizer or with sand before spreading along the row. Raking is an additional help to even distribution. It

can also be applied in a liquid solution. For heavy clay soils the amount of borax applied may be increased up to 3 tablespoons per 100 feet of row. In general, because of possible toxicity, it is safer not to add boron to a soil that has received frequent application of manure or compost.

Emergency spray treatment can be effective if the symptoms are recognized very early in the crop year. Garden centres have preparations for this purpose; since compositions of various boron preparations differ, follow the directions on the label.

Iron Iron deficiency frequently causes chlorosis (yellowing), especially in the tissue between the veins of young leaves. Again, a professional soil analysis is usually the only certain means of accurately identifying the problem. Various iron preparations are sold under differing trade names. Some are appropriate for application to the soil, some as foliar sprays. Each should be used as specified on the label.

Magnesium Plants growing in a magnesium-deficient soil are usually a pale greenish-yellow, although in some plants the leaves may be purplish-red with green veins. Magnesium deficiencies rarely appear, except in soils receiving very little organic matter. Where the pH reading indicates liming is required, available magnesium can be assured over a long period by using dolomite limestone. A simple short-term treatment can be given by adding magnesium sulphate (Epsom salts) as a soil treatment applied as described for boron. The rate should be a ½ cup per 100 square feet for sandy soils, or 1½ cups for clay soils. My method is to add the Epsom salts to a barrel of water and soak the rows of plants.

Sulphur When sulphur is deficient in the soil the plants are often yellowish and stunted. This is seldom a problem, as sufficient sulphur is usually dropped by rain.

Molybdenum This micronutrient is rarely deficient in soils that contain organic matter. Molybdenum seems to be involved primarily in the regulation of various physiological activities within the plant, as are manganese, zinc and copper.

Manganese   To treat the chlorosis (yellowing) that suggests a manganese deficiency, spray with a one percent solution of manganese sulphate or apply to the soil manganese sulphate at the rate of one tablespoon per 100 square feet of soil.

Zinc   Zinc is rarely deficient in gardens of eastern United States and Canada, although it has occasionally occurred in sweet corn and in wet soils. Treatment is as for manganese deficiency, but using zinc sulphate.

Copper   Copper deficiencies are also unusual except in peat soils newly placed in cultivation, or in sandy soils that have been subject to leaching. The crops grown in these soils display similar symptoms to those of iron deficiency. You can correct this by adding 2 to 4 tablespoons of copper sulphate to peat soil or 1½ teaspoons to sandy soil for 100 square feet of garden.

A warning note: It might seem to be much simpler to use a "shotgun" approach in supplying micronutrients. Indeed, preparations have been marketed which do include all of the micronutrients mentioned above. But persistent addition of all of them to soils suitable for vegetables could lead to an imbalance or excess causing toxic effects. Advice from experts in any locality where deficiencies are encountered is preferable to guessing.

Earthworms

I have always associated earthworms with good soil conditions. Somehow, where there were plenty of worms the soil was bound to be good for growing things. My research has led me to understand that earthworms are seldom present in soils that are not rich in humus—but soil which is devoid of earthworms is not necessarily low in nutrients.

In temperate climates earthworms may burrow to a depth of 6 or 8 feet below the surface of the soil, aerating the soil and allowing for better drainage. Their burrows also make it easier for the roots of plants to penetrate the soil.

Earthworms swallow soil as they burrow and deposit it in casts on the surface of the ground. Only the humus encountered in the soil is used as food. In land with a healthy worm population, many tons of valuable nitrogenous fertilizer per acre can be brought to the surface annually.

A high organic content in the soil automatically encourages an increase in the earthworm population. The humus makes for better soil aeration, and the combined benefits of organic matter and earthworms increases the soil fertility.

Certain disease-producing bacteria only thrive in soil conditions where there is no oxygen. With a healthy earthworm population soil conditions remain aerobic, consequently keeping the undesirable bacteria under control.

Worms are bisexual and all produce egg capsules which must be fertilized by another worm. The eggs are laid in sacs beneath the surface of the soil. Mating takes place twice a year, but in rich soil it can be more frequent. To increase the worm population in your soil, after buying them establish "breeding boxes" containing kitchen garbage, manure and green matter. Personally, I rely on keeping the garden soil amply supplied with well-rotted manure and compost. This keeps the worm population happy.

Earthworms are very sensitive to chemicals, so use the latter selectively to maintain the benefit of a thriving worm population.

So what type of soil do you have in your garden? Is it *really* hopeless? Probably not. A systematic approach to building up the soil to a good level of humus and nutrient content and then maintaining it is not an impossible task. But I should point out that it is not a "one-time" project either, and once the soil is understood and has become productive, the upkeep becomes essential if the garden is to *continue* to be productive.

How Plants Grow

A plant is a carefully balanced mechanism which requires specific physical and chemical conditions to keep it healthy and functioning correctly. Each part of a plant plays an individual role and contributes to its overall development, which we call growth. The process of growth is controlled by *photosynthesis*, which in the presence of light is the manufacture of carbon-containing compounds which may be used by the plant. This process requires light, carbon dioxide and water and occurs in all green-pigmented living tissue.

By a process which we call *osmosis*, roots absorb water and nutrients which are transported to the stems and leaves by conducting vessels called *xylem* (see page 40 for illustration.) Manufactured compounds are then moved within the plants by the *phloem*, which are also conducting tissues.

The leaf is the work centre of the plant with its continuous manufacture of compounds and their subsequent distribution within the plant for storage or use in the many biochemical processes which occur. It is designed to absorb light, exchange gases of oxygen and carbon dioxide, release excess moisture, and control excessive moisture loss during periods of stress such as drought. These processes take place in the leaf through structures called *stomata*, or "pores." The opening and closing of the pores is controlled by the guard cells and is dependent on environmental conditions. As their name implies, they are protective mechanisms that prevent excessive stress on the plant during unfavourable weather conditions.

The green pigment within the leaves and some stems is *chlorophyll*, an essential requirement of photosynthesis. Chlorophyll contains carbon, hydrogen and oxygen, as well as nitrogen and magnesium. Deficiencies of various mineral elements inhibit chlorophyll synthesis and cause the development of *chlorosis* (yellowing). In the absence of normal amounts of chlorophyll, the upper leaves quickly become yellow and photosynthesis is reduced.

The utilization of the manufactured carbon-containing compounds (sugars) is called *respiration*, which takes place at all times within the plant, but the rate varies with temperature. The higher the temperature, the more rapid the rate. Oxygen is essential for respiration, which yields carbon dioxide, water and energy. The energy may be released as heat or as chemical energy which is important in causing cell division, absorption of minerals, movement of nutrients and the synthesis of amino acids and proteins. Photosynthesis and respiration are controlled by favourable environmental conditions. Good soil drainage and aeration, sufficient nutrients of the correct kinds, optimum soil moisture and an abundance of sunlight result in growth.

The plant roots absorb nutrients primarily in a soluble form. Commercial fertilizers are usually water soluble, at least in part, and are therefore immediately utilized. Organic fertilizers are not soluble and must first be broken down by soil micro-organisms. The chemical minerals will then be released and become soluble in water. By the time the minerals reach the roots, both the manufactured (synthetic) and the organic fertilizers are identical.

The acidity or pH of soil plays an important role in the availability of nutrients as it affects the activity of the micro-organisms. Most minerals, if present in the soil, are available to the plants when the pH is in the 6 to 6.8 range. When a soil analysis has been made for a home vegetable garden, the recommendations are based on bringing the pH to an optimum level.

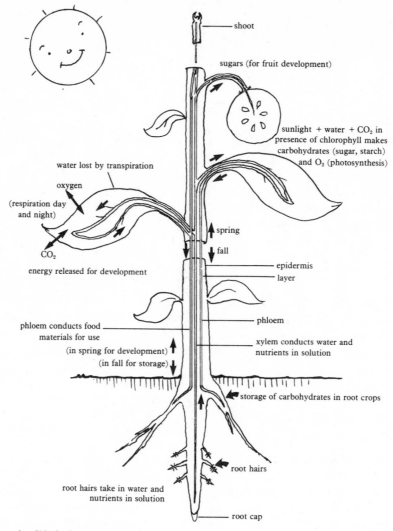

shoot

sugars (for fruit development)

sunlight + water + CO$_2$ in presence of chlorophyll makes carbohydrates (sugar, starch) and O$_2$ (photosynthesis)

water lost by transpiration

oxygen

(respiration day and night)

CO$_2$

energy released for development

spring

fall

epidermis
layer

phloem conducts food materials for use

(in spring for development)

(in fall for storage)

phloem

xylem conducts water and nutrients in solution

storage of carbohydrates in root crops

root hairs

root hairs take in water and nutrients in solution

root cap

Diagram showing simplified plant processes.

A plant grows as a result of an increase in size or number of cells. Cell elongation takes place in many parts of the plant; cell division, or *mitosis*, occurs in certain areas called *meristems*, the most important being the shoot, root tips, lateral buds and the cambium layer. These meristematic tissues are very delicate and sensitive to physical damage, pests and diseases. Stress conditions, which may result in an imbalance or disruption of cell growth, can cause increased vulnerability to disease.

Thickening of stems is the result of the continuously accumulating xylem tissue. The cambium layer surrounding the xylem is increasing by cell division as the stems develop. This can be seen on woody perennials such as the stump of a tree as annual growth rings. Certain cells eventually die but they are continually replaced. In vegetable plants that are growing for only one season, this process is not apparent, whereas in woody plants such as trees and shrubs these cells become support tissue.

Planning Your Vegetable Garden

Working Plan

The size of your plot will govern the type and quantity of crops that can be grown, whether annual or perennial. Before ordering seed, I make a rough diagram marking the rows at 18-inch intervals. This is the standard distance between crops such as carrots, beets and lettuce. For larger plants like tomatoes and cabbage the rows can be double spaced. Vine crops, like cucumbers, need plenty of room and in small gardens a bush variety should be grown.

The rows are best when they run north to south, but this is not essential if all the crops grown are of the same height. Tall crops such as pole beans or corn should be planted at the north side of the garden. Vegetables need plenty of sun, and care must be taken to make sure taller vegetables do not shade the smaller ones.

I like to make two plans for the garden for each season: the first one shows the early crops; the second shows the main and late crops. The first example I give here is only a guide to help beginners get started. No two garden plots are the same, and the vegetable preferences of individuals vary greatly. The second plan is our garden. It measures 140 feet by 40 feet, and provides enough vegetables for a family of six for a year. We do not grow a main crop of potatoes, only the early crop.

This plan for a 9 by 12 foot garden should provide a family of four with fresh salad vegetables during the summer months.

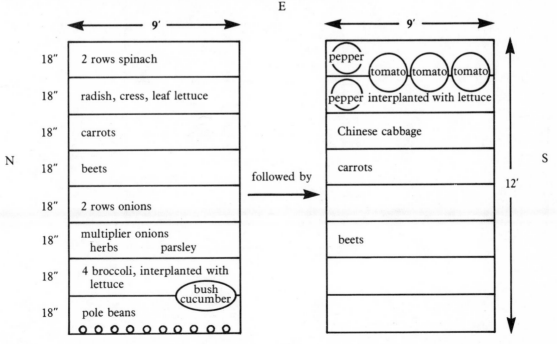

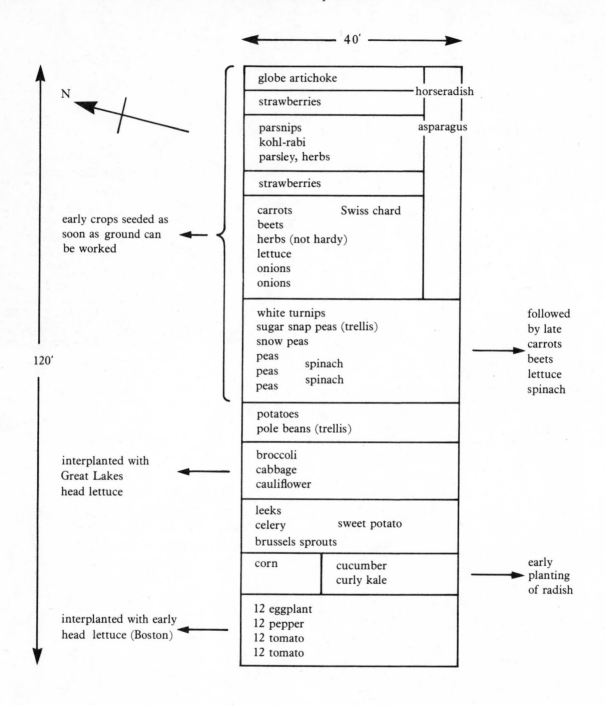

Plan of our vegetable garden for the season during which most of the photos in this book were taken. Our squash, melons, Jerusalem artichokes, rhubarb and raspberries are in another part of the garden.

Intercropping

You can make full use of the entire plot by intercropping. Certain small fast-growing plants such as cress, lettuce, radish and spinach can conveniently be grown in rows between slower-growing larger vegetables such as cabbages, tomatoes or peppers. The fast-growing plants will be harvested before the slow growers are ready to occupy the full space allotted to them.

Other methods of intercropping include planting rows of small fast crops like radishes between rows of onions or peas, or planting fast and slow growers alternately in the same row. Whichever method is used, care must be taken not to overcrowd.

Making intensive use of a small garden by intercropping not only between plants but also between rows. The lettuce (in wire cages — a protection against rabbits) planted between the cabbage will be harvested first. The rows of early onions will be harvested in the summer, leaving ample space for the cabbage.

Lettuce planted between cabbages are ready for harvest now. Note space left between plants will allow for cabbages to mature.

Succession Planting

Succession planting is the term used when a second crop is planted to replace an early crop that has been harvested. This is often practised in small gardens where full use is made of the ground all season. With such intensive use, take particular care to ensure that the soil is enriched with humus and provided with sufficient nutrients. An extra application of fertilizer may be required.

An example of succession planting is an early crop of radish, spinach, cress, leaf lettuce, white turnips, multiplier onions, peas, or kohl-rabi, which may be followed by beans, beets, carrots, late cabbage, cauliflower, broccoli or Chinese cabbage.

It is obvious that in any plot used so intensively it would be hard to maintain a sound crop-rotation plan. Therefore, take great care

Lazy Man's Garden

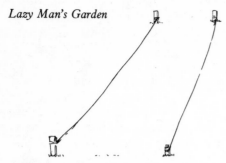

1: *Mark out proposed site with cord.*

2: *Lift sod around area.*

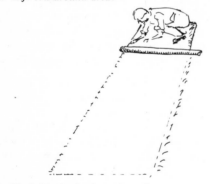

3: *Tuck black plastic under sod.*

4: *Cut holes out of plastic using bulb planter and lift out earth below.*

to avoid the spread of disease by removing any unhealthy plants from the garden and burning or throwing them in the garbage — never in the compost heap.

The Lazy Man's Garden

Many folks would like to have a vegetable plot, but when faced with the task of preparing an area that may now be meadow or lawn, they have second thoughts. No need! A few hours of light work and you'll be ready to plant.

Select an area that gets plenty of sunshine and is free of roots from large trees and shrubs. Be sure it does not get waterlogged during rain storms. A gentle slope is just fine but avoid too steep a location. Where growth is lush and healthy, the topsoil will be deep and the crops so much the better.

The only additional purchase you have to make in preparing the plot is black plastic, which has the desired property of excluding all light and is sold in various widths. When spread over the ground, it prevents growth under the plastic. To allow for tuck-in, it is convenient to make the width of your plot 6 inches narrower than the width of plastic which you select. As for length, it can be as long as you wish. If you prefer a square area, make two plots with a walk of mowed grass dividing them.

Using stakes and your garden line, measure out two parallel lines 6 inches narrower than the plastic. With a spade, cut into the sod about 3 inches deep all round the lines. Turn the edge of the sod away from the plot. Next, get the garden hose and soak the plot thoroughly. Now you are ready to lay the plastic. Start at one end, tucking the plastic under the sod as you return the sod to its original position. You will end up with a film of plastic stretched tightly over the grass and well secured at the edges. The three inches of plastic buried around the plot prevents the lawn encroaching and keeps the plastic sheet from being undermined by the wind. The grass under the plastic will decompose very rapidly, adding nutrients and organic matter to the soil.

The sooner this plastic can be put down in the spring, the better.

In my experience, this garden technique is best suited to transplants. Once weather conditions are ready for transplanting, use a bulb-planter or sharp trowel to pierce through the plastic and remove clods of sod at intervals appropriate for the crop. An "x-cut" 2 inches long can be made in the plastic first to allow easier access to the sod below.

You will now have small holes in the sod in which to set the transplants. It is best if the roots of the seedlings have a good quantity of soil around them. You may have to add a little more top soil to fill each hole.

During the season water and apply liquid fertilizer through the holes in which the plants are growing. Take care not to damage the plant roots with too strong a flow from the hose. Push the nozzle under the plastic and slowly soak the area around the plants. Do not waterlog the bed.

In the fall after the crops have been harvested, you may wish to remove the plastic. The ground underneath is easy to dig, and can be prepared as a conventional garden plot for the next spring. The plastic can be salvaged and re-used; it will have the holes already cut for planting. When it is properly laid down, it is not unsightly and can remain in place for several years before deteriorating.

Crop Rotation

In several sections of this book I refer to the importance of crop rotation. There are two purposes in crop rotation: plant nutrition and control of pests and diseases. Related plants usually prefer similar soil types and remove nutrients from the soil in similar proportions. Planting of related plants such as Brussels sprouts, broccoli, cauliflower or cabbage in the same part of the garden year after year tends to make that soil deficient in the nutrients that the Brassicas have used up. As soon as any one of the essential nutrients is severely deficient, plant growth will be very poor. But if crop rotation is practised so that the same crop family is not planted in the same place for a period of, say, three years, there should be little or no nutrient deficiencies. That is the nutritional purpose of crop rotation. As a example of this, while Brassicas require a considerable quantity of nitrogen, they need very little potash; the reverse is true of beets and potatoes. Furthermore, Brassicas do not send their roots down very far into the soil, which means that plant foods deep down are untouched. This plant food is available for deep-rooted crops like parsnips and carrots which may follow on.

Legumes (peas and beans) pack nitrogen into the soil; Brassicas require plenty of nitrogen. Logically, then, Brassicas should follow legumes. This aspect of crop rotation has been neglected in recent years, but with the sharp increases in commercial fertilizer prices, it may again become recognized.

Better Disease Control

Crop rotation helps control pests and diseases that overwinter in the soil. In general, members of each plant family are susceptible to the same ailments. For example, club root (a fungus disease) in Cruciferae (the cabbage family) will not attack any other family, and if the host plant for club root is rotated to a different section of the garden, there will be nothing for the fungus to feed on.

It follows that if you plant the same family year after year in the same location there will be a build up of soil-borne diseases destructive to that family. This is why I stress the importance of knowing to which family each vegetable belongs.

Based on the above, here is a simple example of a crop rotation plan

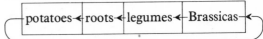

potatoes ◄ roots ◄ legumes ◄ Brassicas ◄

To help you develop your own crop rotation plan, in the section dealing with individual vegetables I have grouped the vegetables in families rather than dealing with them in alphabetical order.

The Naming of Plants

You can grow an excellent garden without knowing the correct names of plants in English, let alone in Latin, but most gardeners run into complicated nomenclatures in pamphlets and seed catalogues. I think, then, that you will find this section informative and helpful.

Since the beginning of time, it has been one of man's characteristics to name things and try to arrange them into an orderly fashion. (Even Noah had the members of the animal kingdom named and grouped into orderly pairs for their forty-day voyage.)

Animals and plants must have proper names which allow us to distinguish between the two major living kingdoms. Similarly, because of the great number of species involved, a nomenclature is needed which will ensure distinctions within the individual kingdoms.

The system for the naming of plants, which has been developed and improved over the years, is a universally accepted one; it encompasses both identification and classification. By the particular name given to a plant, it is possible to identify the group to which it belongs. This is helpful, as each group possesses unique characteristics which separate it from the many other groups. Similarly, it must be possible to classify plants into a particular level within the kingdom structure. This classification would depend on the similarities in the plants' appearances and their genetic relationships.

When a new plant is developed or discovered, it is given a specific botanical name. This name, which by international agreement is in Latin, immediately classifies and identifies it in such a way that botanists who have not even seen it can visualize its characteristics.

One can only imagine the great difficulty and complexity involved in devising a system of rules for naming all the plants in the world.

In the beginning they were arranged into groups by their appearance; the ones with similar features were classed together. The system has developed into a more natural and precise one, using characteristics other than just physical appearance alone. With modern science and technology, we can delve into the actual evolution and gene make-up of the plant. This means that when comparing plant to plant, they can be even more closely grouped together.

To help us understand the many levels within the plant kingdom, imagine a large area of land, a country. Most countries are divided into various major states, divisions or provinces. Within the provinces we find distinct regions in which people have more in common among themselves than they do with those in neighbouring territories. And furthermore, groups are formed within the regions, namely, cities or even smaller, more individual communities. Obviously, the people living in a town have more in common with those in their community than with the people living throughout the larger territory.

The same idea applies to plants. At the top level it is customary to divide all plants into divisions, or phyla. How they reproduce, how their leaves develop, how they conduct water and food are all important but general factors which help to separate plants into these divisions. The divisions that concern us most as gardeners are the bacteria and fungus phyla (Thallophyta) which house all of the garden diseases, and the seed-bearing plant phyla (Spermatophyta) which includes our garden vegetables. All divisions end in "phyta" such as Bryophyta, which we know as mosses and liverworts, and Pteridophyta which includes ferns and other related plants. If we look more selectively at the Spermatophyta division (more commonly referred to as the seed-bearing division), we can see how this major phyla is divided into increasingly specific units.

The first two major subdivisions of this phyla are Gymnospermae and Angiospermae. Plants are placed into either of these subdivisions because they have more characteristics in common with the members of that subdivision than with the plants in the other subdivision. Gymnosperms are plants that have unprotected or naked seeds like the ones you find on a cone scale. All of the coniferous trees are in this subdivision. The Angiosperms, or flowering plants, are the ones with seeds that are protected by a structure or ovary such as a green pepper, orange or apple. In other words, all of our fruit and vegetable crops are in this group.

The flowering plants, in turn, are divided into two classes, which are now beginning to become more scientifically selected as to their common characteristics. For example, if the protected seed, when it begins this development, has one embryonic leaf form, it is classed as a Monocotyledonae (onions, lilies). On the other hand, plants whose seeds form two embryonic leaves (peanut, bean) are called Dicotyledonae. You may have heard these classes referred to by their more common abbreviated names, monocot and dicot.

And so the kingdom continues to be divided, always drawing finer and finer distinctions between plants. Classes divide into subclasses, and in turn into orders, families, genera, species, varieties and cultivars.

For example, cultivars of one variety are much more closely related to each other, genetically and by appearance, than are those members of a whole order.

Gardeners may be forgiven for being confused over the naming of plants in general, as many of them even have several different common names. To be accurate and correct, use the Latin botanical name.

A common practice among commercial growers and seed catalogues is to call a cultivar a "variety." Botanically this is incorrect. Government publications use correct botanical names, but in this book I am occasionally showing both where there might be fear of confusion.

The following family tree shows the "plant kingdom." Don't worry if you can't remember all the names in it. Since horticulture has a universal language, I believe that this information will be useful to gardeners who wish to broaden their interest and knowledge.

Plant Kingdom

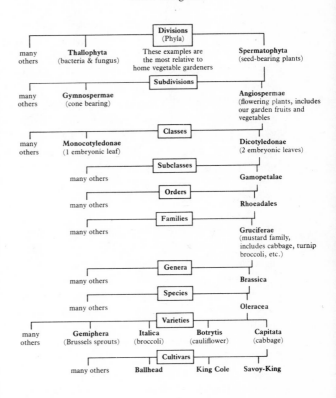

Hardiness of Plants

There are two main categories of garden vegetables: perennials and annuals. The perennials occupy a permanent position in the garden, while the annuals are started from seed each year. In our climate some perennials such as globe artichokes and certain herbs are treated as annuals. Hardy perennials, for example rhubarb and asparagus, once established in a garden can go on growing for many years. The principal factors restricting their vigorous growth are poor soil conditions, lack of moisture, and damage by wind and sun when newly planted. Also, their growth can be arrested if harvested before they have become thoroughly established. In general, hardy perennials can stand the severe frosts of our winters, although they generally respond better to mulching or heavy snow coverage.

Not all annuals can be seeded directly in the garden in early spring because not all species are equally hardy. These are called transplants. Some annuals are tolerant to severe frosts, others to moderate frosts. Some prefer cool growing weather, while others thrive in hot conditions and are unable to withstand even the slightest frost. With these factors in mind, planting vegetables and fruits has to be carefully timed to avoid early season set-backs. The following chart will serve as a guide. (Notice that certain plants are seeded directly into the garden, but the transplants that have been raised under controlled climatic conditions during the preceding weeks are set out as young plants.)

HARDY PERENNIALS

Asparagus	Sea-kale
Raspberries	Strawberries
Currants	Jerusalem artichoke
Rhubarb	Some herbs

All hardy perennials need a permanent place in the garden. When planting, bear in mind that they can remain where planted for many years.

FROST-HARDY ANNUALS

Transplants	Direct Seeding
Broccoli	Beets
Brussels sprouts	Carrots
Cabbage	Chicory
Cauliflower	Cress
Chinese cabbage	Kale
Kale	Kohl-rabi
Kohl-rabi	Lettuce (leaf)
Lettuce (head)	Mustard
Onions	Onion Seed
	Onion Sets
	Parsley
	Peas
	Radish
	Rutabaga
	Spinach
	Turnip
	Some Herbs

Hardy vegetables are planted as soon as the ground can be prepared. With us this is the end of April or early May. In my garden I seed small quantities of the early crops such as beets, carrots and lettuce. I re-seed successive crops to ensure a fresh supply throughout the season. Details are discussed under the description of individual vegetables.

SEMI-HARDY VEGETABLES

Transplants	*Direct Seeding*
Globe artichoke	Chard
Leeks	Celery
	Chinese cabbage
	Endive
	Lettuce (head)
	Mustard
	Parsnips
	Potatoes

Semi-hardy vegetables can be planted two to three weeks before the last frost is expected. I start seeding around the second week in May. Often, if the potato shoots are killed to ground level by frost, there will still be enough material left in the tuber for it to send out new growth and quickly regain its vigour. Possible frost damage may be prevented by mulching.

FROST-TENDER VEGETABLES

Transplants	*Direct Seeding*
Eggplant	Beans
Peppers	Cucumbers
Tomatoes	Muskmelons
Garden huckleberry	Okra
	Pumpkins
	Soybeans
	Squash
	Sweet corn
	Watermelons

Frost-tender vegetables should be planted only after all risk of frost is past. We use May 24th as a guide, but I use my judgement to determine if the soil has become warm enough to assure no set-back. Although one is anxious to get the garden planted out as soon as possible, I have found that, very often, later seeded vegetables grow more rapidly and have a tendency to mature in less time than the earlier seeded ones. When this group is damaged by frost it will not recover and re-seeding will be necessary. The only possible exception is corn.

The preceding classifications may be used to determine the earliest days on which certain vegetables can safely be planted outdoors.

We continue eating the hardy vegetables such as curly kale, broccoli and Brussels sprouts well into the winter. Curly kale (foreground) is the hardiest and will survive hard frosts and snow and has often provided a green vegetable over the Christmas holiday. Parsnips and Jerusalem artichokes also are extremely hardy and can be eaten fresh as long as the ground can be dug.

Purchasing Seeds and Plants

Most experienced gardeners order their vegetable seeds through mail order seed houses. Once you are on a mail order list, the catalogue usually arrives automatically each winter. I receive several catalogues because I order varieties of vegetables that are offered only by certain seed houses. I also like to compare prices and to see what new cultivars or varieties are being offered.

Botanically, the terms cultivars and varieties have different meanings. But, as the difference is unimportant to the home gardener and most seed catalogues refer to varieties where, in fact, they should refer to cultivars, I am using the terms synonymously in this book.

What Is a Hybrid?

A hybrid is a cross between two or more parent plants that are more or less alike. Hybridization is practised by seed growers who specialize in producing new cultivars (varieties) of plants with more vigour, faster growth, disease resistance, and as much as 25% higher yields.

F_1 hybrids (the first generation of a cross) usually produce stronger, better plants and are worth the extra cost. Amateur gardeners will be disappointed if they collect seeds from hybrid plants and expect to obtain identical results the following season. Seedlings will not come true to the hybrid parent. Those interested in learning more about this science should study Mendelian Law and modern books on plant breeding.

Disease-Resistant Seed

When ordering seed, I prefer varieties that are "disease resistant" and where the seed is "treated" with a fungicide. The tiny amount of chemical involved often prevents seed decay and damage by soil-borne diseases. Such conditions are more prevalent early in the spring when the ground is still cold and wet. In our short growing season, several weeks of valuable growing time would be lost by poor germination of the first seeding. Organic gardeners will not agree with using a chemical fungicide, but I feel that, as with many chemicals and drugs, they have their place in our society. However, there is little doubt that such additives should be used only with caution and, in any case, untreated seed is available for the purists. The words "disease resistant" marked on the package mean what they say. They do not state that the plants are immune, only less prone to certain diseases.

Choosing Seeds

Seed catalogues make fascinating reading, and for most of us avid gardeners, many enjoyable winter evenings are spent planning the garden and making decisions regarding the varieties of different crops we plan to grow. For instance, there are over one hundred cultivars of tomatoes from which to choose. The growing habits of each are clearly described in the catalogue, as are the characteristics of other vegetables.

By having the catalogue at home for leisure reading, there is no need to make hasty decisions. You can take days if you wish. I mention this because I consider it to be a great advantage of mail order seed purchases versus store-bought seed. If a gardener only plans to grow a few salad vegetables, this might not be a consideration. For a garden of any size, however, and for those who plan to increase the size of their garden as they gain experience, seed catalogues are invaluable. In addition to information about plants, they contain numerous gardening and cooking tips, as well as a section on garden equipment.

Growing your own vegetables permits you to select varieties of exceptional quality and flavour. The commercial grower is concerned primarily with the durability of the crop during shipping and storage. Avoid varieties recommended as suitable for shipping; they will probably be of a coarser quality.

Another feature to look for in seeds is a variety that will produce a succession of buds and can be harvested over a long period of time. Commercial growers are looking for varieties that will ripen all at the same time to allow for harvesting by mechanical means. Again, these varieties will not have the tender qualities of our home-grown crops, freshly picked for each meal.

Here are some other features to look for in selecting seed:

1. Size of variety when mature;
2. Early or late maturing;
3. Number of days to maturity (after transplanting in garden);
4. Size of fruit;
5. Winter-keeping qualities;
6. Resistance to disease;
7. Untreated seed available for organic gardeners.

I do not intend to give the impression that there is something wrong with seed purchased off racks. Excellent seed is available in garden centres and other stores, but it is important to check that this seed is distributed by reputable seed houses that will guarantee their product. The quality of the seed you plant in your garden will determine, to a certain extent, the quality of the crop produced. If the seed is of poor quality, no matter how good your cultural standards, the resulting produce will be poor.

Gardeners who want to try unusual crops will find that many Chinese, Italian or other ethnic stores carry packages of vegetables and herb seed unavailable elsewhere, usually of excellent quality. I have visited both Chinese and Italian homes and seen superb gardens thickly planted with vegetables unknown to most North Americans.

Most gardeners do not use all the seed in every package every season. The chart on the following page shows the length of time seed can be kept when properly stored.

Purchasing Transplants

Transplants of tomatoes, peppers, eggplant, leeks, celery, Brassicas, and many other vegetables are available in garden centres and from many market gardeners. The novice gardener should be aware that the variety of each plant should be on the label so that he can determine the ultimate size and shape of the fruit or vegetable. For example, Tiny Tim tomatoes are small plants, suitable for hanging baskets, whereas Sweet 100 grows into a large bush abour four feet tall. The fruit on both is the same size.

If you have a seed catalogue, take it along for reference. Otherwise, ask at the nursery for information about the various varieties. Check the plants carefully for signs of stress, disease or insects. If they are not perfectly healthy, do not risk bringing problems into your garden.

Purchasing Plants

Nursery stock of strawberries, raspberries and asparagus is available at garden centres, nursery gardens and through nursery garden catalogues. Always deal with a reputable firm which can guarantee that the stock it is selling you was inspected by a government official during the growing season and certified as disease free. If no appropriate label is attached to the plants, it would be wise to inquire.

When we first moved to the farm we were given different varieties of raspberries by several friends. By accepting these (most gratefully), we introduced a mosaic leaf virus to the garden. The entire raspberry patch had to be dug up and burned, and no raspberries planted in that area for three years. This experience has taught us to be cautious when bringing any new plants into the garden.

GERMINATION AND LONGEVITY OF SEEDS

Crop	T = Transplant D = Direct seeding	Germination Time (Days)	Average Longevity in Years
Beans	D	6–14	3
Beets	D	8–10	5
Broccoli	T	3–10	5
Cabbage	T	4–10	5
Cantaloupe	T–D	8–10	5
Carrot	D	10–17	4
Cauliflower	T	4–10	5
Celeriac	T	10–21	5
Celery	T	10–21	5
Corn	D	6–10	1
Cress	D	2–4	5
Cucumber	D	6–10	5
Eggplant	T	7–14	5
Garden huckleberry	T	5–15	5
Kale	T	3–9	5
Kohl-rabi	T	3–9	5
Leek	T	8–10	2
Lettuce	D	4–8	5
Muskmelon	T–D	4–8	5
Okra	D	10–15	2
Onion	T	7–12	2
Parsley	D	14–28	2
Parsnip	D	15–25	2
Peas	D	6–15	3
Pepper	T	10–20	4
Pumpkin	D	6–10	5
Radish	D	3–10	5
Spinach	D	6–14	5
Squash (winter)	T–D	6–10	5
Swiss chard	D	7–10	5
Tomato	T	6–14	4
Turnip	D	3–10	5
Zucchini	D	3–12	5

Note: Keep seed in an air-tight container in a cool, dry place. Test for germination before planting. Test old seed well ahead of time by counting out a small quantity of seed, planting in growing medium and counting the number that germinate.

Starting the Season Indoors

Growing Transplants

Transplant is the term applied to certain annual plants which need a longer growing season than prevails in your area. A transplant is started from seed either indoors, in a hotframe, in a greenhouse, under lights, or in a sunporch or sunny window long before the outdoor temperature has warmed up sufficiently for the young plants to be set-out. By growing transplants we can extend our growing season by one or two months.

Most experienced gardeners grow their own transplants, but I would recommend that a novice purchase ready-grown plants from a reputable nursery. It is better to start experimenting with transplants after you have gained some practical gardening experience.

The economics of growing transplants should be considered. A small garden where only five or six tomato plants are to be grown does not warrant the purchase of seed and growing medium. On the other hand, the pleasure of growing one's own plants from seed may outweigh economic considerations. I enjoy growing transplants and by doing so am able to select varieties of tomatoes, etc., that are unobtainable as transplants at nursery gardens. Certain vegetables such as globe artichoke may be purchased only as seed through seed catalogues, and therefore growing them yourself is the only way to produce your own crop.

Because I grow my own transplants, I know that from March 15, the date I sow my first seed, until the first week of June, when the last plants are set-out in the garden, I cannot take a holiday. There can be no casual approach to raising these seedlings. A set-back during their early growth may affect the quality of the mature plants. Maybe this is the reason why

purchased transplants sometimed perform poorly — the purchaser has no way of knowing the cause of his poor crop.

The Growing Medium

The growing medium should be sterile and well drained. At no time should the soil be soggy, nor should the seedlings ever be allowed to dry out. A good medium will help avoid these undesirable conditions. Excellent materials are now available through seed catalogues or at garden centres. These include: vermiculite, Pro Mix, Jiffy Mix, Jiffy-7's, fibre pots (to be filled with a soil mix) and many others.

Many of these mixes have no nutrient value, in which case the gardener knows that he must provide a complete fertilizer, added after the plants have developed true leaves. At this point liquid fertilizer should be given at half strength, and the strength gradually increased as the plants grow and are potted-up.

The better-quality mixes have sufficient nutrients to supply the seedling for a few weeks. The package label will state whether nutrients are present and will suggest when feeding should begin.

Ready-made mediums have gained tremendous popularity in recent years. They are labour saving, easy to use and to store, and virtually eliminate the risk of damping-off (see section on starting seeds). Jiffy-7 is the trade name for a compressed, dried peat pellet the size of a checkers pawn. This pellet is enclosed in a nylon mesh and expands about six times when soaked in water, forming a small pot. Jiffy-7's should be left overnight to drain before being seeded.

Experienced gardeners often prefer to make their own growing medium, consisting of:

1 part garden soil (sterilized)
1 part peat moss or leaf mold (sieved)
1 part coarse sand or perlite.

Moisten the peat moss before adding it to the other ingredients.

Sterilizing Soil

Place containers of soil in the oven at 250° to 300° F (121-149°C) for thirty minutes. Use metal pans and cover the soil with tin foil. Allow to cool before using.

or

Put a bushel of soil in a plastic garbage bag. Sprinkle with a solution of 2½ tablespoons of formaldehyde in one cup of water. Close the bag, shake and set aside for three or four days, or until the smell has gone.

Starting the Seeds

Seeds require warm temperatures and moisture for good germination, and sunlight for strong early growth. All gardeners growing seedlings for the first time must be aware of a fungus disease called damping-off, which can wipe out a tray of seedlings virtually overnight. This happens as a result of excessive moisture, poor drainage, fluctuating temperatures and inadequate ventilation. The seedlings topple over and a dark, rotted area can be seen at the soil level, even though the rest of the plant appears to be healthy. There is no hope for recovery. Damping-off can also strike before the seedlings emerge through the soil.

Using seed treated with a protectant is helpful for prevention of damping-off, as is sterilizing soil and growing containers. If any seedlings show evidence of damping-off, the entire crop should be treated immediately with an appropriate fungicide.

I plant three seeds in each Jiffy-7, place them in a container, slip the container into a clear plastic bag and set it in a place where it will have a constant temperature of around 75°-85°F (24°-29°C) until the seeds germinate.

Seeding Jiffy-7 pellets.

Little or no watering should be necessary during this period. Many home gardeners find that the top of their refrigerator provides ideal conditions for the germination of seeds. The constant base heat is just what is required.

Light is not important until the seeds germinate. But immediately the seedlings emerge, the plastic bag must be removed and the seedlings placed in full sunlight or under fluorescent lights. The florescent tube should be kept at a constant distance of about one inch above the tops of the plants.

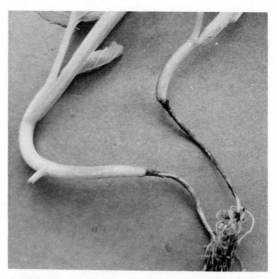

Cauliflower seedlings showing damping-off symptoms.

From now on the seedlings should be grown with day-time temperatures of 70°-75°F (21°-24°C) and a night-time temperature of 60°-65°F (15°-18°C). Twelve hours of light are essential for strong growth. When seedlings do not receive sufficient light, they will become spindly and weak. For another technique, see the section on mini-greenhouses.

When the seedlings are about three inches tall and have developed "true" leaves, snip away all but the strongest plant in each pot with scissors. Pulling out seedlings may damage the tender roots of the remaining plant. Never grow more than one plant in a Jiffy-7.

I prefer Jiffy-7's because from the time the seed is planted until the time the plant is set out in the garden, the root system is never disturbed. No "pricking-off" is required, so time is saved. (Pricking-off is a term used by horticulturalists when transplanting seedlings too small to be moved by hand. A penknife or wooden label is used to lift the tiny seedlings from the seed-bed to the flat or pot.)

Some gardeners prefer to sow seeds in small containers either by broadcasting, that is, scattering, or in drills and covering them with no more than half an inch of soil. The depth of covering depends on the size of seed being sown and should be approximately three times the diameter of the seed. The covering for small seeds should be sieved. After seeding, tamp the soil lightly to ensure that the seed comes in contact with the soil. Then lightly water the container before enclosing it in a clear plastic bag. Once germination has taken place, remove the bag immediately and place the seedlings in good light.

Seedlings grown by this method either in vermiculite or other media must be pricked-off after the first true leaf is formed. Take great care not to damage the root system. Tomatoes, peppers and eggplant seem to prefer individual 3-inch pots; Brassicas do well spaced in flats. Only early Brassicas need to be started indoors; the main crop can be seeded in a cold-frame or garden seed-bed.

Both methods produce satisfactory results.

I am sure other old-time gardeners could tell us of many more techniques. My advice to gardeners is, if your method works for you, stick with it.

Sterilizing Containers

All previously used flats, flower pots and other containers should be sterilized to prevent disease lurking in particles of soil remaining in the containers, which could contaminate the seedlings. It is a tedious job and requires scrubbing the containers, rinsing them with a hose and then dipping them in a disinfectant solution, such as Javex. I prefer to do it outdoors; it is a splashy and messy job.

Miniature Greenhouses

There are a variety of miniature greenhouses on the market today. These vary from simple containers with clear dome-shaped covers, to elaborate models with base electrical heat and fluorescent lighting. We have never purchased either, and, instead, find our homemade type serves our needs most satisfactorily.

We use a plastic kitty-litter tray or a styrofoam flat lined with plastic; three 2-foot lengths of wire; and a large plastic bag of the type used by drycleaners. These miniature greenhouses are excellent for propagating seed and getting the seedlings established. Many homes do not have a room with good conditions for plant propagation and free from

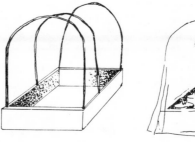

Mini-greenhouse for propagation.

TRANSPLANTS

Vegetable	Where to start seeds	Approximate growing time in weeks before setting out in garden
Eggplant Pepper — Sweet Hot Globe artichoke	Indoors	8-10
Tomato Garden huckleberry Ground cherry	Indoors	Depending on variety 5-8
Leeks Onions Celery Celeriac	Hot-frame or Indoors	8-10
Cabbage — early Cauliflower — early Broccoli Brussels sprouts Red cabbage Kohl-rabi Curly kale	Hot-frame or Indoors	6-8
Squash Melons	Indoors, if early crop desired	3-4

draughts. The climate inside a mini-green-house remains relatively constant and extra light can be given where necessary. It is especially good in very dry houses where the growing medium would be liable to dry out rapidly. When seedlings are well-established, open the bag at one end and allow the air to circulate around the plants. After a few days remove the bag. This will introduce the seedlings to normal household conditions as a step towards facing the outdoor environment.

Frames

Unless seeds are planted directly into the garden, vegetables have to be started under controlled conditions, then subsequently transplanted. Frames are used either to provide controlled conditions for growing seed or as a half-way stage for seedlings between indoors and the garden. Frames can be regarded as a nursery where seedlings are prepared to withstand outdoor conditions in a process generally referred to as "hardening."

Basically, a frame consists of a box, the top of which is made of transparent material such as glass or clear plastic to allow the sun's rays to enter. Seeds or seedlings inside the box can thus be more or less protected from extremes of temperature during their early growth and prior to being planted out when the weather is "set fair."

"Hot-frames" are so named because some form of heating inside the box raises the temperature day and night. Thus, seeds can be planted directly in a hot-frame in early spring when the garden itself is still much too cold. A "cold-frame" merely provides protection from the weather, like an unheated garage, and is ideal for hardening plants originally grown indoors. It is also useful for forcing some early vegetables such as cress, radishes, lettuce and spring onions.

Garden frames can be purchased, but most

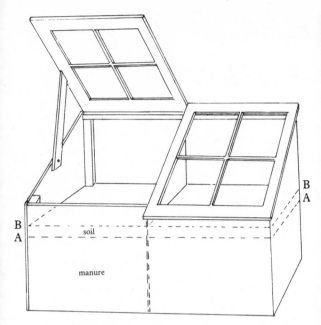

Homemade hot-frame incorporating old storm windows. The box is filled with fresh horse manure (providing heat) to level A-A, and with soil to level B-B.

Hot-frames being filled with fresh, strawy horse manure, topped with a layer of soil. Note in background 45-gallon barrel containing earth is covered to prevent snow entering during the winter.

people make their own, using old storm windows as "lights." These lids, or "lights," as they are sometimes called, can be hinged and should fit the base closely enough to prevent cold drafts damaging the plants.

We purchased one of our frames, containing three windows, very cheaply from the local demolition yard. With a few minor adjustments, permitting the windows to lift up, we have a set of frames that can be moved around the garden as needed.

Frames should face south and be exposed to full sunlight. A wall or fence protecting them from north and east winds is desirable. The "light" should slope towards the south or front of the frame and be approximately 6 inches lower at the front than at the rear. This allows more sunlight to reach the plants and also sheds rain water.

The depth of the frame depends on the purpose which it is going to serve. Generally speaking, deeper frames are more flexible than

On a sunny day ventilation is provided by opening the lids.

This cold-frame has been used as a seed bed. The seedlings have hardened and some already transplanted into the garden.

shallow ones. If flats of small seedlings are set out in a deep frame, they can be placed on raised boards when small and the boards lowered as the seedlings grow. The seedlings should be within a few inches of the glass.

Cold-frames are heated by the sun, but cool off at night. Therefore, tender plants should not be put out in them until all danger of severe frost is past. The plants can be protected from mild frost at night by covering the "lights" with old rugs, sacks or carpeting.

A cold (unheated)-frame can be converted into a hot (heated)-frame by either installing electric cables, or placing the frame on a bed of fresh horse manure. We prefer the latter method. Not only does it produce steady heat

(unaffected by any possible electrical failure), but over a period of several months the manure breaks down and can be worked into the garden in the fall, adding humus and enriching the soil.

The manure should be strawy and not more than one month old. Nowadays it is not always possible to find a stable that beds their horses in straw, often wood shavings are used instead. Such a mixture is acceptable. As you make the hot bed, tread each layer down firmly or beat it with a fork. As the "breakdown" of the manure takes place, the height of the hot bed will be reduced. The manure should be at least 18 inches deep. Watering the fresh manure makes it heat up very quickly.

If the hot-frame is to be used for direct seeding, cover the manure with 4 to 6 inches of soil, the surface of the soil sloping at the same angle as the "light," with approximately 6 inches between the soil and the "light." When the frame is prepared replace the "light," but prop it open to allow steam to escape. In five or six days the seed may be sown. The soil temperature should be 75° to 80°F (23° to 26°C). A soil thermometer permits accurate temperature reading, and eliminates guesswork for a novice gardener, but I have always relied on my own judgement.

Electric cables purchased from garden centres are an alternative method of heating a hot-frame. They are easy to install if the instructions are carefully followed. The cables should be covered with 6 to 9 inches of soil. Prior to seeding, allow 24 hours for the soil to reach a uniform temperature.

When hot-frames are needed in early spring, the garden plot is still frozen. Therefore, you must plan ahead in the fall by storing sufficient soil in a location where it will remain dry and thaw out early. We prepare this soil on a warm day by sieving it into 45-gallon drums which we cover over.

Many gardeners now prefer to use an artificial soil mixture as a substitute for soil. It is costly, but reduces the risk of soil-borne diseases, has good drainage and is free of weeds.

The correct ventilation and watering of the frames is most important: the risk of burning seedlings on a sunny day is just as great as the risk of damage by freezing. Ventilation needs care. On cold, sunny days it may be sufficient to open the lights very slightly. On warm, still days the "lights" may be lifted during the day and replaced at night. During very hot, sunny weather it is often necessary to protect the seedlings from the direct rays of the sun. We use an old bamboo blind, which filters the sunlight perfectly. Newspapers or old sacking are acceptable, but might be blown away by the wind unless firmly anchored.

I place the bamboo on top of the "light," then prop the "light" open with a stick, which allows sufficient ventilation. It does not take long to learn to operate a frame, and my experience has taught me that when I plan to be away all day, I must always place the bamboo on top of the glass before leaving. Dull mornings often turn into hot, sunny afternoons, and if seedlings have a severe set-back from overheating, they never fully recover. Naturally, as the plants become stronger, they can be exposed to more direct sunlight. Before seedlings are set out in the garden, the frame should be kept completely open day and night for about a week.

Water in the morning, taking care to ensure that the moisture has reached below the roots of the plants. In very hot, dry weather it may be necessary to water again at mid-day. Avoid watering at night, as damp night conditions are conducive to fungal infection.

Avoid using icy cold water. I use stored rain water when possible because it is the same temperature as the atmosphere. Tap water with the chill removed is perfectly suitable. Try to avoid using water that has been conditioned by a water softener.

Some local gardeners have successfully grown lettuce in their cold-frames in September for early spring use. The seed germinates and before winter sets in sturdy young plants have formed. These are protected by the "lights" during the winter and re-emerge in the spring to produce a very early crop.

The Greenhouse

A greenhouse is a glorified hot-frame and plays no essential role in the home vegetable garden. We have one because gardening is our hobby, and it enables us to enjoy gardening year round and to grow annuals for the flower garden.

The cost of heating our small greenhouse has risen dramatically over the last few years, even though we insulate it with bubble plastic. I would recommend to anyone considering this large capital outlay that they inquire about the latest technological developments in this field. Many improvements such as double glazing have taken place since we purchased ours.

Hot- and cold-frames, a sunny porch or fluorescent lights are all that are required to grow vegetable transplants.

An unheated sunporch facing south can usually be converted into a greenhouse by mid-March, after the severe cold of the winter is past. Some form of heating is usually required for dull days and cold nights, and a fluorescent or Gro-light is of benefit if seedlings are becoming leggy due to lack of sunlight. Bubble plastic insulation applied to the glass on the inside is a great heat saver and is available from greenhouse suppliers. It is easy to install.

First, mist both the glass and the bubble side of the plastic with a mixture of one tablespoon of glycerine and 24 fluid ounces of hot water. Apply the bubble side to the glass and it will adhere. In the spring remove this insulation and store it for use the following winter. When it is left on the glass all summer, it deteriorates rapidly.

A warm, sunny window can provide ideal conditions when only a few seedlings are being grown. Make sure there are no drafts which could injure young plants.

All germinating seedlings benefit from base heat. Electrically controlled propagating mats are available in various sizes. They take the guesswork out of growing seeds, but most gardeners manage well without them. They are nice to have but not an essential.

After a year or two of experimenting, most home gardeners find a satisfactory way to grow their own transplants. It sounds far more complicated than in fact it is.

Hardening Transplants

Hardening the transplants means gradually introducing the plants to the great outdoors. Start by giving them an hour or two each day, being sure not to set them in a draft. Increase the outdoor time gradually until, weather permitting, the seedlings can remain outdoors day and night. This usually takes one or two weeks.

The ideal method of hardening plants is to set the flats in a cold-frame. This eliminates hauling them in and out of the house. Just put them in the frame and adjust the lid daily according to the weather conditions. If there is any risk of very cool weather or frost, a cover can be thrown over the lid at night. Another idea is to put the flats in the garden cart; it can be pushed outdoors during the day and brought in under cover at night.

The hardening of plants is very important, but with experience a gardener soon learns to judge when his transplants are ready to be set out permanently. Even though plants may look sturdy and ready for the garden while still in a controlled environment, this transition period is critical in preparing them for both the lower temperature and humidity conditions that prevail outdoors. Without the hardening process a great many transplants could be lost.

Watering must be carefully monitored at this period. When outdoor, flats tend to dry out in the wind and sun. Some days they may even need watering twice. A set-back at this stage in growth may cause poor fruiting later on, even if the plants appear to have recovered perfectly.

Overwatering also has an adverse effect. As much damage is caused by allowing plants to become waterlogged as is caused by drying out; the roots of plants need oxygen. Watering should be done early enough in the day to allow quick drying of the soil surface.

A disadvantage of purchasing transplants is that you have no way of telling whether the nursery plants have had any early set-backs. Also, it is often hard to find plants of the variety you wish to grow. Mislabelling of seedlings by growers is by no means uncommon. Many gardeners have been disappointed to find that the crops they eventually harvest bear little relationship to the ones they had been told they were buying.

These flats of transplants started indoors have been brought out to be hardened in a cold-frame.

The Season Outdoors

When spring comes and warmth is in the sun, I have a tremendous urge to start working outdoors. There will still be snow in shaded areas and where drifts have lain, but gradually the ground thaws out, dries and work can commence.

The Spring Clean-up

The first outdoor job that we tackle is a general "clean-up." Although we tidy the grounds in the fall, it is surprising how much debris accumulates during the winter. Our debris is organic, but in city gardens there may be all kinds of litter that has blown in and become covered under a blanket of snow. As well as being good for the garden, this early spring clean-up is cosmetic.

Although you may be anxious to get started on the job, it is very important not to walk on or start work on lawns and grass paths while the frost is still coming out of the ground. Lawns can be severely damaged at this stage, requiring a great deal of unnecessary work to get them back into shape. Wait until they are dry, and your footsteps leave no depression.

Rake the lawn with a grass rake. This removes the dead grass which has often formed a thick mat, and any leaves or debris that may have been missed in the fall. If the growing points of the grass do not receive air and light, they will suffocate and die, leaving bare patches. If winter-kill has caused damage to the lawn, now is the time to re-seed.

Hedges also need to have leaves and grass removed from the base of the bushes. This allows air to circulate and the growth of the hedge to remain thick at ground level. Straggly hedges are badly maintained hedges. Spring hedge care is very important; it is in the spring that all plants make their strongest growth.

Removing Mulch

All plants that have been mulched in the fall for winter protection should have the mulch gradually removed, exposing the growing points of the plants to light and air. The mulch can be spread on the ground around the plants to control weeds. If, subsequently, a heavy frost is anticipated, the mulch can be replaced temporarily. It is late frost that is the most usual cause of damage to strawberry blossoms. In home berry patches we can usually protect against this.

Preparing the Garden Plot

The vegetable garden plot takes much longer than the lawns to reach a workable condition. Do not walk on it if you "sink in." Test the soil by picking up a handful, rolling it into a ball and then "flicking" it with your finger. If the soil disintegrates like breadcrumbs, it is ready to work. If it breaks in small lumps, it is still too wet.

Clay soil takes longer to dry out in the spring and should not be handled while still sticky or gummy.

Another way to judge if the soil is ready to work is whether or not it sticks to the fork, spade or blades of the rotary tiller. If it does, you're too early.

Never work a garden plot before the soil is ready. Ground worked too early in the spring will remain lumpy all season, and the resulting crops will be of poorer quality. In most gardens some sections dry out much earlier than others. (Our first seeding of hardy annuals is planted in these areas.) Some years when a late spring is encountered, it is hard to maintain good crop rotation practices, but as long as the previous year's crops were healthy this is not

In early April the garden plot is still too wet and cold to work. Preparatory work has begun in the frames.

too serious. However, if any disease was encountered, refrain from growing any member of that plant family in the same location.

If no manure or compost was available to spread on the garden plot in the fall, now is the time to do it. We also apply a complete fertilizer in granular form and till the two into the ground together. I will not suggest the amount and ratio of fertilizer to use, as the specific needs of every garden will differ. The only way to ascertain the exact requirements of your garden is to make a soil test. We do not consider this essential every year. If the crops were excellent the previous season there may be no need for either a soil test or additional fertilizer, but if the crops were poor, an accurate and complete soil test should be made. The growing crops will always let you know if the soil conditions do not meet their requirements.

Small garden plots can be dug by hand.

Some gardeners use a spade; others, like myself, prefer a fork. The finished results are the same. The soil should be "friable" or "in good tilth," which means its texture should be like breadcrumbs. This is the type of soil every gardener desires, aims at maintaining or, in gardens with poor conditions, tries to develop over the years.

When the ground is being worked, take care to remove any quack grass, dandelion or other noxious perennial weeds. Annual weeds may be turned under, where they will decay, adding humus to the soil. Destroy quack grass roots; they will create havoc in the compost if there is any life left in them.

The soil is turned over leaving a nice smooth surface which can be raked before seeding. (A small guest looks on approvingly.) Note the cart full of quack grass to be removed and burned.

Seeding

You are now ready to make a seed bed. The soil will be loose in texture. Rake it with the garden rake to level and pulverize the top inch or so, which will aid in germination. Seed can remain dormant a considerable time if buried among clods or put into ground that has been hardened by too much tramping or a heavy rainfall.

Before sowing the seed, use the garden line to keep the rows straight and evenly spaced. The space between rows depends on the crops being sown. To open up a drill or shallow trench for the seed, use either the handle of a rake or one corner of the blade of a draw hoe. The depth of the drill will vary with the type of seed being sown. After the seed has been sown it must be covered. Use the garden rake to draw soil over the seed, then, with the prongs flat on the ground, tamp until the soil is in close contact with the seed. This prevents the soil from drying out too rapidly, and the emerging plants being deprived of essential moisture and nutrients.

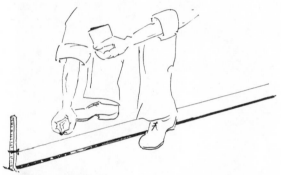

Seeding in a drill

Covering seeded drill with board

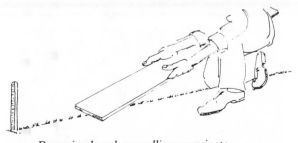

Removing board as seedlings germinate

Sow seed in accordance with the directions given on each packet. Small seeds can be trickled out of the seed package; larger ones can be spaced out one by one.

Novice gardeners are inclined to plant seed far too thickly, and most of the seedlings have to be pulled up and thrown away. With the ever-increasing cost of garden seed it would be a saving of both money and labour to sow the seeds at the distance recommended. In gardens where space is limited, more intensive planting can take place. In this case it is best to intercrop, seeding rows of fast-maturing vegetables between the rows of slower growing main crops, or between main crop plants. Crops grown in such crowded conditions must be thinned and weeded carefully, and given extra fertilizer.

Labelling

Label each row after you plant the seed. A common practice is to push a stick into the ground at each end of the row and use the empty seed packet as the marker. This is fine unless the wind blows it away, or rain washes out the print. I prefer to use plastic labels and write on them with indelible ink. One year I used the wrong marking pencil, and all the writing was washed off in the first rain!

I like to mark each label with the date of seeding, name of variety and the seed house. This way I can keep a record of the performance of different varieties.

Covering the Seeds

To prevent soil drying out in anticipation of a hot, rainless spell, cover the seeded rows with an old board or something equivalent until the seed shows signs of germination. This technique is especially good every season for slow germinating crops like parsnips and parsley.

Old boards placed between the rows of vegetables are handy for the gardener to step on when the soil is wet. This prevents footsteps compressing the soil and saves shoes from getting muddy.

Plant Support

Crops such as peas and pole beans should have the necessary support erected at seeding time. Plant supports are discussed later in detail under the individual vegetables. It is important to ensure that plants do not get blown over and lie on the ground. Adequate support prevents disease, allows air to circulate and sunshine to penetrate.

Setting Out Transplants

The early broccoli, cauliflower and cabbage plants that were started indoors should be hardened by now and ready to set out in the garden. The day before planting out, thoroughly moisten the soil in the flats. The best weather for planting out is a cool, rainy day. If you must plant out in hot weather, wait until the cool of the evening. In addition, give the young plants some protection from the sun for a few days. Artificial shade can be provided in many ways. Examples are inverted flower pots or cedar shingles stuck firmly in the ground at an angle.

Before removing plants from a flat, divide them by cutting in sections with a knife as you would a pan of brownies. Using a trowel, lift each plant out singly with as much soil around the root system as possible. The less the roots are disturbed the better. Plant each seedling in a trowel-made hole, the lowest leaves flush with the soil, and the soil made firm above the roots. With Brassicas and onions, I like to work diazinon crystals into the soil before planting as a precaution against root maggot. Paper collars can be used to prevent damage by cutworms.

Hoeing

The early garden will now be under way, and it will not be long before signs of life spring up all over the ground — unfortunately the annual weeds are the first to emerge. All gardens with good soil also grow excellent weeds. These must be hoed as soon as possible.

Preparing to plant young seedlings outdoors. You need a trowel, a roll of plaster-board sealing tape (or equivalent paper), a broad-bladed knife to separate the soil into "cubes" and flats of hardened transplants. Not shown but also needed is a garden line and a tin of diazinon crystals.

Before planting, mark your bed with a garden line. Work in diazinon crystals with the trowel around the hole where you will plant. Wrap paper collar around the stem of the plant. Plant the seedling, ensuring that the collar is partly buried and partly above soil level.

When the weeds are still only an inch or so tall, it is time to hoe them. This is best done when the top of the soil is dry and the weather hot and sunny. In these conditions the weeds will shrivel and die, whereas in moist, cool conditions they might re-establish themselves. The importance of having straight, well-marked rows is clearly understood when doing the first hoeing. Weeds germinate faster than vegetables. If you are unable to identify the vegetable seedlings, you can always stretch a line between the markers and then hoe safely between rows. Hoeing at this stage is very light work and saves hours of labour in the long run. Unless the ground is mulched it will be necessary to hoe frequently, but the work will be easy and quick each time if the weed seedlings are still tiny.

Thinning

The gardener who makes two blades of grass grow where only one grew before is doing an excellent job. But the gardener who tries to crowd his vegetables is making a grave error. Vegetables need space, within reason, to produce high-quality crops and avoid disease.

If seed is planted too densely the seedlings will be weak and spindly . . . and the need for more space will become greater with subsequent growth. Thinning will be necessary and must be done according to each plant's requirements. Pull out surplus seedlings complete with their roots, causing as little disturbance as possible to adjacent plants. This is easiest to do when the soil is moist . . . and the remaining plants can be made firm again in the ground.

The thinnings need not always be wasted; beets, carrots, and onions, for instance, can be used in the kitchen. Thinning should not take place in one operation, but in stages over a period of time, providing the house with a regular supply of early crops. We find these young vegetables far more tasty than their mature brothers (or sisters!).

Weeds and Weeding

There are hundreds of weeds that thrive in our gardens in spite of our cold winters. These are, for all general purposes, divided into two categories: annuals and perennials.

The annual weeds do not pose a serious problem if the emerging seedlings are hoed down before they go to seed. Pursale, for example, which has minute seeds, can produce over 190,000 seeds per plant each season. These seeds can remain viable for many years

Plant supports are neatly erected to accommodate seedlings already beginning to show up. Note the martin house in the background. The martins will, we hope, keep the garden area mosquito-free during the season.

Seedlings emerging, but well marked by plastic labels. Hoeing keeps weeds down until we mulch between the rows.

A row of Brassica seedlings are hidden by this jungle of annual weeds. The pigweed shown here harbours mosaic disease, and aphids carry this to other plants. The problems next year for this garden's owner will be dreadful.

when plowed under the soil. The same can be said for many other weeds. For this reason, and because they harbour pests and diseases, I stress the importance of hoeing down emerging weed seedling and maintaining as weed-free a garden as possible.

The perennial weeds can be a far greater problem to eradicate. There are some with vigorous, fast growing, underground root stocks, which are able to send up new shoots at many places throughout their length. If these are tilled into the ground, each segment grows and potential plants are distributed all over the garden plot. Quack grass (an unsolicited import from Europe) is the most common member of this group. There are also perennial weeds with deep taproots. If the entire root is

not removed, any remaining sections left in the soil are sufficient to grow new plants — witness the notorious dandelion.

Perennial weeds should be burned. If you want to throw them on the compost heap, leave them in the sun first to wither and die. Be certain they are completely dead. Quack grass roots growing in a compost heap give the gardener many unnecessary hours of hard labour.

In the spring and early summer I like to weed the garden in the rain or just after a rainfall. To weed when the ground is wet, place a board between rows to stand on so that the ground does not become compacted. I know that removing weeds from between the seedlings during a soft rainfall will do little or no damage to the tender young roots of the crop, whereas weeding the rows in dry weather can cause considerable damage.

Later on, when the crops are so advanced that working between the rows would cause me to brush against the plants, I wait until the foliage is dry to prevent the possible spread of disease.

The golden rule concerning weeds in the garden plot is to hoe emerging annuals and to remove and destroy all perennials. Do not put them in the compost until they are very dead.

It is self-evident that all weeds compete with crops for available nutrients in the soil. We wage an unending battle against weeds and have found that mulching is a tremendous help.

Mulch

What is a mulch? In its simplest terms it is the gardener's version of what has been happening on the floor of our forests over many decades. Trees collect around them an accumulation of leaves, twigs, branches, and dead plant materials that have decayed through a natural process and created top soil.

In our gardens we attempt to reproduce nature's work with what we call a mulch. This consists of any material that can be applied to the soil surface without causing injury to the plants. Such a covering not only prevents growth of weeds between cultivated plants, but also reduces soil moisture evaporation.

While mulching does create some extra labour initially, in the long run it is a great saver of time and effort, and it almost certainly produces better crops. A real advantage to mulching is that the labour it saves comes at a time when I am busy processing the produce. Without this mulch I would be devoting time to watering or weeding.

For several years we have been experimenting with different types of mulches. Basically, we use whatever is easily available to us, provided that it is aesthetically suitable for the different areas of the garden. For example, we use sawdust for the raspberries; plastic film for the melons; compost, well-rotted manure, hay and grass clippings for the vegetable garden. We do not apply fresh garden and household refuse directly as a mulch. We prefer to compost it first and spread it after one or two years. Our method allows us to have a much neater garden than the ones where all refuse is used directly in the garden as a mulch.

Because we prefer to rotary-till the entire garden in the spring and fall, we apply only sufficient mulch during the season to conserve moisture and control weeds. People who apply a very deep mulch never cultivate their gardens. In the spring they rake away enough mulch to plant their crops. This is the method advocated by Ruth Stout, author of several organic gardening books, which I have read and enjoyed thoroughly. I have utilized her methods wherever possible in my garden; however, I cannot overcome my preference for a neat, nice looking plot. Her garden had a wild look which fits into the rugged countryside where she lived.

Ruth Stout made the added claim that deep mulching also controls cut worms, slugs, root maggots, and in fact virtually every underground pest. While I can confirm that her soil was in excellent condition and produced beautiful crops, I am unable to verify her stand on pests. She may well be right.

Grass clipping laid over newspaper makes an excellent mulch. The clippings are spread thinly to prevent overheating and added to as more become available.

Wood shavings are being used as mulch around a young tomato plant. A further application of shavings will completely surround the plant.

TYPES OF MULCHES RECOMMENDED

Hay (spoiled)	Sometimes available free from farmers after being damaged by rain. An excellent mulch, but may introduce annual weeds.
Lawn clippings	We apply thin layers on top of newspaper. If applied too thickly, they may heat excessively.
Leaf mold	Made by composting leaves raked in the fall.
Manure	Obtained from farms or stables. Excellent mulch containing nutrients. If too fresh, may burn plants.
Mushroom compost	Available from commercial mushroom growers. Slight nutrient value. An excellent mulch. Weed free.
Peat moss	Purchased from garden supply stores. A fine texture and good appearance, but has a tendency to dry out and become impervious to water.
Black plastic	Purchased from garden supply stores. Practical for large gardens, but unattractive and liable to be blown about in windstorms if not securely anchored. Does not break down into soil as do organic mulches.
Sawdust	Usually obtained free from sawmills and lumber yards. A good general mulch. May cause a nitrogen deficiency which can be corrected by fertilizing.
Straw	Obtained from farms. Coarser and more durable than most kinds of hay. A good mulch.
Newspaper	This should be laid flat on the soil several layers deep and weighted down with other organic materials such as grass clippings to avoid being blown away. Do not get distracted by reading the old news which somehow always acquires renewed interest when it is lying on the ground!

When planning to incorporate the mulch in the soil each year, consider the types of mulches that can be used. For example, if heavy layers of newspaper are used for several years, it might cause a build-up of lead in the soil. Similarly, too much sawdust might cause a lack of nitrogen. We attempt to rotate the mulches as we do the crops. I am sure most home gardens have a variety of mulches just as we do. Where the richest nutrients are applied one year, that is where the heaviest feeding crop will be planted the next.

We test the soil from several locations in the garden most years, but this is not really necessary. If the ground is not producing excellent crops, the plants will tell you that the soil is not right, and you must take appropriate steps to correct the nutrient deficiencies.

Care of the Surroundings

If lawns or grass paths surround a vegetable garden, they need to be kept trim. Not only does this give the garden a more pleasing appearance, but it discourages mosquitoes and blackflies, which prefer damp, thick vegetation, two sufficient reasons to make most gardeners groom their property. But the most important aspect is in the eradication of host plants for the pests, or "bad-guys," with whom we wage a constant battle.

Many weeds belong to the same plant families as our vegetable crops. If we allow these weeds to grow wild around the vegetable plots, we are providing protection and food for the pests, hence diseases, which we are trying to eliminate from our gardens.

In large gardens where a farm tractor is used for cultivation and no cut lawns surround the vegetable plot, the surrounding area should either be tilled and kept black, or grass and weeds cut low.

Our vegetable garden plot is surrounded by cut grass paths. In order to prevent the grass encroaching on the plot it is necessary to keep the edges straight and trimmed. This is a tedious job, but so greatly improves the visual aspect that we consider it time well spent. This job needs to be repeated several times during the season.

It is my experience that the things that are wrong or untidy in a garden are far more likely to attract the eye of the beholder than those that are in good order. I prefer my garden to be remembered for its good features rather than the bad ones. Straight rows of vegetables and straight grass edges may sound unimportant, but they tell the difference between well and poorly kept gardens.

Summer Work

Summer work in a garden is continuous. The frost-tender main crops must be seeded and frost-tender transplants set out in their final locations. The hoe is busy controlling weeds

The edges of the surrounding grass paths are kept trimmed and straight. This can be done by a sharp spade or an edger. Here a mechanical edger is being used. Note the plastic labels at the ends of rows.

and any available mulch should be spread between the rows. This stage of gardening is tremendously rewarding. The growth of all plants is very rapid, and harvesting of early crops will be well under way. As the ground is emptied it should be dug and enriched for succession plantings.

In late May or early June the seeds of late Brassica crops should be sown in a cold-frame or a seed-bed in the garden. These seedlings will be ready for transplanting into the garden by early or mid-July. The culture is the same as for early crops.

Inspecting for Ailments

When crops are growing actively, it is wise to take time each day to wander through the garden inspecting the crops for any signs of distress. If wilted plants or leaves, chewed leaves, gun-shot damage to leaves, blossom-drop or any other unusual symptoms are noticed, the plant should be closely examined, the cause of the problem determined and the necessary steps taken to prevent further damage.

The arrival of white butterflies indicates that their eggs will soon be laid on the undersides of Brassica leaves. These eggs hatch out as caterpillars that chew cabbage and broccoli. As soon as I see those butterflies I start my dusting program. Some gardeners prefer to spray.

An old-timers' method to control caterpillars in cabbages is to sprinkle pickling salt down in among the leaves, making three or four applications during the growing season. At my home we used to spray the cabbages with a solution of a handful of salt to a bucket of water. To the best of my recollection it worked remarkably well.

It is interesting also that the use of soaps was popular fifty years ago as a remedy for pest control. This method appears to be coming back into favour because of its ability to kill specific pests while not affecting the "good guys" such as bees, lady bugs or parasitic wasps.

Watering

For optimal growth, plants must always have an adequate supply of moisture at root level. Ascertain the depth of moisture in the soil by actually checking physically with a garden fork. If watering is needed, make sure each watering is sufficient to reach below root level. If watering is done from overhead, do this early enough in the day to allow the foliage to dry off before nightfall. Seepage watering can be done at any time, day or night.

Do not move among the plants when the foliage is wet, either from dew, sprinkling or rain, because this can cause spread of disease or rust spots on beans.

Harvesting

As the season progresses, crops ripen and harvesting becomes a daily routine along with garden maintenance.

Most perishable crops must be harvested when still in prime condition. Sugar or snow peas left on the vine only one day too long will be coarse and stringy, as will overripe kohlrabi. Many people are turned against certain vegetables because, on their first encounter, those vegetables were of inferior quality or poorly cooked.

The heat of the summer is promoting lush growth, but the garden must not be allowed to dry out. We sometimes place a sprinkler on top of a step ladder and let it soak the surrounding area. Individual plants get liquid fertilizer.

Harvesting Blue Lake pole beans that have grown well over the top of the 6-foot trellis. They provide a heavy crop which is harvested over an extended period.

Compost being spread in the area no longer occupied by plants. Cleaning up debris by burning is in some situations preferable to composting.

Well-rotted manure being rototilled into the soil. Some late frost-hardy crops (Brussels sprouts, leeks, carrots) continue to mature pending harvesting.

Putting the Garden to Bed

By mid-August many of the main crops will have been harvested, leaving empty spaces in the garden. In areas where frost is not expected until late September, these spaces can be re-seeded with fall crops of lettuce, Chinese cabbage and spinach. Once you know your garden and its climatic variations, you will be able to judge how many crops you can grow successfully. In northern areas re-seeding in mid-August is out of the question.

Frost-tender annual herbs should be harvested and dried before there is any risk of frost. Hardy perennial herbs may be cut back and the prunings dried if needed. Cutting back shapes the plants and prevents them from becoming straggly.

Chives can be cut back, potted-up and brought into the house for winter garnishes. They will shoot up again in no time. Parsley can also be potted-up and brought indoors. I like to leave the rest of the parsley row in the garden as, being a biennial, it will usually grow

again in the spring to provide the house with an early crop before finally going to seed. Other frost-tender perennial herbs such as rosemary and oregano should be brought indoors in good time. I like to keep mine permanently potted, setting the pots out in the garden during the summer.

As soon as the various vegetable crops are over, the debris should be cleaned up and taken to the compost heap. Any annual weeds still in the ground should be hoed, and the perennial ones removed and destroyed. Now is the time to start transferring the well-rotted compost to the garden and spreading it in the vacant areas. If manure is available, all the better. This process continues throughout the fall while the late crops are gradually harvested. Root crops can remain in the ground until October — a light frost is said to improve the flavour of some.

Broccoli, Brussels sprouts, cabbage, celery, Swiss chard, curly kale, leeks and spinach can withstand quite a lot of frost. I like to leave these crops in the garden as long as possible.

We usually continue eating freshly picked produce well into November.

The hardiest of these are Brussels sprouts and curly kale. They stay in the ground all winter for the simple reason that the ground has frozen over before I have finished harvest-

A picture of dejection as our "groundhog repeller" surveys the garden after the first snowfall.

ing them. The other vegetables should be dug up before the ground freezes and brought into the cool room, or root cellar. We can usually eat our own fresh vegetables until Christmas.

Parsnips can remain in the ground all winter, ready to be dug as soon as the ground thaws in spring. I always bring enough into the cool room to supply us during the winter months. We have never been successful overwintering carrots and leeks in the garden. I am sure this is because our garden is too wet the following spring, and it is at this stage that these vegetables rot. However, I know people who do overwinter these crops in this way, and I believe it is because their gardens dry out quickly in the spring.

Some gardeners leave tilling the ground until spring. We prefer to do it in the fall as well. I am convinced we get better results. I know we

save time in the spring when so much has to be done all at once. This end-of-season digging or tilling, incorporating mulch into the soil, should be completed before freeze-up when the ground is dry. Cultivating wet soil leaves it in hard clods.

The surface should be left rough or in ridges so that the frost may penetrate more of the ground. Freezing breaks up soil into small particles, leaving it more porous. It also helps to kill the eggs of many insects by exposing them to sun, wind and birds.

Once the ground has frozen, mulch can be applied to plants that need protection. Asparagus, sea-kale, strawberries, raspberries, rhubarb, globe and Jerusalem artichokes all benefit, as well as many herbs. Rhubarb benefits most from a heavy application of well-rotted manure. It is a rich feeder.

Rodents can do severe damage to the garden in winter. I protect young trees with either plastic tree guards or by painting the bark with a bitter-tasting repellant. In the raspberry patch, I place jam jars on their sides partially filled with mouse poison. This latter technique eliminates any fear of birds picking up the "seed" but deals most satisfactorily with mice.

After all the leaves have fallen they should be collected and, unless needed for leaf mold or winter mulch, added to the compost heap. Leaf mold is an excellent substitute for peat moss and is weed free.

When all the organic waste available has been added and the compost heap is complete, it should be finished off with a final layer of soil and a sprinkling of high nitrogen fertilizer. There will be plenty of internal heat in it in the spring — an ideal location for growing cantaloupe.

If the crops in your garden have not been satisfactory and you have never had the soil analyzed, now is the time to do it. When we first started developing our present garden we sent soil away for a full analysis. This enabled us to apply nutrients in the correct proportions. Now we test only when the crops tell us their nutrient needs are not being fully met.

Diseases and Pests

In the preceding part of this book I have attempted to describe the practical aspects of vegetable gardening with particular reference to methods which seem to suit us best.

The next part of the book deals with disease and pests. Sooner or later we all run into gardening problems arising from plants clearly sending out distress signals. I believe that at that time you will find it useful to compare such problems with those described or illustrated here. In this way the cause of the problem can be identified and dealt with.

Because prevention is better than cure I have summarized many of the control measures needed to deal with gardening problems before they arise.

Readers will already be familiar with my views on the use of chemicals. Rotenone powder, which is an organic product, is our general purpose pesticide, and we use it as a preventative as well as a cure. I have also touched on the reviving interest in insecticidal soaps. The potential of this old-time remedy was scientifically proven some years ago by Dr. George Puritch while working in his laboratory at the Pacific Forest Research Centre in British Columbia. Since then, the Victoria-based firm of Safer-Agro-Chem Limited has developed and marketed a number of product lines. I have found their preparation designed to kill aphids and mealybugs very effective in my greenhouse. Research is now being aimed at the control of carrot fly, root maggots and caterpillars. There are also plans to combine fatty acids with petrochemicals to deal with other insects difficult to control, among these earwigs and leafhoppers. Hopefully, a new pesticide industry is on the horizon which will make use of fats and oils derived from plant and animal sources. While such research appears to be reaching a point where mass production can be contemplated, I cannot comment on such products from practical experience in the garden. For this reason, the chapter on pest control which follows later in this section does not refer directly to insecticidal soaps, but gardeners will no doubt be interested to follow new developments in this field.

It should also be noted that our scientific knowledge of plants is undergoing rapid change. As a result, we now appreciate that plant life is not as simple as it was once thought to be. From the gardener's point of view, it is important to know something of the way plants grow, because this has a direct bearing on how plants become the victims of disease.

Plant Diseases

Plant diseases can be roughly divided into three categories: physiological diseases due to improper nutrition, which we have already discussed; infectious diseases caused by micro-organisms; and diseases caused by pests like insects, slugs and nematodes, which bite or bore their way into the plant. This section is concerned with infections, although all types of disease are interrelated. A weak plant suffering from a trace element deficiency is more likely to succumb to a fungus attack than a healthy one, and insect pests often introduce viruses during their ravagings.

Diseases are naturally spread by wind or rain drops carrying infectious particles from one plant to another. Birds and animals also aid dissemination by carrying plant material and soil with them as they move about. Insects, as we shall see, play a major role in spreading virus infections, and even the gardener, tramping between the rows of plants, may cause bruising and so increase the risk of infection.

The incidence of disease is greatly affected by the weather, and conditions of temperature and humidity which favour one disease may discourage another. All we can be sure of is that no two years will be the same.

A pathogen is an agent which causes disease. It is usually a microscopic organism, and plants are susceptible to attack by three main kinds of pathogens: fungi, bacteria and viruses.

Most infectious diseases in plants are caused by fungi, microscopic cousins of the familiar mushrooms and toadstools. To begin with, we will take a general look at what happens when a fungus invades a plant. When a spore lands on a plant, it germinates, producing very fine branching threads called hyphae. These hyphae penetrate by boring through the outer epidermis of the plant, or growing through the breathing pores (stomata), or through a wound. Once inside, they branch and grow, excreting substances which dissolve the cell walls so that they can feed on the plant tissues.

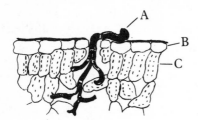

*Cross section of a leaf showing
infection by a fungus*

A: *Fungus spore producing hypha, which is penetrating leaf through pore (stomata).*
B: *Leaf epidermal cells.*
C: *Leaf cells with green chloroplasts.*

After the infection is well developed, some of the hyphae near the surface of the plant will organize themselves to produce millions of tiny new spores which are easily borne away by the wind to start new infections on neighbouring plants. Late in the season the fungi stop their attack and develop tough resting structures, or special spores, in the dead tissues of the plants

they have killed, or in niches under the bark of trees or perhaps in the soil. In this condition they wait out the winter. The following spring new hyphae develop which produce a new crop of spores to start the cycle of infection over again, if the weather conditions are favourable. In this way there are often two stages to the spread of disease in the garden. First, the arrival of unwanted spores, perhaps only a few which may land on a single plant; this is followed by secondary spread throughout the growing season to other plants of the same family growing nearby. Not all fungi attack the aerial parts of the plant. Some live on dead organic matter in the soil and, when they come in contact with a susceptible root, they will invade it and spread through the whole root system and up the stem.

It is very important to understand that many, but not all, of the fungi which cause plant diseases are able to live on dead plant material when there is no suitable living plant around to attack. This is the reason for the crop rotation and garden hygiene we have talked about. It would be foolish to plant new young plants in a part of the garden where a pathogen is suspected to be lurking in the soil; we know it is there because the plants of the same family which grew there last year were diseased. To repeat the planting would lead to a build-up of infection in the soil that might take years to eradicate.

All this sounds as if a plant is doomed to certain death when attacked by a fungus. Not so. It can fight back and is able to produce antibiotic substances with which it tries to stop the fungal advance. If it is successful it is called a resistant variety. It can also develop thickened, corky layers in the cells surrounding the advancing infection, and so wall off the area and starve the invader.

Fungal Diseases

These diseases are mainly grouped according to the symptoms exhibited by the plants, although identical symptoms may result from infections by quite different fungi. For example, if the root system is extensively damaged or the water-conducting tissue of the stem affected, the main symptom will be general wilting, with no indication of which fungus is causing the trouble. On the other hand, some diseases are so characteristic, such as potato blight or corn smut, that they are immediately recognizable.

Let us now take a brief look at some of the types of diseases commonly seen in the garden.

Leaf spots and anthracnoses. As the names suggest, these fungi are characteristically confined to the local areas of the plant where the infections take place. The fungi do not usually penetrate deeply, and the host plant is able to build a barrier around the site, leaving necrotic (dead) patches. If too many of these necrotic spots occur on a leaf it may die, and if too many leaves die the plant becomes defoliated and dies too. This is rare, however, and most plants continue to grow, although with impaired vigour. Anthracnoses are not confined to the leaves and cause blackened, burned-looking irregular spots on any part of the plant. These infections may be severe, especially on peas and beans, where the fungus

Leaf spot on parsnips.

also may invade the pods and so infect the seeds. If these seeds are kept for planting the next year, disaster will follow; the young plants will be systemically infected, and those that survive will not produce a crop worth harvesting.

Wilt diseases. Fungi which are not confined to the superficial tissues of the plant but penetrate deeply may interfere with the water supply of the shoots and thus induce wilting. This may be partly due to the physical blocking of the xylem by the fungal hyphae, but it is mainly a result of chemical reactions of substances released by the growing hyphae which interfere with the mechanisms for water transport in the plant. If the fungus invades at a point on the

Eggplant severely infected with Verticillium wilt compared with healthy specimen.

stem, only the shoot above that point will wilt, but when the roots or stems at soil level are attacked (root and collar rots) the result is wilting and collapse of the entire plant.

Blight diseases. This term is used to describe infections which progress rapidly so that shoots, or even whole plants, which appear to be healthy one day may be dead within forty-eight hours. Late blight of potatoes is the classic example. The coincidence of a cloud of wind-borne spores with a period of humid weather spells trouble for the potato patch. Potato blight is one of the few fungal diseases

Late blight on tomato leaf.

Late blight on two outer petioles of celery. Central petiole is healthy.

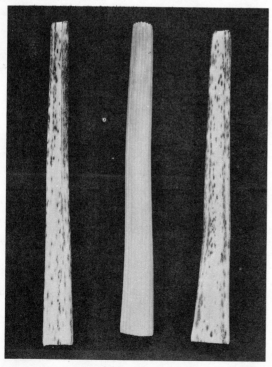

able to cause extensive epidemics and was the reason for the infamous Irish potato famines of the nineteenth century

Mildews. These diseases are exceedingly common on a great variety of plants and are recognized by the white powdery effect which they produce on the leaves, stems, and sometimes flowers of the host plants. They are different from the fungi we have talked about so far, in that they are "obligate parasites," that is, they are unable to grow on dead plant remains and only attack living hosts. They usually make their appearance when the plants are reaching maturity, and do not kill but cause discolouration and weakening.

Rusts and smuts. These descriptive names embrace a group of highly specialized and destructive pathogens. Fortunately, only two of them appear to plague us in the vegetable garden: corn and onion smut. Both rusts and smuts produce their spores gathered in large masses in pustules or galls situated below the epidermis of the host. This finally breaks open to reveal the orange-red rust spores or sooty-black smut balls. Smuts infect only the actively growing tips of the host plant, the fungal hyphae keeping pace with its growth and frequently dying out in the older parts of the plant. Often there is no indication that the plant is infected until the galls form and break open.

Rusts do not pose a problem in the vegetable garden, except for infections on gooseberry and currant bushes. The infections may not be severe in themselves, but the bushes serve as alternate hosts for the white pine blister rust which has killed so many of these beautiful trees, and so they present a hazard we should not countenance in our gardens, unless we are prepared to keep a sharp watch for signs of rust. If it appears, eradicate the bushes.

Botrytis grey mold and miscellaneous rots. This category is not really concerned with diseases so much as with nuisances.

Botrytis is an ever-present fungus which isn't much of a pathogen itself, but it is very quick to enter a wound or to attack weakened plants, especially when they are crowded and ventilation around them is poor. It grows rapidly, reducing plant tissues to a soft mush covered with a grey fuzz.

Some fungi will cause rots in the root storage organs, as well as attacking the aerial parts of the plants, but these types of rot are more often of bacterial origin. Another nuisance which should be mentioned is potato scab (not actually caused by a fungus) which spoils the appearance of the tubers though not affecting their eating quality.

"Damping off" of seedlings is a soil-borne infection which occurs when seedlings are planted too close together in humid conditions. The fungus weakens the young stems at soil level, causing the seedlings to fall over and die. This is a greenhouse infection and rarely troubles seeds sown in the open.

Bacterial Diseases

So far we have considered only fungal pathogens, which are the cause of the most troublesome infections in our gardens. Bacterial diseases play a relatively minor role. This is quite the reverse of the situation in the animal kingdom in which bacterial diseases cause severe and widespread illnesses, and fungal infections are superficial or rare.

Bacteria are tiny single-celled organisms, so much smaller than the fungi that they can barely be seen under the light microscope. They grow by dividing into two daughter cells that rapidly regain the size of the original cell and divide again. Their numbers multiply much faster than the fungi, and one bacillus may become several million within a few hours. With a few exceptions bacterial pathogens live in the soil, feeding on nutrients released during the breakdown of organic matter. They do not produce airborne spores and so do not spread readily from garden to garden, but generally gain entry into the plant through natural pores, or through wounds or holes caused by boring insects. They often follow, and complicate, infections initially caused by fungi. Many species of bacteria are able to invade a wide range of host plants and do not have to confine their attentions to a single plant family, so there are few characteristic bacterial diseases to describe, happily for us.

Bacterial soft rots.   These affect the underground storage organs of many vegetables such as turnips, carrots, and onions, as well as the succulent parts of cabbages, broccoli and celery, etc. Infection always takes place through a wound, caused perhaps by careless hoeing or by slugs. While the growing leaves may not at first show signs of what is happening below the ground, they will wilt and die as the rot progresses. We are all familiar with the sight of the occasional carrot whose inside has rotted to a pasty white mush which has washed away in the rain, leaving only the resistant rind to show what might have been.

Crown galls.   Galls are a plant's response to invasion by fungi, bacteria or insects. The plant cells at the site of invasion are stimulated to start dividing in a somewhat haphazard fashion and the result is the production of irregular, tumour-like growths, sometimes of enormous size. Crown galls, as the name suggests, are produced on the crown of the plant just at or below soil level. The bacteria which cause them differ from the soft rotting organisms in that they are unable to produce the substances which dissolve the plant cells and so rot the tissues. Instead, they excrete substances which stimulate the plant cells around them to divide in an uncontrolled manner. Crown galls are not a great source of economic loss and are mainly seen on raspberry canes and fruit trees.

Fireblight.   A most destructive disease of apple and pear trees, as well as some ornamental trees. These bacteria do not live in the soil but overwinter in small cankers on the bark of the tree. In spring the renewed growth of the bacteria causes the cankers to ooze a sticky, sweet fluid, attracting the bees which are pollinating the blossom at this time. The insects carry the bacteria to the flowers and the germs are able to penetrate the soft tissues, entering the wood and causing severe wilting, first of the branches, and then very quickly of the whole tree.

Viruses

Viruses can, and do, infect all animals and plants, even including the very same fungal and bacterial pathogens which we have just been describing. They are very tiny infectious agents, so small that they cannot be seen under the light microscope, and they are different because they are not really "alive" in the usual sense of the word. Unlike other micro-organisms, they cannot grow and divide by themselves. A virus particle consists of a central core of nucleic acid, which is the material responsible for the genetic code, surrounded by a protein coat. It does not have any of the organized structures necessary for the life of a true cell, and so the term particle (or virion) describes it very well.

If viruses are so small and inert, how do they get about and cause diseases? In the case of plants they are mostly carried by leaf-sucking insects such as aphids. When an aphid feeds it sucks up sap from the plant; it then wanders around and tries a fresh area, usually near the growing buds and young leaves. When the insect pierces the epidermal cells, it dribbles in a little saliva before it starts to feed and, if it has been previously taking sap from an infected cell, some of the virus particles it has imbibed from that cell will be dribbled into the new cell with the saliva. Once inside the host the virion sheds its coat, the nucleic acid is then exposed, and it is able to influence the genetic code of the host cell and instruct it to make new virus particles. If the virus is a very forceful one, it can order the host cell to stop its normal activities and direct all its energies to making virus particles, until it bursts and dies, releasing the millions of new virions it has made. At the other extreme, the virus may cause little or no disruption in the host cell's activities, ensuring only that a few new virions are made which lie dormant in the cell.

Mild mosaic symptoms on two outer leaves. Centre leaf is healthy.

The interactions between the host and the virus determine what symptoms appear on the infected plant. Most viruses can only multiply within a single susceptible species, or family of plants, because the cells of unrelated plants are able to resist instructions given by the viral genetic code. A virus which can cause severe symptoms on a potato plant may not cause any signs when inoculated into a tomato plant, although the host cells will then replicate, that is, reproduce identical virus particles. We then have the confusing situation of apparently healthy "carrier plants" harbouring a potentially virulent virus without showing any symptoms, while providing a reservoir from which travelling insects can spread infection. These carriers are just as likely to be weeds as other related garden plants.

To add to the confusion, no exact criterion exists for the diagnosis of a plant virus disease. None of the symptoms is exclusive, but the commonest is probably the mottling of leaves in different shades of green and yellow, which is described as "mosaic." This symptom is unfortunately also found in various deficiency diseases. Sometimes there is a yellowing, or chlorosis, which may become generalized over the whole leaf or may be restricted to chlorotic areas arranged in concentric circles called "ring spots." Some virus infections produce dark-green bands bounding the veins, while in others the veins appear translucent. Various types of leaf curl and crinkle are also characteristic of virus infections, as is the appearance of necrotic spots. Viruses may prevent the elongation of the stem so that all the leaves grow in one place, producing symptoms known as "bunchy top" and "rosette." Other infections result in a proliferation of shoots described as "fern leaf" and "witches broom." The best advice is to pull up and burn plants showing any abnormal growth patterns and mottled leaves; they may be sources of virus infection in your garden.

Another condition attributable to viral infection is the so-called degeneration of plant stock. This occurs in plants such as raspberries, strawberries and potatoes, in which next year's plants are propagated from the roots or stems of the old plants. When the stock becomes infected by a mild or slow virus, as it almost inevitably will, a progressive deterioration in the condition of the plants will be seen in subsequent years. A similar type of transmission of virus from one generation to another may take place during grafting if either root stock or scion is infected.

In recent years some of the plant "yellows" infections previously attributed to viruses have proved to be yet another diverse group of pathogens called spiroplasmas. This is the only mention we will make of them, since they are insect-transmitted, and as far as the home vegetable garden is concerned, they behave like viruses.

Pests

This is only a general guide to common garden pests; later sections on individual vegetables include a greater variety of them, along with advice on their control.

Aphids are a continual menace in the garden. They attack virtually every plant and weed, sucking the juices from stems, leaves, flowers and roots. They not only spread disease, but also secrete honeydew which attracts ants and provides suitable conditions for the growth of sooty mold.

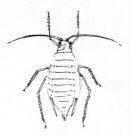

Aphid.

There are many different types of aphids which vary in size and colour. These insects have a complicated life cycle and produce many generations in one season. The eggs overwinter in the soil and hatch in the spring.

It is essential to control these pests, a relatively easy task. Douse with a strong jet from the garden hose or a bucket of soapy water, or dust with rotenone. Also, the defenceless aphids have many natural predators, the most important being the lady bug beetle.

Earwigs. The European earwig is now a pest in many parts of our area. It attacks fruits, ornamentals and many vegetables including raspberries, beans, carrots, celery, corn, lettuce and potatoes. The adults are about three-quarters of an inch long and reddish-brown in colour. The males have a large pair of curved pincers at the rear end which are, in fact, harmless. The female lays eggs in the soil, and when the young are about one-quarter of an inch long they leave the nest and search for food. Nocturnal, they hide during the day in crevices and on plants with closely packed leaves. A second batch of eggs may hatch in July. In seasons when the insect is very numerous, the earwigs can become a nuisance in the house as well as in the garden. As adults they overwinter in the soil.

Earwig.

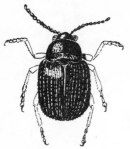

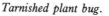

Flea beetle.   *Leafhopper.*   *Tarnished plant bug.*   *White grub.*

Flea beetles derive their name from the fact that they jump like fleas when disturbed. There are many types of flea beetles; all attack the foliage of plants. They can carry with them virus diseases, and the holes they chew in leaves are open invitations to fungal and bacterial infections. The adults overwinter in garden refuse and in spring eggs are laid in the soil, the larvae emerging at planting time to feed on germinating seeds. They are a particular problem during a long, cool spring when germination is delayed. The fall garden clean-up is most important, as is the control of insects during the growing season.

Leafhoppers attack most of the common garden vegetables. There are many species of this pest. They are usually pale green to yellow in colour, are wedge-shaped and measure half an inch in length. When plants are disturbed, the winged adults can be seen hopping around while the wingless nymphs scurry under the leaves. Damage is caused by the hoppers sucking the juices from the plants, transmitting diseases and laying scores of eggs on leaves and stems. Several generations occur each season, and therefore regular insect control is essential.

The tarnished plant bug can damage most of our vegetable and fruit crops, as well as many ornamental plants. They inject a poison into the plant that causes many varying injuries. A blackening of the leaf tips on the various plants is the first important signal of their presence.

The adult bug is tarnish-coloured, flat, oval shaped and measures a quarter of an inch in length. The distinguishing feature is a clear, yellow triangle containing a black dot on the lower part of each side of the bug.

Dust with rotenone immediately the blackened leaf tips or the bug itself are noticed.

Whitefly Whiteflies are rarely a serious problem outdoors, but in the house or greenhouse they can cause considerable damage if not controlled. These pests are seldom noticed until the plant is disturbed at which time they fly out in a cloud.

They are sucking insects that feed on the sap of the plants, leaving a sticky secretion called honeydew, which is an ideal breeding ground for sooty mold. This mold or fungus can easily be detected with the naked eye, and the gardener, alerted to the fact that whiteflies are probably the cause, can be on the lookout.

It is not easy to control whiteflies in the garden. Spraying the undersides of leaves with a strong jet of water may help. If the infestation is severe and causing distress to the plants early in the season, it would be advisable to consult your local agricultural representative.

Whiteflies found outdoors late in the season are unlikely to damage the crop. Indoors, they must be controlled by repeated spraying with a recommended insecticide.

White grubs are the larvae of the June bug (sometimes called May beetle). The life cycle is complex and provides the grub two summers in which to feed on the roots or tubers of plants. During the first season the June bug lays eggs in grassy areas where they hatch in about two weeks' time. The grubs spend the first summer a few inches below the soil sur-

Ground beetle.   Lady bug beetle.

face, feeding on roots and burrowing quite deeply to overwinter. As the second season begins, they again come to within a few inches of the surface, where they remain, feeding on available material. They burrow again in the fall to spend a second winter underground. The third season they pupate in early summer and remain in the soil as an adult for the third winter. The fourth season they emerge as June bugs, and the life cycle starts all over again. White grubs are most often found in gardens that are being newly developed from lawn or sodded areas. After a garden has been worked for a year or two, white grubs are not a problem.

"Good Guys"

The good guys in our gardens are the predators and parasites which feed on harmful insects. Among the predators are the ground beetle and the lady bug or beetle.

Ground beetles are large, black, fast-moving beetles, whose long pointed jaws are ideal for grasping other insects. Both adults and larvae feed on several garden pests.

Lady bugs are small, orange, hemispherical beetles with a varying number of black spots, but the norm is twelve. This welcome visitor to the garden dines constantly on aphids and mealybugs. Be aware that lady bugs can be mistaken for Mexican bean beetles and squash beetles, which, respectively, have eight and seven dark spots on each front wing.

Praying mantises, snakes, toads, and aleo-

chara are also among the many fairweather friends in our gardens. Biological control of insects is a relatively new field that is developing rapidly. Readers who are interested in investigating further should obtain the most up-to-date information available.

Dusting Against Pests

Gardeners use many different techniques to achieve the same ends. Some prefer to spray rather than to dust. I dust because it is quicker. I find that I can dust the whole crop in the time it would take me just to prepare the spray. Because the crop must be re-treated after each rain, spraying is very time-consuming.

I first saw the "sack" method of dusting crops when visiting an old-time gardener in our area. It was so fast and efficient that I immediately adopted his technique. I use rotenone powder (derris) which, although poisonous to fish, is relatively safe to animals. (We do not have a stream or pond nearby, so no worry over killing fish.)

As soon as the white butterflies are seen dusting should commence. Put a scoop of the powder in an old sack and walk along beside the rows shaking the sack over each plant by giving the bag a downward jerk. Always work

The potential damage caused to plants by the cabbage caterpillar is referred to in many parts of this book. When you see the white butterflies tracing a happy dance around the garden, it is time to give the cabbage tribe a dusting of rotenone.

up-wind and apply the dust when the leaves are wet from either rain or early morning dew. It is a good idea to protect yourself against risk of inhaling the dust; a scarf over the nose and mouth will suffice. And don't forget to wash all vegetables before eating.

I could, however, change my mind about dusting if spraying with insecticidal soap proves to be as effective and safe as is claimed. Such soaps, containing new, soluble fatty acid salts, are being developed for use in vegetable gardens against a variety of pests. I particularly like the fact that these products are biodegradable and leave no residual effect.

Disease and Pest Control in the Garden

The foregoing plant problems that may occur in your garden can be controlled to a major extent. The following summary of controls will also remind the reader of some of the gardening practices recommended in earlier parts of this book.

Spring

1. When raising seedlings indoors, use sterilized soil (or medium) and containers.
2. Use only top quality virus-resistant seed treated against fungus infection if available.
3. Only plant small fruits carrying disease-free government certification.
4. Plant only seed potatoes that are government certified disease-free.
5. Space crops and rows to allow for good ventilation and avoid overcrowding as plants grow.
6. Practise crop rotation.
7. When rotating crops, make sure that the new plants are not susceptible to the same diseases as the ones they replace.
8. Use paper (or other) collars on transplants to avoid cutworm damage.
9. Use only well-rotted manure or compost.
10. Use fertilizers and lime with caution. A soil analysis is recommended.
11. Certain sprays must be used early to be effective (for example to fight the cucumber beetle).

Summer

1. Practise the best possible garden sanitation. Pull up and destroy (do not compost) diseased plants as soon as noticed.
2. Control weeds in and around the vegetable plot. They can harbour fungi and virus-carrying insects.
3. Water only as needed. In some cases watering "from above" may be damaging and "seepage" is recommended.
4. Maintain adequate moisture level in ground at all times. When watering, soak the ground thoroughly. Never apply light sprinklings.
5. Do not walk around rows of plants, brushing against them when they are wet.
6. Keep plants and particularly fruit off the ground (by staking or other means).
7. Do not overfertilize, particularly with high nitrogen levels.
8. Watch raspberries for signs of cane borers. Prune 6 inches below tell-tale entrance holes, or until pith is no longer discoloured.
9. Pull pea vines as soon as main crop is harvested.
10. Compost all post-harvest litter unless infected.
11. Prune fruit to minimize crowding of foliage in centre of bush, thereby allowing sunlight to enter and air to circulate.
12. Spray or dust Brassicas regularly with rotenone, particularly when white cabbage butterfly is seen. Also spray or dust potatoes for blight and beetles.

Fall

1. Remove and burn old raspberry canes as well as weak, spindly new growth.
2. After crops are harvested, remove remaining debris to the compost heap. Burn any diseased materials.
3. Spread well-rotted manure or compost on vacant areas. Cultivate.
4. When harvesting crops for winter storage:
   a: take care not to damage produce;
   b: dry roots and tubers outdoors in sunshine before storing;
   c: store at recommended temperatures.

Part Two

Vegetables, Fruits and Herbs

Apples	163	Kale, Sea	109
Apricots	164	Kohl-Rabi	106
Artichokes, Globe	93	Leeks	85
Artichokes, Jerusalem	93	Lettuce	96
Asparagus	129	Lovage	155
Aubergine	134	Marjoram	156
Basil, Sweet	157	Marrow, Vegetable	111
Beans, Broad	123	Melon	114
Beans, Fava	123	Mint	156
Beans, Lima	123	Muskmellon	114
Beans, Navy	123	Okra	131
Beans, Pole	122	Onions	87
Beans, Runner	123	Oregano	156
Beans, Shelling	123	Parsley	149
Beans, Snap	122	Parsley, Parsnip — rooted	150
Beans, Soy	124	Parsnips	150
Beets	90	Peaches	164
Blueberries	165	Peanuts	127
Broccoli	102	Pears	163
Brussels Sprouts	103	Peas	124
Cabbage	104	Peas, Edible — podded	124
Cabbage, Chinese	106	Peas, Snow	126
Cabbage, Red	104	Peas, Sugar Snap	127
Cantaloupe	114	Peppers, Hot	135
Carrots	146	Peppers, Sweet	135
Cauliflower	105	Plums	163
Celeriac	149	Potatoes	139
Celery	147	Potatoes, Sweet	99
Chard	91	Pumpkins	111
Chicory, Witloof	96	Radishes	108
Chives	153	Raspberries	169
Chives, Garlic	154	Rhubarb	132
Corn	117	Rosemary	156
Crabapples	163	Rutabaga	107
Cress	108	Sage	157
Cress, Water	110	Savory, Summer	157
Cucumbers	113	Sea-Kale	109
Currants	165	Soybean	124
Dill	154	Spinach	91
Eggplant	134	Spinach, New Zealand	92
Endive	95	Squash	111
Endive, French	96	Strawberries	172
Escarole	95	Tarragon	158
Garlic	85	Thyme	158
Gooseberries	165	Tomatoes	136
Grapes	176	Turnips, Summer	108
Ground Cherry	142	Turnips, Swede	107
Horseradish	154	Turnips, Winter	107
Huckleberry, Garden	141	Watermelon	115
Kale	106	Zucchini	115

AMARYLLIDACEAE:
The Onion Family

Garlic: *Allium sativum*

Garlic is a herb native to southern Europe and was transported to many other parts of the world at a very early period in history. The ancient Egyptians held it in great esteem, while the Israelites in the wilderness lamented to Moses about the lack of garlic. The Romans fed it to their labourers to strengthen them and to their armies because of its health-giving properties. It was probably the Romans who introduced garlic to the rest of Europe. In North America we consider garlic to be a culinary herb of some importance. The juice of a small clove greatly enhances the flavour of many dishes.

Garlic is easy to grow if it is planted as early in the spring as the ground can be worked. Cool temperatures for early growth are essential. However, at the late stage of growth garlic can tolerate hot weather, and for this reason it can be planted in the main garden where it will get full sunshine. In too shady a location bulbs will be poorly formed. A mature garlic bulb consists of a number of bulblets, or cloves, each of which can be planted. One such bulb will produce enough cloves for the average home gardener to plant. Because few seed catalogues include garlic, many gardeners use bulbs purchased at the supermarket for propagation.

These cloves should be planted with the fat end down, one or 2 inches deep and 4 to 6 inches apart. The soil should be well-drained but with a high organic content. An area that was well-manured the previous year is perfect. As the bulbs reach maturity, withhold fertilizer and water. The plants will look like onions and will be about one foot high.

During the summer the leaves can be cut and added to salads or used in cooking. The main harvest will take place after the tops have died down. The bulbs should be pulled up and left lying on the ground until the tops are completely dry, then brought into a shed and cured like onions. Some people like to braid the stalks and hang them up; others prefer to cut the tops off and keep the bulbs in an airy container.

Garlic is subject to most of the same ailments as onions, but seems to be more disease-resistant.

Leeks *Allium porrum*

The leek is a plant native to southern Europe and the Near East. Records indicate it was revered by the early Egyptians who grew it among the vegetables under general cultivation. The Romans are believed to have introduced leeks to Britain, and Saxon writings record them as being considered valuable food. To this day, leeks are very popular in Europe and the British Isles, and should be seen far more often in North American kitchen gardens.

The leek that grows wild in eastern North American forests has a very pungent odour and is in no way similar to our garden variety.

The cultivated leek is the aristocrat of the onion tribe, being both mild and delicate in flavour. Many novice gardeners find leeks hard to grow, and the instructions given on most seed packages are not sufficient to produce a good crop.

Leeks need a long growing season to mature. To assure a good crop, the seed must be started eight to ten weeks before planting-out time. Leeks can tolerate light frost and can be set out in the garden about two weeks before the last frost-free date. For people who do not have a hot-frame, start the seed indoors in the

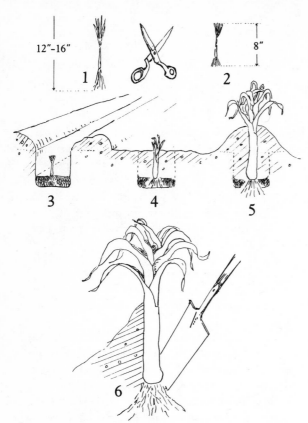

1. *Leek seedling removed from seed bed.*
2. *Seedling with top and root trimmed prior to transplanting.*
3. *Leeks planted in trench. Good soil should be placed on top of well-rotted manure or compost.*
4. *Fill trench as plant grows.*
5. *Hill leeks as necessary to ensure blanching.*
6. *Dig carefully, removing soil first, to avoid damaging mature plants. Leeks develop a strong root system.*

same manner as other transplants. I use a hotframe and sow the seed quite thickly in drills. Because germination is often irregular and poor, it is easier to thin the rows if necessary than to have insufficient plants. The seedlings remain in the frame until they reach the size of a thin pencil and are ready to be planted out in the garden.

The best results are obtained by planting leeks in a trench dug with a spade. Dig a trench 8-10 inches deep and the width of the spade. Pile the soil on either side of the trench. If the topsoil in the garden is shallow, do not make the trench so deep. Well-rotted manure or compost should be forked into the bottom of the trench and some good soil placed on top of it. Use a small pointed stick or pencil to make holes for planting. Trim the tops and roots of the seedlings before planting. Keep well-watered. Fertilize the plants every two weeks with weak liquid manure or fertilizer (5:10:5). As the plants grow, gradually fill in the trench with the soil from either side, leaving the green fan-like growth exposed. If the trench is not deep, hill the plants to blanch them. Unblanched leeks are tough and lack good flavour.

Some harvesting may be done as soon as the plants are large enough. Leeks can withstand quite a hard frost when mature and should be kept in the ground as long as possible, digging only as needed for immediate use. I dig all our plants before freeze-up, and put a four-week supply in the crisper, the rest in the freezer. Gardeners whose land dries out early in the spring can leave a crop in the ground over winter, and have freshly dug leeks the following spring.

Leeks do not require processing before being put in the freezer. All they need is careful washing to remove any sand particles from between the leaves. The thick, white stems should be cut into 2-inch lengths, bagged and frozen. The more tender of the green tops can be thinly chopped and frozen for later use in soups.

It is the long white stems of the leek that we eat. These can be sliced finely and used as a substitute for onions in salads, or cooked.

Boiled leeks in cream sauce. Cut the leeks into whatever lengths you desire. I prefer them about 6 inches long. Steam or boil until tender, using as little water as possible. Strain and keep this water. Make a cream sauce, add the water and a dash of sherry and serve hot.

Leftover leeks and mashed potatoes can be combined, creamed in the blender and diluted with chicken stock and/or milk to make a delicious soup that can be served either hot or cold. A garnish of chives or parsley completes the dish.

The first harvest. Remaining crop continues growing. Leeks are harvested August through November.

Onions: *Allium cepa*

Of all vegetables the onion is the most widely used. It may be eaten raw, cooked as a vegetable on its own, or as an important addition to many thousands of recipes. Onions are believed to have originated in southwest Asia, although various members of the onion family are known to be native in many other parts of the world. The Greek historian, Herodotus, has recorded that in the Great Pyramid of Cheops there is an inscription which states that 1,600 talents of silver were paid to supply the workers with onions, garlic and radishes. The Egyptians held the onion in exceedingly high esteem and worshipped it as a deity, believing the layers of the bulb represented the various spheres of the earth, heaven and hell. They were aware of the rich food value of the onion and gave the workers a daily ration.

The onion belongs to the Amaryllis family and is closely related to garlic, leeks and chives. Nowadays we have a wide range of varieties to choose from, but before selecting seed, consider the method of cultivation to be adopted. There are three methods commonly used in growing onions: by sets, by seed and by seedling plants.

Onion sets. The simplest and most dependable method of growing onions for the novice gardener is the onion set. These are small onion bulbs that have been grown under controlled conditions from seed the previous year. The sets should not exceed a ³/₄-inch diameter; ¹/₂ inch is the ideal. Large sets are likely to "bolt," that is, mature too rapidly, and go to seed. The onion, a biennial, has a tendency to form seed in the second year of growth.

Sets are planted in drills deep enough to cover the bulbs. I plant two drills about 6 inches apart. Some people prefer drills 12 to 18 inches apart to allow for cultivation between rows. If the sets are to be grown as the main crop for winter storage, allow 3 to 4 inches between bulbs. If you want small, early green onions, plant them more densely, harvesting as desired.

For winter storage we grow main crop onion sets. There are now many varieties on the market offering such differing characteristics as colour, shape, size and keeping quality. Some new hybrids can be stored for as long as eighteen months.

If any of the plants go to seed, break off the seed blossom, and use these onions quickly for they will not store well.

Multiplier sets will produce very early spring onions. These sets each have several cloves or bulblets that can be divided and planted individually. Each set or bulblet will send up a cluster of very tasty young shoots ready to harvest in three to four weeks. Successive plantings should be made for about six weeks or as long as the bulblets remain firm.

Seed. Onion seed can be sown directly in the garden as soon as the ground can be worked. If the seed is sown thickly, thin the seedlings when very young and use the thinnings as scallions or green onions. If the plants are left growing in crowded conditions, the bulbs will be very small. With certain varieties these small bulbs, when cured, can be used the following year as sets. If the plants are thinned to a space of 4 to 6 inches, they will form large bulbs, suitable for storage.

A forest of healthy, growing onions. They were seeded in rows 18 inches apart directly in the garden in late April.

Drying onions in the garden prior to bringing them into a shed. Those in the foreground were planted as "sets." Some have gone to seed and will not keep long in storage.

Onion seedling plants. These should be started indoors in February or March. When large enough to handle, transplant the seedlings into flats and harden before transplanting into the garden when danger of severe frost is past. These seedling should be the size of a pencil and be spaced 6 inches apart in the rows. Very large onions can be grown this way, but they require a great deal more time and effort.

It is important to prepare the ground thoroughly before planting any onions. The soil should be fertile and high in organic matter. Work in well-rotted manure, compost and wood ash if available. A sprinkling of 5:10:5 or 5:10:10 fertilizer also helps. If clay conditions prevail in the garden, make a raised bed to ensure good drainage. Onions are very sensitive to wet, soggy ground. Onions are one of the few crops that you can grow in the same bed several years running; it is therefore well worth putting extra work into the preparation of the bed, especially important in gardens with poor soil conditions.

Onions are heavy feeders and benefit from additional fertilizing. A balanced fertilizer or weak liquid manure can be given after the plants are growing strongly, but not when the bulbs have started to form. For their early growth onions prefer cool weather conditions and plenty of moisture (but not sogginess),

during which time they make a strong leafy growth. Then in July and August, during hot, dry conditions, they form a large bulb.

Green onions and scallions can be grown in partial shade but the bulbs must have full sun. Onions are sensitive to day length, and should attain maximum top growth before the days become shorter.

As the onion bed is rich, fertile and moist, it is also an ideal place for weeds. Weeding the rows by hand, when the weeds are small, is a relatively simple job. If the weeds are allowed to grow sufficiently large that the root system will interfere with the onion, damage will occur when weeding. Hoe between the rows.

In late summer or early fall the onion tops will start to die down naturally, so there is no need to bend them over. If you decide to give them a little help, be careful not to bruise the necks—this will shorten storage life. When the tops have died down, pull the bulbs out of the ground, place them in rows and leave them to dry in the sun for several days. Next, bring them into the garage or tool shed, spread them out and leave to cure for several weeks. If you intend to "braid" them before hanging them, leave the tops on; otherwise, cut them off one inch above the bulb.

Before there is any risk of freezing tempera-

Onions drying in a shed. Curing takes two to three weeks.

tures, bring the bulbs indoors and store in a cool, well-ventilated and dry area. Only certain varieties are recommended for winter storage.

Problems and Controls

Onion maggots. The most serious problem usually encountered with the onion family is the onion maggot. The first sign of something amiss is when the plant begins to wilt. Experienced gardeners detect maggot damage very quickly and take immediate steps to remedy the situation.

Onion maggots are the larvae of a small fly, which lays its eggs on the soil surface around the onions. The maggots are about 1/3-inch long and burrow into onion bulbs, killing the young plants. My method of controlling maggots is to work diazinon crystals into the soil before planting onions. If I notice any wilting plants later on, I remove and destroy the damaged bulbs and water the row of healthy onions with liquid diazinon. There are other products on the market for controlling maggots and new developments will be reported in government pamphlets.

Thrips. Small, yellowish sucking insects called thrips may attack the leaves of the onion family. If the leaves have a mottled appearance, look for thrips. They can be controlled satisfac-

torily by dusting or spraying with a recommended pesticide.

Onion smut. This fungus can live in the soil for years. It only attacks young seedlings (not sets), usually in cool, damp seasons. Onion smut is not often encountered in home gardens. If it should occur, make sure you do not plant onion seed or seedlings in the same soil for several years following — in fact, it would be safer not to plant onion seeds at all for a few years. The fungus can be identified by a blackening of the small seedling and can be avoided by planting disease-resistant sets.

Downy mildew. This fungus disease occurs during cool, wet weather. It is a light-coloured, downy coating that will cause the leaves to yellow and die. It can be easily controlled by several applications of a recommended fungicide. As soon as the mildew is noticed, begin treatment.

Thick neck. While harvesting, you may notice that some of your onions have not died down properly and will have quite a thick neck. These onions will not cure, and should be eaten first as they will not last in storage. The term "thick neck" describes this condition.

(We ran into an unexpected problem during the curing stage. A family of squirrels discovered our onions in the garage and made off with a large part before we noticed it. Fortunately, we found their cache in a box in the rafters above.)

Onion bulb infested with maggots.

CHENOPODIACEAE:
The Beet Family

Beets: *Beta vulgaris*

Beets, or beetroot as it is known in England, is native to southern Europe. It is a coastal plant, and although it does best in a sandy loam, it will thrive in any good soil. Beets do well in full sun but can tolerate partial shade. As with all root crops, the soil should be worked to a depth of at least 8 inches and be free of clods and stones. Well-rotted manure dug into the soil enriches it, allowing better germination and rapid growth of the plants. The more rapid the growth, the better quality of the beets. Each beet seed will produce a cluster of three or four plants. Plant about ten seeds per foot of row at a depth of half an inch. Cover and tamp firmly. Allow 12 to 15 inches between rows. Germination takes eight to ten days. If the weather is dry and hot, I cover the row with a board, removing it at the first sign of germination. This prevents the seed and soil from drying out at the critical stage. When the seedling are 4 to 6 inches high, thin them, using the thinnings as greens. Subsequent thinning should be done as the roots mature and become crowded in the row.

Beets are at their prime when they are young. Harvest them when they reach about 2 inches in diameter. Also, the tops may be eaten either in salads or cooked like spinach. Make successive plantings every two weeks until mid-July.

Beets benefit from a light application of salt worked into the ground before seeding, not more than an ounce per square yard. I also give my plants one more treat when they are 4 to 6 inches tall: one tablespoon of salt to one gallon of water — I give the plants a good soaking. This should be applied only when the plants are actively growing and the soil is moist.

Never allow beets to dry out or they will become "woody."

There is now a golden beet on the market. This variety is especially valuable as a dual-purpose vegetable. While the root is still growing, the leaves may be picked and used like spinach. The root does not "bleed" and will not discolour other ingredients in a salad. Beets are now available in various shapes and sizes, with maturing times ranging from 40 to 80 days.

I would recommend that the novice gardener study a seed catalogue before purchasing any seed, and avoid novelty varieties in the first year.

Beets do not have many problems. Our worst enemy is a very pretty goldfinch which pecks holes in the leaves.

Harvesting beets in mid-season.

In overlimed gardens black spots, dry rot and scab may occur on the roots because boron is less available to the plants in sweet soil. A soil test will determine the pH level, which should read between 6.0 and 6.8.

Beets taste better when freshly harvested, so pull only enough for immediate use. However, when the main crop is ready, the beets should be harvested and frozen, pickled or stored in the cool room for winter use.

To freeze, cook thoroughly, cool before dicing and put in plastic bags or containers in the freezer. For the cool room, either pack in boxes of sand or in ventilated plastic bags. I prefer the latter method and find the beets remain firm for several months.

Chard: *Beta vulgaris cicla*

Chard, also called Swiss chard, is a close relative of the beet, and also native to southern Europe. For best results the soil should be rich in organic content and have good drainage. The seeds should be sown ³/₄-inch deep and thinned to a distance of 8 to 12 inches. Allow 2 feet between rows. Chard can tolerate partial shade, and prefers cool temperatures.

In our garden we grow four plants, which is ample for our needs. Chard is rather like rhubarb in appearance, having a long thick stalk and a large leaf. Both the stalk and the leaf are eaten. The stalk is cooked like celery and the leaf used in the same manner as spinach, either cooked or in salads. Chard will grow to a height of 2 to 2½ feet, and will produce well into the fall as only the outer leaves are cut or pulled, leaving the rest of the plant in the ground to continue growing.

There are several varieties available. Some have green or white stalks, while the colourful rhubarb chard with its bright crimson stalks and crumply leaves is very appealing to the eye, and may be grown in flower beds.

Chard is relatively free from troubles. Aphids and leaf miners are sometimes a problem, but can be controlled by rotenone.

Chard in late season.

Spinach: *Spinacia oleracea*

Spinach is one of the earliest vegetables known to man. A most important green vegetable, it is very rich in vitamin A, high in ascorbic acid, riboflavin, plus some thiamine, and also rich in iron and calcium.

Spinach is a fast-growing, cool-weather crop and must be seeded directly in the garden as soon as the ground is prepared. I like to grow spinach in beds three rows wide with the rows 6 inches apart and the beds 18 inches wide. Some gardeners prefer to grow spinach in single rows 12 inches apart. Another method is to broadcast the seed in a prepared seed bed, then rake it in and tamp it down. Successive plantings may be made during early spring, but not during the summer because plants "bolt" to seed in hot weather. Plants must be kept well-watered, and the addition of a high nitrogen fertilizer to the soil before planting is helpful.

A healthy row of spinach ready for harvesting in early June.

When watering the growing plants, use liquid manure or a high nitrogen liquid fertilizer. Wait until early August before planting seed for fall crops — light frost will not hurt spinach.

Spinach can tolerate partial shade, but I have found that when grown in full sun, growth is more rapid and the quality of the crop much better. I start harvesting the leaves about six weeks after seeding, or when they are sufficiently mature. This will vary from season to season. I pick only the outer leaves and allow the plants to continue growing until they show signs of going to seed. The entire crop is then harvested by cutting the stems at ground level, usually about ten weeks after seeding. This is the crop that I process for the freezer.

It is unusual for the home gardener to have problems growing spinach, but if the seed is planted late in the spring and a hot season follows, the plants will bolt (run to seed). Also, if the plants are allowed to dry out, the same condition will result.

New Zealand Spinach: *Tetragonia expansa*

This is not, in fact, a member of the beet family but belongs to the Aizoaceae, the carpet-weed family. It is included here because, for culinary purposes, it is treated like spinach.

Unlike ordinary spinach, this plant thrives in hot weather and produces throughout the summer. It is called a perennial spinach in the seed catalogues, but I have found that hard frost will kill it. Many home gardeners grow New Zealand spinach and enjoy it; it is not, however, a favourite in our house. This is simply a matter of taste, probably because there are so many other more luscious vegetables which thrive in the hot weather and mature at the same time as the New Zealand spinach. Two or three plants would be sufficient for the average family, as this variety of spinach becomes a small prostrate bush spreading about 2 feet in all directions. For use, pick the tender young leaves at the tips of the branches and cook in the same manner as ordinary spinach. When eaten raw in salads, it may leave a dry taste in the mouth.

Problems and Controls

The leaf miner is common to both beets and chard. It is a small, white maggot that burrows into the tissue of the leaves, causing considerable distress to the plant. The main vein of the leaf will show discolouration, and the leaves will be misshapen and wilted.

The web worm larvae attack the undersides of the leaves. These insects are not generally considered serious problems and can be controlled by spraying or dusting.

Spinach yellows is a virus disease spread by aphids. You can recognize it by a mottling and yellowing of the leaves and stunted growth of the entire plant. The best control is to purchase disease-resistant seed, and if aphids are seen, dust or spray the plants. Any diseased plants should be burned. Generally speaking, beets, chard and spinach are easy crops to grow and are not normally disease prone.

COMPOSITAE:
The Sunflower or Thistle Family

Globe Artichoke: *Cynara scolymus*

The globe artichoke is a gourmet vegetable only recommended for the garden where space is not a concern and the gardener enjoys experimenting. I have tried growing them on a number of occasions — some years I have a most successful crop; others, a failure.

The globe artichoke is a perennial plant native to the Mediterranean region and the Canary Islands. Therefore, it must be grown in full sunlight. It closely resembles a thistle and attains a height of 2 to 3 feet. The flower buds are the edible portion of the plant. In our climate it is treated as an annual, but in milder areas globe artichokes may survive the winter if heavily mulched after freeze-up. Globe artichokes must be started indoors in early March using the same method as for other transplants; if the transplants become too large for the Jiffy-7's or flats, it may be necessary to pot them up individually. Don't grow too many; ten plants in the garden should be ample for the average household.

Transplant outdoors the third week in May if the weather is warm. Allow 3 feet between plants, as well as between rows. Artichokes need rich soil and plenty of water. Feed regularly with a balanced fertilizer. Unless care is taken, the buds become infested with insects. Keep dusting with rotenone to discourage the moth laying her eggs.

The first or main bud should be ready to harvest by early August, after which side shoots will produce smaller buds that are just as tasty as the original.

Harvest the buds when the petals are still tight by cutting the stem 2 to 3 inches below the bud. This stem is also edible. Wash thoroughly and soak in cold, salted water for thirty minutes before cooking. Cook in boiling water

Globe artichoke ready for harvest. Notice the secondary bud which will be left for a later harvest. In spite of dusting with rotenone, the leaves show signs of damage by the flea beetle; however, the buds themselves are free of injury.

until the stalk-end is tender when prodded with a skewer. Drain upside down. Serve hot with melted butter, or cold with a salad dressing or Hollandaise sauce. If the buds open and are no longer edible, these flowers can be air-dried and used in flower arrangements.

Jerusalem Artichokes: *Helianthus tuberosus*

A native tuberous perennial weed of eastern North America and the Pacific coast, the Jerusalem artichoke grows in moist, peaty soils.

Nobody seems to know why it is called "artichoke"; it is in no way similar to the globe artichoke. (It is, however, a member of the

When we are ready to "do" the artichoke patch, I bring the garden cart and a spade. First, I pile the old mulch along the edge of the bed. Then I dig systematically, throwing the tubers, which will have begun to "shoot," into the cart.

The new planting, fertilized and watered, soon begins to "take off." No more attention is needed except for the occasional watering in very hot, dry weather until the fall.

After the first frost the tall, sunflower-like plants are cut down to about one foot and covered in mulch. (The old mulch will probably have "broken down.") Thereafter, I dig tubers as I need them until Christmas. The tops are carted away and can be composted.

sunflower family.) Neither has it any connection with the Holy Land. The name "Jerusalem" is probably derived from the Italian word *girasol* (turning to the sun), so called by the Italian sailors who reputedly brought the tubers back to Europe after being introduced to them by the North American Indians.

The Jerusalem artichoke is far better known in Europe and the British Isles than it is in its native North America, and deserves far more attention in the home garden when space is available. It is exceedingly easy to grow and seems to have no enemies. The only disadvantage of this vegetable is that unless allotted a large separate area of the garden, it can take over the whole plot and become very hard to eradicate. These sun-loving members of the sunflower family will send up a strong upright stem and grow to a height of 8 to 10 feet.

For these reasons I plant it in a 10 by 10 foot plot, treat it as a perennial and do not rotate. Instead, I ensure that sufficient nutrients are provided through manure and fertilizing. The tubers are the edible part and are planted like potatoes, 12 inches apart in rows with 1½ to 2 feet between rows. They do well in any soil, but best in a light, sandy loam enriched with well-rotted manure. After planting, I water the bed thoroughly if it is dry, then apply a mulch. The mulch controls the weeds and retains the moisture so that very little care is needed before harvesting in the fall. Frost improves the flavour and quality of the tubers. Dig only the amount required for immediate use and continue harvesting all through the winter if conditions permit. We often dig tubers at Christmas when it is necessary to clear the snow and mulch away.

In the spring, continue harvesting until the tubers begin to sprout. Then, dig up the entire bed, removing the tubers; dig in more manure or compost; add a complete fertilizer (a few handfuls sprinkled lightly over the area) and re-plant in rows. You are sure to have plenty of tubers left over; keep these in plastic bags in the cool room or refrigerator until used. The artichokes you keep to eat should be the size of medium potatoes. The tubers are nobbly, and

Harvesting Jerusalem artichoke tubers.

for this reason the smaller ones are very tedious to prepare for the table. They are best kept for seed.

Artichokes in cream sauce. To prevent discolouring, peel thinly under water to which is added one teaspoonful of lemon juice or white vinegar; add one teaspoon of lemon juice or white vinegar to cooking water; simmer until tender; strain; serve in white sauce.

Jerusalem artichoke soup. Prepare artichokes as in previous recipe; use stock for cooking; when tender puree in blender; thicken with flour, cornflour or arrowroot (blended with milk); season to taste. Mashed potato added to the puree gives a better consistency.

Jerusalem artichoke salad. Slice thinly or grate; sprinkle with lemon juice and add to salads.

Boiled artichokes. Wash thoroughly; place in a saucepan; cover with boiling water; simmer until tender when prodded with a skewer (about twenty minutes). Serve the same as potatoes.

Endive and Escarole: *Chicorium endivia*

Endive is believed to have originated in East India, spreading throughout Europe and the Orient at a very early date in history. The ancient Egyptians used it as a vegetable and the Greeks as a salad and pot herb.

The endive we know today differs little from its ancestor, and is used mostly in salads. There are two major varieties: "green curled" which has very curly, serrated leaves; and the "broad leafed Bavarian" which has large, closely packed, upright leaves and is usually marketed under the name escarole.

The general culture of these two varieties is similar to that of lettuce. Endive does best in well-drained soil enriched with plenty of well-rotted manure or compost. Never use fresh manure as this would cause the flavour of the endive to be rank and the growth too lush. Endive is a cool-weather crop which can tolerate partial shade and requires about three months to mature. The seed should be sown as soon as the ground has been worked in the spring. Sow only a small amount at one time, but make subsequent seedings every two weeks or so, as with lettuce. Thin the plants to one foot apart after they have developed sufficiently. Endive can be sown in a seed-bed and the seedlings transplanted to the main garden. Both methods are equally satisfactory.

The flavour of endive is rather bitter unless the plants are blanched three weeks prior to harvesting. When plants are nearing maturity, cover them with an inverted flower pot or with a box or boards. Usually three large flower pots or boxes are all the home gardener requires; this gives a succession of plants being blanched. One large head of endive supplies the average family with ample salads for a week. Plants ready for harvesting should be cut before going to seed. Endives can also be served cooked or steamed in the same way as spinach.

As endive is a cool-weather crop, it is best grown early in the season and again as a salad crop for late fall use. Sow the last seeds towards the end of July or early in August. Endive can tolerate fall rain and early frost, since the late crop is protected from frost by blanching. If a severe frost is anticipated, apply extra protection.

Endive is easy to grow and can extend the home-garden salad season well into the fall after other crops are over. Slugs are its main enemy, and in unfavourable weather conditions stem-rot may occur.

French Endive, or Witloof Chicory:
Cichorium intybus

French endive, or chicory, is a biennial native plant of Europe and the Orient. It is extremely popular in France and other European countries and ranks high in the gourmet class of vegetables. The shoots can be eaten either raw in salads or cooked. For the ultimate in flavour and tenderness, blanching is desirable.

The cultural requirements are similar to those of lettuce, endive and escarole but, since it is a biennial, the roots can remain in the ground all winter to send up shoots in the spring to provide an early vegetable for the household. These shoots should be blanched too. The plant is normally more vigorous in the second year than the first.

At my home in Ireland, French endive roots were brought into a shed in the fall after the first season, packed closely together in boxes of soil and "forced" for winter use. I have tried this method in our basement here, but found the work involved did not give an adequate return. It was a constant battle with the cat which decided my indoor boxes of soil were there for her convenience, and the job of carrying soil up and down the basement stairs seemed like too much hard work. We grew enough for several delicious dishes, but not sufficient to justify repeating the experiment.

The roots of French endive (chicory) can be processed and used as a substitute for coffee. Essence of chicory is sold in liquid form and is more popular in Europe than in North America.

Cooking French endive.   Cook endive shoots slowly until tender. Steaming is the best method, but if this is not possible use a minimum amount of water. Strain, set in an open casserole, cover with cheese sauce and place under the broiler until brown. Cooking time is about twenty minutes.

Lettuce: *Lactuca saliva*

It is said, that the effect of eating too Much Lettuce is "soporific" I have never felt sleepy after eating Lettuces; but then, I am not a rabbit — They certainly had a very soporific effect upon the Flopsy Bunnies!

Beatrix Potter

There is no doubt that lettuce is the most popular salad plant. Rabbits seem to like it too! Ask anyone whose garden has been visited by that unwanted gardener!

Lettuce is among the earliest of recorded vegetables, popular with the Persians and Romans as early as 500 BC. It is a cool-season crop, and it is likely to "bolt" to seed if grown in the heat of the summer. There are a great many varieties listed in our seed catalogues, and have only slight differences in their characteristics, namely: number of days to maturity; size of head; texture of leaf; resistance to disease or drought.

For practical purposes the varieties can be divided into four groups: loose-leaf lettuce; crisp heading lettuce; cos or romaine lettuce; and butterhead, or Boston, lettuce.

Loose-leaf lettuce   is the most popular variety with home gardeners because it is so easy to grow. It does best in a light fertile soil and can tolerate full sun in the spring and fall. Lettuce will, however, bolt in the heat of the summer. Therefore, the summer crop can be grown in partial shade. The first seeding is made early in the season, the end of April or the beginning of May, and successive seedings are made every two weeks until July. You should only sow as much as your household can use in a two-week period, usually about 4 feet of row. Allow 18 to 24 inches between rows; cover seeds lightly and thin seedlings (using these in a salad) to 6

(Above.) An early July view of the garden shows very rapid growth after the soil is warm. We have been eating fresh produce since May and will continue to do so until freeze-up.

(Below.) Main crop broccoli transplants are intercropped with Boston lettuce. The latter will be harvested before the broccoli needs the space. The heavy mulch controls weeds and conserves water.

The crisp, crinkly leaves and delicate flavour makes the Savoy cabbage my favourite, both raw and cooked.

A basket of freshly harvested globe artichokes.

Leeks are the mildest and most delicately flavoured of the onion group. Easy to grow, using the right methods.

The compact growth of a bush vegetable marrow makes this squash suitable for small gardens.

Black seeded Simpson is a fast growing early lettuce, suitable for transplanting or direct garden seeding.

inches apart. If any difficulty is encountered with seed germination, particularly during hot weather, try refrigerating the seeds for a couple of days prior to planting. Normal germination time for all lettuce is four to eight days.

Crisp heading lettuce has dark-green outer leaves and a light or blanched heart. When fully grown it can measure 12 or 15 inches

broccoli plants. The lettuce will have matured before the Brassicas need the space, and as the Brassicas grow they give the lettuce some shade which is most beneficial. I do not even attempt to grow head lettuce during the summer heat.

Cos or romaine lettuce is recognized by the upright character of the plants with their hearts of long, slender leaves. The texture appears to

Butterhead lettuce ready to harvest between young pepper plants. Note heavy straw mulch.

Cos or Romaine lettuce.

across. Plant seed indoors in April or in the hot-frame for very early plants. Plant seed in the cold-frame or seed-bed in May for successive crops. Transplant to the garden when small sturdy plants have formed, allowing 12 inches between plants in rows 18 to 24 inches apart.

In my garden, I do not give head lettuce a separate row. Instead, I plant a seedling between each of the cabbage, cauliflower and

be coarse but, in fact, is sweet and tender and will stand up much better to intense summer heat than other types. Culture is the same as for crisp heading lettuce.

Butterhead or Boston lettuce has a very tender texture to the leaves and may be either seeded directly or grown as a transplant. It is very popular in the home garden but will not stand up well to intense summer heat. Freshly picked butterhead lettuce is hard to beat!

All lettuce must be kept well-watered, and regular application of liquid manure or high-nitrogen fertilizer aids rapid growth. This is essential for top-grade lettuce. Never permit the lettuce plants to dry out; the quality of the crop will be permanently damaged. For fall use, plant seed at the end of July or early August and treat in the same manner as the spring crop.

The most usual way to eat lettuce is raw or in salads. But you will often find that you have more than you can use before it goes to seed, so why not treat it like spinach. Your spinach crop will be over by the time lettuce is ready to "bolt." In France, lettuce is frequently served braised as a hot vegetable.

Braised lettuce. Remove the coarse outer leaves; cut the head into quarters; place in saucepan, adding a very small quantity of hot stock or thickened gravy; simmer for about eight minutes or until tender; add seasoning and serve.

Problems and Controls

Slugs. Lettuce has few insect enemies; the most common is the slug. To control, use slug-bait or, better still, flat dishes of stale beer set in the ground with some kind of cover to keep out the rain. Slugs love beer and drown in it.

Slug.

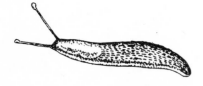

Fungi. There are many soil-borne diseases which attack lettuce. The most common of these are three fungi, all of which cause rotting of the lower leaves and stem.

To avoid fungi, purchase disease-resistant seed and rotate your crops. Allow good circulation of air around and under the plants. Remove and destroy any diseased plants. Remember to remove all old plant refuse. Maintain dry soil around plants with shallow cultivation.

Water the plants early in the day in order to allow the foliage and soil surface to dry out before night.

Dig sweet potatoes after the vines have been killed by the first frosts. However, dig only as many as you need for immediate use and try not to damage the skins of the tubers.

CONVOLVULACEAE:
The Morning Glory Family

Sweet Potatoes: *Ipomoea batatas*

The sweet potato is native to the tropics of America. It should not be confused with the yam, which comes from Africa and is not generally considered edible by modern man but rather an animal fodder. Many supermarkets sell "yams," but these are incorrectly named since they are, in fact, sweet potatoes.

Sweet potatoes require a very long, hot growing season. We grow only one or two hills in our garden, just for the fun of it. The tubers do not have time to ripen sufficiently for winter storage so must be eaten soon after being dug. Nowhere in Canada are sweet potatoes an economic crop. But growing some plants is an excellent way to involve children in gardening. In February or March, look in the supermarket for a tuber whose "eyes" look alive or, better still, have already started to sprout. Store-bought tubers have been treated with a gas to inhibit sprouting, but there are always a few in each shipment that remain viable. Each tuber will have as many as 50 eyes.

Place the tuber in a glass of water in such a way that only the bottom half is immersed in the water. The top half, where it was joined to the plant, is exposed to the air. The bottom will develop roots and the top, shoots. These shoots can be cut from the "mother" and rooted in water or moist peat moss. After hardening, plant them out in the garden or in a large container. The "mother" tuber can be left to grow as a house plant or vine. Sweet potatoes are very frost-tender, so don't be in a hurry to plant them outdoors; the first week in June is time enough in our garden. Be sure that all danger of frost is past and that the soil has warmed up.

Unlike most garden vegetables, sweet potatoes prefer a slightly acid, sandy loam. A sunny area in the garden where other vegetables have not done well will often suit them fine. As with all root crops, work the ground deeply before planting the sprouts. A handful of complete fertilizer is beneficial too.

The sweet potato is a vine with trailing and rooting stems. One hill of three plants will occupy an area of 3 to 4 square feet. Some varieties need more space than others, but with a store-bought tuber, it is impossible to know which you are growing. If the season is good, tubers will form wherever the stems put down roots.

Mulching after the ground is really warm conserves heat and controls weeds.

The leaves can be eaten in salads and the tubers harvested after the tops have been killed by the first frost. Dig only as many as you need for immediate use. Our experience is that they will keep better in the ground than in the refrigerator. The entire crop should be used within a few weeks after the foliage has been killed; otherwise, the tubers will rot.

Sweet potatoes are not a guaranteed crop and should be given a very low priority in gardens where space is limited. If grown in a container, bring indoors before there is any risk of frost and allow the tubers to continue growing until mature. Sweet potatoes are a novelty crop in Canada.

Problems and Controls

There are various diseases and pests to which sweet potatoes are susceptible. However, when growing only a few plants, these will not be a problem to home gardeners in temperate zones. Any insects noticed can be controlled by dusting or spraying and diseased plants removed from the garden and destroyed.

CRUCIFERAE:
The Mustard or Cabbage Family

The cabbage-like members of this family are thought by most people to be related crops. However, I have found many gardeners do not realize that turnips, radishes, cress and sea-kale also belong to this category. Cabbages and most of the other vegetables in this family are members of the Brassica genus and have much in common with regard to cultivation and susceptibility to pests and diseases. The cultivation of cress, radishes, sea-kale and watercress is different from the other Cruciferae and is treated under their separate headings.

The Brassicas

For the novice gardener a little information on the background of this group will help to understand their culture. The cultivars we grow in our gardens today are mostly horticultural hybrids whose common ancestors were native to Europe and the Mediterranean region.

All the Brassicas are sun-loving, cool-weather crops and will vary in quality according to the season. When purchasing seed, decide whether early, mid-season or late varieties are required. Early crops must be started indoors as transplants. Late crops can be seeded directly in the garden and either thinned or transplanted.

Brassicas will grow in a wide range of soils, but do best when the pH level is around 6.5. If the soil is acidic, it should be limed. The ground should be fertile, high in humus and with good drainage. The organic matter should be worked into the ground during the fall, prior to planting. We try to locate the Brassicas in the area occupied previously by legumes because they need the nitrogen that the legumes pack into the soil. During the growing season it is very important never to permit the

ground to dry out; a lack of moisture, even for a relatively short period of time, will cause a serious set-back, especially to the cauliflower. Sudden heavy rain or watering after a dry spell will cause cabbages to grow rapidly and split. If there is sufficient humus in the soil and the soil is kept moist, these conditions are less likely to occur.

In highly fertile soils additional fertilizing at planting time is unnecessary. In poor soils an application of 10:10:10 at the rate of up to 4 pounds per 100 square feet is beneficial. After three or four weeks, when the plants are growing well, they benefit from a side dressing of a high nitrogen fertilizer or a watering with liquid manure.

Our experiences have shown that mulching is a definite help in conserving moisture and controlling weeds. Brassicas should never be allotted the same location in the plot in successive years, nor for two croppings in the same season. When possible allow three years to elapse before replanting Brassicas in any one section of the garden. This helps prevent a recurrence of any disease which might remain dormant in the soil. We have found it is convenient to group all the Brassicas together in the garden; by doing so, the pest control program for Brassicas is confined to one area. For blemish-free crops, pest control is essential.

Problems and Controls of Brassicas

Cutworms. Newly transplanted Brassicas are extremely vulnerable to attack by the cutworm. These dull-grey grubs come out of the soil at night or on cloudy days and chew the stems of the plants at ground level. To the uninitiated it might appear that the stem has been broken by a cat or dog, but on close inspection you will see it is not actually a break. Sometimes the cutworm will chew only part way through the stem. These plants seldom survive. After feeding, cutworms rest during the day in the cool soil below the plant. I always dig down, find the culprit and destroy it, preventing the same cutworm from doing further damage.

Paper collars are the simplest protection against the cutworm. These collars should be fitted around the stem to give protection both above and below soil level.

Cabbage root maggot.   Damage to the roots of Brassicas, turnips and radishes is caused by the larvae of a fly that lays her eggs in the soil beside the plants. These small, white maggots feed on the developing roots, and the first indication of the presence will be a wilting of the entire plant. With experience a gardener will soon learn to identify this particular wilt. When damaged plants are pulled and the roots inspected, the maggots will be visible. The whole plant should be destroyed.

The cabbage root maggot can be controlled by working diazinon crystals into the ground prior to planting. Subsequent watering with liquid diazinon is recommended. Another control is to lay a thick mat of paper around the base of the plant, which prevents the fly from depositing eggs close to the plant.

Cabbage caterpillars.   When I first notice white butterflies fluttering around the garden, I know that unless I take the necessary precautions immediately, it will not be long before the caterpillars are chewing the Brassicas. This butterfly lays her eggs on the undersides of the leaves and, unless deterred, the resulting caterpillars will make the crop unsightly and unappetizing.

Prevention consists of either spraying or dusting. I prefer the latter as I find it far quicker. The process must be repeated after each rain or overhead watering.

The cabbage looper feeds on all Brassicas, as well as lettuce, turnips, tomatoes, radishes, peas and potatoes. This pale-green 1½-inch-

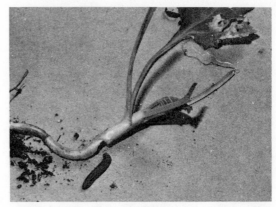

Cutworm having Brassica dinner.

Wilted cauliflower leaves indicate root maggot infestation.

Aleochara attacking cabbage root maggot.

long caterpillar alternately loops and stretches its body as it moves along, hence its name. It overwinters in the pupal stage on the leaves of its favourite plants, including many weeds. For this reason the fall clean-up in the garden is entremely important and can help keep the succeeding crop looper-free. However, if cabbage loopers do appear, the easist control is to

Cabbage looper.

knock them off into a bucket of salty water. Government pamphlets will suggest what insecticide should be used. I personally use rotenone.

Black rot is a seed-borne bacteria that causes rot of the stems and veins of the leaves. This problem can be avoided by using disease-free seed and resistant varieties.

Black leg is a soil-borne fungus that attacks seeds and seedlings. It can be recognized by a blackening of the stems at the surface of the soil. The best control is by using sterilized soil in the seed bed and observing crop rotation.

Cabbage yellows is a soil-borne fungus which results in the plant becoming lifeless yellowish-green a few weeks after transplanting. Control is by purchasing yellows-resistant varieties and by practising crop rotation.

Club root is a soil-borne fungus which produces gall-like swellings on the roots of Brassicas and stunting of the entire plant. This disease thrives in acid soils and once established in a garden is hard to eradicate. Prevention consists of maintaining a soil pH of 6.8 to 7 and following crop rotation procedures.

Broccoli: *Brassica oleracea italica*

As the botanical name denotes, broccoli was introduced to us from Italy and has only been a popular vegetable in North America since the 1920s. Broccoli is easy to grow, and plants will remain productive for three to four months, or as long as the gardener keeps harvesting the young shoots. Broccoli transplants can be set out in the garden as soon as the ground has been worked. When the plants are hardened, they will not be damaged by light frost. Protection against cutworms and root maggots should be provided.

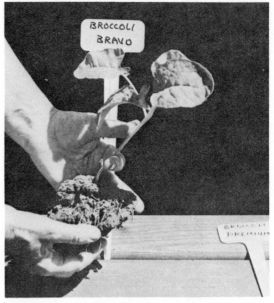

Broccoli seedling. Note the strong root growth which should be disturbed as little as possible.

Broccoli interplanted with lettuce.

There are several varieties on the market. We grow the sprouting broccoli, starting the plants early indoors. This one planting keeps us supplied throughout the season.

The large, central flower head of broccoli ready to be harvested. Smaller secondary heads will grow on side branches if the plant is left in the garden.

Brussels sprouts ready for harvesting. The lower sprouts should be broken off now to allow the upper ones to develop. Note that the upper leaves have been slightly damaged by caterpillars, but the sprouts are perfectly healthy.

Sprouting broccoli is a green vegetable that produces a large central flower head. This head must be cut when still compact, leaving the rest of the plant in the ground to branch and produce a constant supply of secondary shoots. With subsequent cutting these shoots become smaller, but are just as tasty as the main shoot.

Broccoli is an excellent vegetable for the small garden, much easier to grow than cauliflower, and provides a very long harvest season. Broccoli can be eaten raw in salads or with dips, cooked, or processed for the freezer. It is a most delicious vegetable, very rich in vitamins, especially the leaves.

A common complaint of broccoli growers is the little green caterpillar that so quickly turns people against eating this vegetable. If the controls mentioned earlier are observed, this should not be a problem.

Brussels Sprouts: *Brassica oleracea gemmifera*

Brussels sprouts derived their name from the Belgian city of Brussels where they have been grown since approximately the fourteenth century. They are not currently popular in North American gardens, possibly because World War II veterans stationed in England were served an abundance of this vegetable. Sprouts deserve more recognition, and should provide the family with a fresh green vegetable well after the main crops have been harvested, and right up until severe freezing occurs. In fact, the flavour is improved by a frost.

Brussels sprouts is an erect plant with a single stalk that grows about 3 feet high and develops sprouts in the axils of the leaves. The sprouts are like miniature cabbages, measuring one to 2 inches in diameter. Because the sprouts develop first on the lower portion of the stalk, break off the adjoining leaves, thus allowing the sprouts more room to mature. Harvest when they are still tightly closed by breaking the sprout away from the stalk with a sideways jerk, or by cutting with a knife. The plant will continue to push out new leaves at the top, and a new sprout will form in the axil of each leaf.

A healthy, mature ball-head cabbage showing no sign of pest damage.

A healthy, mature Savoy cabbage. In this variety the leaves are crinkly.

In areas like ours, where the growing season ends in early November, I find it is best to pinch out the growing point of the plant in mid-September to force the remaining sprouts to mature. In milder areas this growth should be left untouched.

Brussels sprouts can be stored for four to six weeks at a temperature slightly above freezing. To do this, the entire plant must be dug up and hung upside down in the storage cellar.

Brussels sprouts have a distinctive flavour. They are rich in vitamins, as well as iron and calcium.

Cabbage and Red Cabbage: *Brassica oleracea capitata*

There are literally hundreds of varieties of cabbage, which vary in colour, size, shape, texture, days to maturity and resistance to various diseases. The experienced home gardener knows that at the same time as his early cabbages are maturing, there is also an abundance of other vegetables. So it is wise not to plant too many early cabbages; six green and six red are enough for most families. Plant more of the late winter storage types, the kind that will keep in the cool room until well into the New Year.

If early cabbages are grown and the space is not required for another crop, harvest by cutting off the head with a sharp knife, leaving the stalk and root still growing. Cut a cross on top of the stalk with the knife, and in October four small cabbages will have formed, providing a second crop from one plant. It is important to continue your pest control program on these second crop plants.

With so many varieties available, it is hard to decide which to grow. Our favourite is Savoy, both early and late. I consider it to be the "King of the Cabbages." We also grow red cabbage, which we eat raw in salads, cook in the German style and pickle for winter use.

New cultivars are constantly appearing on the market, mainly available through seed catalogues. Some advantages of new hybrids are improved flavour and the ability to remain mature in the garden for a couple of months without splitting.

Red cabbage — German style. Shred finely one medium cabbage. Soak in salted water for about half an hour. Melt bacon fat or butter in a large saucepan. Add one medium onion, chopped. Cook until transparent. Lift the cabbage out of the water and put into the saucepan. Cook slowly for one hour with the lid on. Add two apples, cored and thinly sliced. Continue cooking for another hour. Stir occasionally. There should be enough juice to prevent sticking, but if the cabbage is drying

out, add a little water. It is more usual for there
to be too much juice, in which case remove the
cover and allow the moisture to evaporate.
Dissolve 2 tablespoons of flour and 4 tablespoons of brown sugar in 4 tablespoons of
vinegar. Add this to the cabbage and simmer
for another ten minutes or until thick. This
recipe freezes well.

Cauliflower: *Brassica oleracea botrytis*

Cauliflower is the least dependable of the Brassicas for the home gardener to grow. They are
always treated as transplants. The early crop
must be started indoors or in a hot-frame in
March or April and hardened before being set
out in the garden. Late spring frost will not
damage the hardened plants. Cauliflower is a
cool-weather crop, and the quality of the early
plants will to a great extent depend on the
season. The earlier they are set out in the
garden, the better. At no time should the
plants be allowed to dry out, because this
checks the growth of the heads, causing them
to become runted and button-like.

The late crop can be seeded in an outdoor
seed-bed in May and transplanted into the
garden during the summer. I like to transplant
these seedlings at intervals as they mature.
This provides an extended harvest of
cauliflower during the fall. They should be
transplanted on cool, rainy days and shaded
from the sun until re-established.

Most people prefer pure white cauliflower.
To obtain this purity, it is necessary to blanch
the head or curds. Shortly after the button-like
head appears, bring the outer leaves up and
over it and hold them together with a rubber
band or length of twine. The curds will continue to grow, and will remain white because
the light has been excluded. Cauliflower heads
must be harvested before the curds begin to
"rice" and discolour. It is very easy to remove
the rubber band to check, and essential to cut
the heads when they are ready. After harvesting, remove the remainder of the plant from
the garden, and if free from disease, put on the

*Cauliflowers with their outside leaves gathered together
by rubber bands. This helps the flower to bleach and
prevents unwelcome visits from the cabbage butterfly.*

*A fine example of a white cauliflower curd ready to be
harvested.*

compost heap. Some gardeners, including myself, prefer to burn the stalks; they take too
long to break down.

There are new self-blanching varieties on
the market, as well as a green-curded one, but
neither of these have proven especially popular
to date. As with cabbages, new varieties are
constantly being introduced. Again, the seed
catalogues are the best source of information.

Chinese Cabbage: *Brassica chinensis*

This cabbage originates in China and is a cool-weather crop. If exposed to summer heat and long days it will quickly go to seed.

For the best results plant seed directly in the garden in late July or early August. Thin the seedlings to 10 inches apart and keep them well-watered. From seeding time to harvest will be between 60 and 80 days.

Chinese cabbage is usually served as a salad, but can also be cooked. The flavour is milder than regular cabbage.

Kale: *Brassica oleracea acephala*

Kale is also known as borecole collard, cow or green cabbage, German greens, or curly kale. It has been under cultivation for many centuries and is probably the ancestor of the various Brassicas grown today.

Curly kale ready to be harvested. The growth can be noted from the plastic marker which is about 9 inches above ground.

Kale is definitely not a hot-weather crop and should be grown for late fall harvesting. It is the most hardy of all the Brassicas and can usually be harvested throughout November in our area. Three or four kale plants warrant a place in the garden to provide the family with fresh late garden greens. Kale is very high in nutritive value; rich in vitamin A, thiamine, and ascorbic acid.

Plant seed directly in the garden in late May or early June preferably in a sunny location. I find it best to thin the seedlings several times over a period of weeks, ending up with the four strongest plants about 18 inches apart. The plants will become sturdy bushes about 3 feet tall. The leaves are picked as required, leaving the plant to continue growing.

Kale has no serious enemies. If holes are noticed in the leaves, a light dusting with rotenone will control the chewing insests.

To cook kale, wash the leaves, chop them and cook in a covered saucepan until tender. With young leaves this takes about ten minutes.

In some parts of England boiled potatoes and cooked kale or cabbage when fried together are known as "Bubble and Squeak." It is a remarkably tasty way of eating leftovers, and a little chopped onion gives added flavour.

Kohl-Rabi: *Brassica caulorapa*

This vegetable derives its name from the German words "Kohl," which means cabbage, and "Rabi" which means turnip. Kohl-rabi is a Brassica with a turnip-like swelling of the stem above ground level. The swollen part should be eaten while it is still young, juicy and tender. Most kohl-rabi sold in supermarkets are well past their prime and are stringy and coarse. We enjoy eating kohl-rabi raw with a dip or with salads. When cooked, they can replace summer turnips.

Kohl-rabi is one of the easiest Brassicas to grow. Plant the seed directly in the garden as soon as the ground is worked. Thin the seedlings 4 to 8 inches apart. Harvest in about two months, before the swelling reaches the size of a tennis ball. Keep the plants free from weeds. Never permit the ground to dry out as this will cause even small kohl-rabi to become woody.

To ensure a good-quality crop, make successive small plantings every couple of weeks until the weather gets hot. Kohl-rabi grows best in cool seasons and can tolerate partial shade and light frost. Whether Kohl-rabi is grown as an early or late crop, it is important to maintain rapid growth.

The pests are the same as with the rest of the cabbage family. Because kohl-rabi is a fast-maturing crop, its space can be replanted with fall crops such as carrots, beets, late spinach, chinese cabbage or lettuce.

"Dip" for kohl-rabi.   Add one packet of dried onion soup to 2 cups of sour cream or yogurt. Add fresh herbs in season as desired. Thin if necessary with milk or cream. Allow to stand for several hours before serving. This gives the dried soup time to swell and thicken the dip. Cut the kohl-rabi into sticks.

A row of kohl-rabi between broad beans (left) and parsnips (right). This area was well-mulched.

Rutabaga:
(Swede Turnip or Winter Turnip)
Brassica napobrassica

The turnip is a root vegetable known to have been grown by the Romans. Probably it was introduced to other parts of Europe and the British Isles during the Roman occupation. The first mention of turnips in North America was in 1540 when Cartier, on his third voyage, sowed turnip seed in Canada.

Rutabagas have a protruding neck and a mass of roots that grow from the base of the vegetable. Their smooth, hairless leaves are covered with a bloom that gives a bluish appearance, and the flesh is a yellow-golden colour. A most important feature for home gardeners to know is that rutabaga are slow-maturing roots for winter storage.

Rutabagas do best in a well-limed soil. The seed should be sown directly in the garden in the spring at the same time as semi-hardy annuals. They prefer full sun. Allow 20 to 24 inches between rows, and thin the seedlings 4 to 6 inches apart. Further thinning will be needed as the plants grow. The seed should be planted half an inch deep. Light frost will not damage rutabagas; in fact, many people claim fall frost improves the flavour of the mature roots. Turnips are vulnerable to the same diseases and pests as the other members of the mustard family.

Unlike parsnips, rutabagas cannot be left in the ground over winter, but should be dug on a warm, sunny fall day and left on the ground for a couple of hours until the roots are dry before being brought into the cool room. This also allows any wounds that may have occurred during harvesting to heal over, thus protecting the roots from possible infection. Some people enjoy the young green leaves as a spring vegetable, but I find the flavour rather strong.

Mashed rutabagas.   The flavour of mashed rutabaga is greatly enhanced by adding a pinch or two of curry powder. Cooked rutabaga can be frozen if cool-room space is not available.

Summer Turnip: *Brassica rapa*

The leaves and stems of summer turnips are hairy and coarse, and the flesh is usually white. They are a cool-weather crop and should be sown directly in the garden as soon as the ground has been worked. Like rutabaga, they dislike an acid soil and should, if possible, be grown in an area that has recently been limed. Early culture is the same as for rutabaga, but white turnips mature rapidly and should be harvested when about 3 to 4 inches in diameter. If allowed to grow larger, they will be coarse and stringy. Seed can be sown again in late July for a fall harvest. Do not try growing summer turnip in the heat of the season; the resulting crop is seldom worth the trouble. Turnips taste better if they come to maturity quickly. Therefore take care not to let the soil around them to dry out.

Most, but not all, summer turnips are white fleshed. Seed catalogues give clear descriptions of varieties. The most common problem we have encountered with both rutabaga and turnips is the root maggot. To guard against this I work diazinon crystals into the ground before seeding. As members of the cabbage family, they are subject to the same ailments and to the same crop rotation program.

White turnips are eaten cooked and served in either a cream sauce or with butter and parsley.

Cress: *Lepidium sativum*

Cress, or pepper grass, is very simple to grow. Sow a short row of seed outdoors as early as possible in the spring. Sprinkle the seed thickly in the row, cover lightly and tamp with the back of a rake. Germination is rapid, usually two to four days, depending on the temperature. The plants will be ready for cutting in three to four weeks or when about 4 inches tall. Make successive plantings throughout the summer. Keep the soil moist, otherwise the plants will go to seed very quickly. Cress can be grown in full sun or partial shade.

It is delicious in salads and sandwiches.

Radishes: *Raphanus sativus*

Radishes are very easy to grow in the early spring; they do best in cool weather, and the first seeding should be made as soon as the ground can be worked. Radishes can tolerate light frost and partial shade. Successive plantings can be made at two-week intervals until mid-June. Seed thinly to eliminate the need for constant thinning later. The plants will be ready to harvest in three to four weeks. They prefer a well-worked, well-drained, not too rich soil. The plants should never be allowed to dry out, or they will become woody. Daily watering is necessary in dry weather. Radishes taste better when they are brought to maturity rapidly. Thinning is most important; overcrowding prevents their roots from swelling into juicy, crisp vegetables. We do not bother growing radishes in July and August because they dislike hot, dry weather. Unless the summer is cool, radishes will be inferior and woody.

The tastiest radishes are grown in the hotframe in early spring. The flavour is not as sharp as those grown outdoors and the texture much finer.

Because the radish germinates so quickly, it is often planted with slow-germinating seeds to mark the row. The radishes will be harvested before the other crop requires the space to grow. When used as a row marker, the seed should be sown sparsely.

Radishes are not prone to many pests and diseases. The most common pest is cabbage root maggots, which can be controlled by working diazinon crystals into the soil before planting. If aphids attack the leaves, dust with rotenone.

Freshly picked radishes are very high in vitamin C. We treat them as one of the main ingredients of salads, rather than as a garnish. I have heard that the juice of thinly sliced radishes sprinkled with sugar is an old remedy for colds and sore throats.

Sea-Kale: *Crambe maritima*

This perennial plant is native to the seacoasts of western Europe and Asia Minor. It was always considered an important vegetable at my home in Ireland. The fleshy, celery-like shoots provide a most succulent dish early in the spring before the asparagus comes in. I have been growing it with great success ever since we moved to Evergreen Farm. It is a hardy perennial, and should be given a permanent site in the same manner as asparagus and rhubarb.

Sea-kale is not an economic plant for a small garden, but gives excellent returns for many years when a sunny location and rich soil can be spared in the larger home garden.

I grew my stock from seed purchased from Perron's Seed House in Quebec. It is not easy to locate seed in Canada, and a would-be grower might have to send to England. There are no restrictions against seed coming through the mail.

Sow the seed outdoors as soon as the ground can be worked. Scatter thinly in drills one inch deep; cover and tamp. Seed takes about twenty days to germinate. Before the seedlings become congested, thin them out to 6 inches apart. A year from sowing, the seedlings are fit to plant in their permanent positions.

In some areas it may be possible to purchase sea-kale roots, which are available in the spring. The roots will be 4 to 8 inches long. They should be planted 2 feet apart, upright in the ground, and the tops covered with about

Tops of mature sea-kale roots in very early spring after mulch cover has been removed. Roots can be divided at this stage.

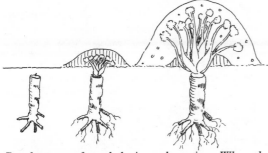

Development of sea-kale in early spring. When the shoots appear, they should be blanched with a mulch (as shown here) or a box or flower pot to exclude light.

Flower pot removed to allow harvesting of young shoots.

one inch of soil. Only one bud should be allowed to remain at each root-top; the others should be removed with a knife. The object is to keep each plant single.

It is extremely important to know which is the top and bottom of root cuttings. The com-

A gourmet spring dish of sea-kale.

mon practice is to cut the tops square, and the lower end slanted. When propagating your own stock always follow this practice. Sea-kale is extremely easy to propagate from root cuttings. Pencil-thin cuttings will take a year to establish themselves and produce a crop. They are very hardy.

As the sea-kale will remain in its permanent position for many years, the ground should be prepared thoroughly.

Sea-kale in its wild form is a coastal plant

and accustomed to salty conditions. Seaweed is to its liking, and anyone close enough to the coast to obtain this superb fertilizer should use it. Growers not able to find free seaweed should enrich the ground with well-rotted manure or compost. The soil must be well-drained; heavy clay ground should be well-worked and have sand, rubble or ashes added to ensure good drainage. If necessary the bed can be slightly raised. I find a heavy mulch of straw or hay is most beneficial. Leave it on all year round.

The shoots and leaf stalks require blanching (see Glossary) before eating to prevent them from tasting coarse and strong. The blanching covers can be placed over the plants in the late fall or early spring. I use old flower pots or boxes — anything that will exclude all light.

As the shoots develop in the spring, check the plants regularly and harvest by cutting with a sharp knife. Harvesting can continue over a period of four to six weeks. After that, remove the covers, feed the plants with a complete fertilizer, and allow them to grow freely.

Sea-kale suffers from very few problems. The most common is slugs. These can usually be attracted by slug-bait or dishes of stale beer. If drainage is poor the roots may rot.

Sea-kale can be served hot like asparagus, or raw in salads, like celery. In Europe it is considered a gourmet dish. This little known and seldom grown vegetable deserves more attention, especially in the home garden.

Water Cress: *Nasturtium officinale*

A European water plant which has become naturalized in the cold, shallow streams of northeastern United States and eastern Canada, water cress is extremely hard to grow unless a cool, permanently flowing stream is at hand. Once established, this perennial plant will last for many, many years.

Water cress must not be confused with the common garden nasturtium that belongs to a completely different family.

Water cress is not a plant for the average home vegetable garden.

CUCURBITACEAE:
The Gourd Family

Squash, cucumbers, pumpkins and melons all belong to the same family, generally referred to as "cucurbits." They all need the same cultural treatment and fall prey to the same pests and diseases.

Cucurbits prefer full sunshine and a slightly acid soil. I have never worried too much about soil acidity with regard to cucurbits, because I always grow my squash on the old compost pile where they thrive. For gardeners who do not have a compost heap and grow their cucurbits in the main garden, they require a soil that is high in humus content, fertile and well-drained.

Cucurbits are heavy feeders and benefit from additional feeding during the growing season. I use liquid manure when available, but otherwise a complete fertilizer.

The soil should be kept moist at all times, since drying out will cause the fruits to be stunted. Preferably soak the soil rather than sprinkle from above. Mulching conserves moisture as well as controlling weeds.

Outdoor Seeding

Here is a method you can try as a headstart on melon seeding. In our area, we use old car tires to give protection to melons and cucumbers seeded directly in the garden. A week or so before seeding time, place the car tire in the garden, fill with water and cover with clear plastic securely anchored to the ground. The sun's rays will heat the water and the mini-greenhouse will remain warm day and night. If frost is anticipated, an additional cover such as a sack will give the necessary protection. This method allows us to start melons outdoors several weeks before it would otherwise be possible.

Squash and Pumpkins: *Cucurbita species*

Generally speaking, squash are divided into two groups.

Summer squash is harvested when the fruit is still immature and tender. Included in this category are:

zucchini
summer scallop squash
straightneck
crookneck
vegetable marrow (immature)

Winter squash are for winter storage and should be ripened on the vine until the skin is hard. Exposure to frost damages keeping quality. Included in this category are:

butternut
buttercup
pepper squash
hubbard
pumpkins
spaghetti squash
vegetable marrow (mature)

There are also many novelty varieties

Squash and pumpkins are grown in either bush or vine form. Summer squash usually occupy less space than their winter counterparts, but culture of both types is the same.

Being native to tropical Central America and Mexico, they are very frost-tender. The seed should not be planted until all danger of frost is past. In northern areas it may be necessary to start plants indoors. In our part of the Ottawa Valley, direct garden seeding around May 24th has always proven successful.

For small garden plots bush squash are the most suitable. Even these will spread 3 feet in all directions. Do not overcrowd. Plant about ten seeds to each "hill." After true leaves have developed, thin out the plants by snipping with

A compost heap consisting of household scrap, farm yard manure, garden debris and leaves makes a good base on which to grow squash. As seeds in each hill germinate, squash vines sprout and begin to run.

The entire compost heap is covered with green growth as the squash vines spread out. We watch carefully for any sign of pests; fortunately, there were none.

scissors, leaving only the strongest three. Vine squash require a great deal of space as the vines often ramble 20 or 30 feet. Allow 8 to 10 feet between rows, and 4 to 6 feet between hills. The distance between the squash depends on the variety grown.

The area allotted to squash can be used early in the season to produce the fast-maturing, early cool-weather crops such as spinach, radishes, lettuce or cress. These crops will be harvested before the squash need the space. The squash will remain in the garden until the leaves are touched by frost. Vines can be trained to climb on a trellis or fence. After a number of fruits have set, the vines should be pruned and kept under control. The fruit may need support if larger fruiting varieties like Hubbard are grown.

Squash grow best in rich, fertile soil and need plenty of moisture, sunshine and heat. Most gardens have a compost pile, and it is here that I recommend growing squash. Last year's compost pile is ideal; there is still plenty of heat being generated, which the squash love, and the unsightly heap will rapidly be covered by the vines and hidden from view.

Prepare the seed-beds by making indentations in the compost and filling these with 4 to 6 inches of garden soil before planting the seed. Allow 4 to 6 feet between hills.

Take care to select varieties of squash that are suited to the individual garden. It is usual for home gardeners to grow several varieties of both squash and cucumbers. Those who save their own seeds should realize that with *cucurbitaceae* the next year's plants might not produce the type of fruits they had hoped for. There is always a strong chance that cross-pollination has taken place, and consequently the seed grown the following year may not come true to the parent. Also, insects and bees pollinate the gourd family. Any amateur gardener interested in keeping seed should study this subject in more depth before experimenting.

It is a common myth that cantaloupe and cucumber cross-pollinate, producing a mongrel fruit during the current season. It is the seed from any cross-pollinated fruit that will produce the mongrel the following year. When seed is purchased from a reliable seed house, you can be reasonably certain of the results.

Many novice gardeners are disappointed that so many of the blossoms on their squash plants never develop into fruit. If they look more closely at the plants, they will notice that some blossoms are borne on long stems, others on short stems. The former are male flowers, the latter female. Only the female flowers develop fruit. There will be ten or twenty male flowers to every female.

Squash seed can be kept for about five years if stored in a dry, dark, cool place.

Pumpkins and squash fall heir to the same ailments as do other members of the gourd family. To help prevent disease, keep weeds under control or, better still, mulch the ground. Burn the old vines in the fall. Do not add them to the compost pile. Do not grow members of the gourd family in the same place the following season.

Cucumbers: *Cucumis sativus*

The cucumber originates in Asia and is a very frost-tender annual vegetable. There are dozens of varieties to choose from. The vines of some cucumber crawl on the ground or can be trained to climb; other types are compact bushes suitable for a small garden or a patio planter. The fruits vary in size and texture; some are for eating fresh, others for pickling.

As with all gourds there will be ten to twenty male flowers to every female. Only the female flowers produce fruits.

In northern climates the seed may be started indoors, but I have not found this necessary in our area. We achieve the best results by direct garden seeding using the car-tire method.

Cucumbers need rich, well-drained soil, plenty of moisture, sunshine and heat. Additional feeding with 5:10:10 when the young plants are established promotes rapid growth.

Cucumbers can be planted in "hills" or

(Left) The male gourd flower is supported by a thin stem on which no fruit will grow.

(Right) The female flower is supported by a bulbous neck of butternut squash. As the fruit grows and matures, the blossom will shrivel and fall.

rows. Do not overcrowd; allow plenty of space for the vines to run.

Cucumbers are subject to the same ailments as the rest of the cucurbits. The plants should be checked daily when young, and if any signs of insect attack or disease are noticed, immediate action must be taken. Left unchecked, the vines can be damaged beyond recovery in a matter of days.

Climbing cucumber hanging from chicken-wire netting.

Muskmelon, Honeydew Melon and Cantaloupe: *Cucumis melo*

The muskmelon is native to Persia (Iran) and neighbouring areas. Muskmelons are known to have been cultivated as far back as 2400 BC. Over the years cultivation of melons gradually spread westward around the Mediterranean. Melons became a common fruit in Spain by the fifteenth century, and Columbus brought muskmelon seeds on his second voyage to the New World.

Today melons and cantaloupe are an important crop in the United States. They are not often grown commercially in Canada, but should be included in home gardens wherever three frost-free months are enjoyed.

There are a number of varieties to choose from; the dates listed in the seed catalogues are from transplanting time to harvest. Although melons are usually grown as transplants, I find it easier to plant the seed directly in the place the vines are to grow, using the car-tire method as described earlier. This is done either on a compost heap that is still generating heat, or a hot bed made from fresh horse manure and located in the garden plot. First, dig a hole the width of a car tire and about one foot deep. Fill it with some fresh horse manure; replace about 4 inches of soil; place the tire on top; fill the rim with rain water; plant the seeds inside and cover with clear plastic. Thin to the three strongest plants.

The mini-greenhouse shown in the illustration can be started in early May, and the protection removed on hot sunny days after all risk of frost is past. The plants will grow rapidly and not have to suffer a set-back from transplanting. We have also found mulching beneficial. Allow a 4 by 4 foot area around each hill.

Prior to planting, apply a complete fertilizer (5:10:10) and work it into the soil. Feed again with liquid fertilizer when vines start to run, and give a final feeding when the fruits have started to form. The fruits should be ripening in mid-August. Test by lifting the melon and seeing if it breaks away freely from its stem.

Squash seed has been planted in hills on the compost heap. A tire is placed on each hill and the rim filled with water.

Tires covered with light plastic to create a warm, humid atmosphere.

Canteloupe seedlings emerge, and plastic cover is removed during the day.

The harvest of cantaloupes is exemplified by this picture — a most satisfactory and heavy crop of healthy fruit. It may become necessary to protect the fruit from frost damage. We protect our cantaloupe bed against early frost, thereby extending the season for ripening.

Compost heap covered with cantaloupe. The ridge poles hold up plastic sheets to protect against early fall frost.

A zucchini hill consisting of three plants gives the appearance of a large, single bush.

Vine-ripened fruit are the most tasty, but to avoid frost damage it may become necessary to cut and harvest earlier. We protect our cantaloupe bed against early frost, thereby extending the season for ripening.

Muskmelons are very nutritious and a strong source of vitamin C. The deeper the colour, the higher the vitamin A content.

Melons are susceptible to the same problems as the rest of the gourd family. Check the plants daily for any signs of insect damage or disease.

Watermelons: *Citrullus vulgaris*

The watermelon is probably native to Africa, and has been grown in the southern United States since the latter part of the seventeenth century. Varieties have now been developed which are suited to our colder climate. The would-be watermelon grower should check which varieties grow best in his area.

Watermelons are very frost-tender. The cultural requirements and ailments are similar to those of muskmelons.

Zucchini: *Cucurbita pepo*

Zucchini has become a very popular vegetable in the home garden. It is easy to grow and, if

kept harvested, will produce fruit until the first frost. The most suitable type for the home garden is a bush variety. The seed can be planted directly in the garden, and we have found the car-tire method very satisfactory. This gives us about a two-week start over seed that has no protection.

Plant about ten seeds inside the ring, and after they are well-established, thin, leaving only the three strongest plants. Remove the car tire when all danger of frost is past. The plants will become good-sized bushes, with large leaves on long stems. Allow a 4×4 foot square for each clump. Harvest the fruits when they

Several zucchini fruit growing behind female flowers.

are very young and tender, and not more than 6 inches in length. Zucchini grow very rapidly and need to be harvested every day.

Soil and cultural requirements are the same as for other squash. One hill of zucchini provides the average family with an ample supply commencing six to eight weeks after seeding.

Problems and Controls

During the early stages of growth, cucurbits are particularly vulnerable to attack by insects and the resulting spread of certain diseases. The plants should be checked daily and if any signs of distress or insects are noticed, immediate steps must be taken to prevent further damage.

Squash vine borer.

Squash vine borer   tunnels into the stem of the plant causing the leaves to wilt. It can easily be detected by a small pile of sawdust-like material surrounding the entry hole. The stem should be slit lengthwise, and the borer removed and destroyed. The vine stem can then be hilled up with soil so that it can re-root.

The mature state of the squash vine borer is

a day-flying moth that resembles a wasp. It lays its eggs on the stems in which the larvae make holes. It is interesting to note that butternut squash is resistant to this pest, while acorn and green Hubbard are quite susceptible. Dusting or spraying will keep the borer under control.

Squash bugs are hard-shelled, black and brown on top and yellow underneath. They are about half an inch long. The adults overwinter in garden refuse and emerge in the spring just in time to attack young plants, and for the females to lay their eggs on the undersides of the leaves.

The red-brown eggs can be seen in clusters, and the leaves should be picked off and destroyed. To control, spray or dust when the bugs are first noticed.

Squash bug.   *Striped cucumber beetle.*

Striped cucumber beetle   is a yellowish bug with three black stripes. It overwinters in garden debris, becoming active in early spring. The female lays her eggs in the soil, and the larvae feed on the roots and stems of plants. When mature, the new adults feed on the upper growth of the plants. The cucumber beetle is responsible for the spread of bacterial wilt and cucumber mosaic. These beetles can cause serious damage very rapidly and must be controlled by spraying or dusting as soon as they are seen.

All cucurbits are susceptible to viruses, fungi and bacterial diseases. Control consists of purchasing disease-resistant varieties, practising crop rotation, controlling weeds and insects, dusting with the appropriate chemicals and generally observing good garden-hygiene practices.

GRAMINAE:
The Grass Family

Corn: *Zea mays rugosa*

> *"Oh the corn is as high*
> *As an elephant's eye"*
>   *Oklahoma*, Rodgers and Hammerstein

Although sweet corn is the only member of the grass family we grow in our gardens, many other members such as wheat, oat, barley, rye and rice form part of our daily diet.

Corn is very popular in the home garden even though it occupies a large amount of space for the quantity of food produced. North Americans know well the delicious flavour of freshly picked cobs.

The earliest records of corn came from Guatemala, where the Indians are known to have grown it during the eighth century. Columbus saw it in Cuba in November 1492, and recorded "a kind of grain called 'maiz' of which was made a very well-tasted flour." In 1498 corn was brought by Columbus to Venezuela, and also recorded later in Chile and Peru. It is believed to be native to tropical America. In 1535, when Cartier visited Hochelaga, now Montreal, he recorded "that town was situated in the midst of extensive cornfields." Corn seems to have been grown all over the American continent by the Indians. The first mention of corn in gardening books was in the 1830s.

Sweet corn is grown on all types of soil. A well-drained, fertile, sandy loam is preferred. The richer the ground, the sweeter and more tasty the crop. Corn has a deep, strong root system, and it is therefore very important to prepare the land thoroughly before planting. In addition to humus, work in 6 to 8 pounds of 5:10:10 fertilizer per 100 feet of row. If no humus is available, increase the fertilizer by 2 to 3 pounds. Additional feeding during the growing season is beneficial.

Corn is a sun-loving warm-weather crop, and if seeded too early, can be damaged by frost after germination. Germination will also be poor if the soil is wet and cold, so it is best to delay planting until the conditions are suit-

I planted two rows of corn 3 feet apart and thinned them by snipping seedlings with scissors, leaving them 6 to 8 inches apart.

Growing seedlings of corn mulched with grass clippings. The variety "Peaches and Cream" is excellent for the home garden.

able. Sweet corn can be planted either in drills or hills. In drills, the thinned seedlings should be spaced 6 to 8 inches apart. In hills, allow three plants to each, with 18 to 24 inches between hills. I prefer drills. However, in either case, keep the rows 3 feet apart.

In our garden corn is the only vegetable we grow where pollination is done by the wind. Planting corn in a block of short rows, rather than one long row, allows better circulation of pollen around the plants. Without complete pollination, the cobs will have gaps without kernels. If several varieties (for example, early mid-season and late) are grown, each variety should be in a block.

Corn grows to a height of about 6 feet, depending on the variety. It should be given a location in the garden where it will not shade other plants. It is not a good crop to grow in very small gardens because it does not give a large enough return for the space it occupies. However, in an intensively planted garden, the area where the corn is grown can be occupied early in the season by crops such as spinach, lettuce, radish and cress. I have also visited gardens where the squash has been grown

successfully in the corn patch. The disadvantages of this kind of intensive planting is in controlling pests and diseases. I prefer to grow the corn by itself.

Corn is a heavy feeder and benefits from additional fertilizer during the growing season. Apply a balanced fertilizer either in liquid form or as a side dressing. Signs of distress such as yellowing leaves or stunted growth often mean lack of the necessary plant nutrients. If these symptoms should appear, apply a fertilizer and water the crop if the weather is dry.

The plants should never lack moisture, because if they do, the quality of the crop will suffer. The healthier the growth of the plants, the more succulent the flavour of the cobs.

To extend the harvest season, plant early, mid-season and late varieties. These can be planted simultaneously, but will mature in succession.

The advantage of home-grown corn is that it can be harvested while the kernels are still plump and the juice is milky. Pick when the silks have turned brown, and the ear is firm and full. You can have the pot boiling before picking the cobs and have them eaten before the sugar in the kernels has had time to turn to starch. If you've never eaten freshly picked corn, you're in for a treat.

Here the rows of corn have begun to mature. First the pollen-producing tassels appear on the plant. Three to four days later, silks begin to show on the corn ear shoots. Usually we harvest after the silks have turned brown, two or three weeks after they first appear.

A friend and I make light work of harvesting.

Problems and Controls

The corn borer can be very destructive, attacking the stalks and ears of corn. Its presence is indicated by castings outside tiny holes, broken tassels and wilting stalks.

The flesh-coloured, inch-long worms overwinter in old stalks, pupate in the spring, and emerge as moths to lay eggs during the summer. Control can be maintained by dusting with insecticide at regular intervals, beginning when the plant is about 18 inches tall.

Corn borers have never been a problem in our garden, and I have yet to find it necessary to initiate a dusting program.

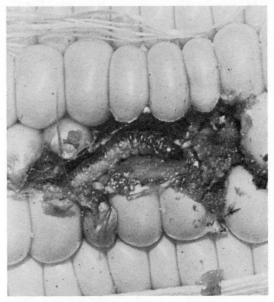

European corn borer.

European corn borer.

Corn earworms are stocky, striped worms about 2 inches long. These pests do not usually overwinter in northern climates, but adult moths migrate with warming temperatures. The females lay their eggs on the silks, and the emerging larvae enter the ears and feed on the kernels.

Earworms can be controlled by dusting the silks lightly but thoroughly as part of your regular dusting program, or by applying a few drops of mineral oil to the tip of each ear as the silks are first appearing.

Corn smut is a most unpleasant-looking fungal disease that produces large, grey-black boils on the ears. These boils contain a mass of spores that are spread by the wind if the boils are allowed to break open. They should be removed and burned immediately they are noticed to prevent them from infecting the rest of your corn, as well as your neighbour's. If these boils are allowed to burst, the spores can remain viable for up to seven years! Unfortunately, fungicides are not an effective control, but planting treated seed helps.

Corn smut.

Birds sometimes eat newly planted corn, but using a treated seed usually prevents this. Scarecrows and glitters help to frighten birds away from mature cobs.

Raccoons can be distracted by music from a radio placed in the corn patch overnight, or by the presence of a good dog.

LEGUMINOSAE:
Beans and Peas

Supports for Beans and Peas

Many vegetables need some kind of support to prevent them from being blown over by the wind or collapsing under their own weight. Climbing vegetables such as sugar snap peas, snow peas and pole beans can reach heights of 8 feet or more and definitely need support. Supports are usually constructed from whatever materials are at hand and according to the whims and skills of the gardener.

If brushwood is available locally (brushwood is the thinnings from shrubberies or woods), it makes an excellent inexpensive support. To stand firm in high winds, the brush must be pushed into the ground with some force.

An economical and practical trellis can be made by 2 inch by 2 inch cedar posts, 8 feet high, and a combination of clothes lines and twine.

For years we used cedar poles, sometimes reinforced with metal posts, to which we attached chicken wire. The vines climbed up these poles, but as the season advanced, they nearly always had to be supported by guy wires to prevent the trellis from collapsing inwards under the weight of the vines. I dislike guy wires — they have a habit of either tripping or decapitating the unwary.

Hopson trellis. I am indebted to Anne Hopson of Carsonby, Ontario for introducing me to a trellis designed by her engineer husband, and tested with success over many years. Basically, the Hopson trellis, illustrated here, consists of a series of A-frames which incorporate open-ended boxes at top and bottom; the frames are connected by a ridge pole at the top and one at each side at the bottom. The upper ridge poles

Trellis using 2-inch by 2-inch cedar posts.

An alternate method of staking peas is the use of brushwood or prunings from trees and shrubs.

have 1½-inch galvanized nails set every 4 inches along the top, while the lower poles have similar nails along the outer sides. The ridge poles slide into and are pinned firmly to the open-ended boxes by means of 5-inch nails. The entire trellis is itself secured to the ground by 2-inch by 2-inch stakes, 18 inches long. These are driven through a small box fixed to the lowest cross pieces on each A-frame. Once the trellis is in position, lace binder twine securely between the upper ridge pole and the base, using the galvanized nails to keep the twine correctly spaced. These trellises withstand extremely high winds even when loaded down with heavy vines.

The wood used for this is one inch by 3 inch cedar, or equivalent treated wood. Such trellises can be made to any size, but ours are 6 feet high and 3 feet wide. The ridge poles are all 9 feet long. There are numerous pictures of these trellises in this book, and I think you will agree that they are practical and look attractive. Unless you make them yourself, they are not cheap. However, they should last a good many years, if well-treated.

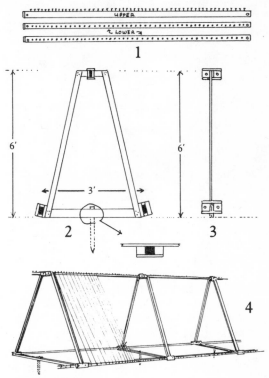

The Hopson Trellis
1. *Ridge poles*
2. *A-frame elevation (front)*
3. *A-frame elevation (side)*
4. *Trellis assembled and extended*

Trellis used by the Central Experimental Farm in Ottawa consists of stout cedar poles supporting open nylon netting.

Planting bean seeds at the base of a Hopson trellis.

Harvesting bush beans. One row is of the green and the other of the wax variety. The crop is usually prolific, but picking requires constant bending down — a disadvantage for most folks.

Pole beans starting to climb the Hopson trellis. Note mulch of grass clippings.

Bush Snap Beans: *Phaseolus vulgaris*

The most common bean grown in the garden plot is the bush snap bean, a native of Mexico and Central America. It may be green or golden in colour. If picked frequently, the bushes will continue to produce over a long period of time. There are a great many varieties of bush beans, both green and wax, available through the seed catalogues. It is often a help to the novice to inquire from a knowledgeable local gardener as to the varieties to be found satisfactory in the area.

Beans grow well in full sun in most gardens as long as the ground is well drained. Too fertile a soil will produce lots of leaves but few beans. Snap and pole bean seed should not be planted until all danger of frost is past, and the ground has warmed up. A 60°F (15°C) soil temperature is required for good germination. Bush beans will become a thick 2-foot-high hedge when mature. Allow 3 feet between rows. Make a drill one inch deep and space the seed 2 to 4 inches apart. Cover with soil and firm down with the back of the rake. I always plant treated seed, but if untreated seed is used, it should be planted more closely and then, if necessary, the seedlings thinned. With untreated seed, germination is not always as reliable.

I often hear people complaining that they have so many beans they don't know what to do with them. My suggestion is to plant half the quantity in the first seeding and the rest two or three weeks later, thereby staggering the harvest. A 25-feet row will yield 15 to 18 pounds of beans.

Beans are easy to grow. The safest way to avoid problems is to purchase top-quality disease-resistant seed; never grow beans in the same location two years running; burn all plants that have any sign of disease; never work around the crops when the leaves are wet.

Pole Snap Beans

These beans are similar in appearance and flavour to their bush counterpart. However, you can harvest a larger quantity of pole beans from the same space. I also find pole beans are much less tiring to harvest. The culture is the same as for bush beans but, as their name denotes, they are climbers and must be given a trellis or poles to climb, installed before the beans are planted. Be sure to place them where they will not cast a shadow on the rest of the garden. Pole beans take slightly longer to mature than bush beans, but when picked regularly, continue producing until frost. We have found the variety "Blue Lake" is very rewarding in our area.

We grew two pole bean varieties at the same time. The Blue Lake occupied the two sections in the distance and Scarlet Runners the nearest section in the foreground. We found the Blue Lake much more bountiful. Harvesting from a trellis is very simple as the beans are easily seen. Note the Scarlet Runners in the foreground are still in flower, while the Blue Lake are already producing.

A row of broad beans in early spring. Note mulch of hay and grass clippings.

Scarlet Runners: *Phaseolus coccineus*

Scarlet runners are a visually attractive addition to the garden, often planted around a porch or arbour in the flower garden or against a fence as a screen. The 8- to 10-foot vines produce brilliant scarlet flowers, which become 6- to 10-inch long, flat pods. These must be harvested when tender, before the beans mature.

Scarlet runners are best served frenched, or thinly sliced, and are excellent when cooked. The culture is the same as for pole beans.

Bush or Pole Lima Beans:
Phaseolus lunatus (also known as butter beans)

Limas are usually grown for the beans (rather than the pods) which can be eaten fresh, or allowed to remain on the vine until mature, then harvested, dried and kept for winter use. They can also be picked when immature and cooked in the same manner as snap beans.

The culture is the same as for other bush and pole beans. The important difference is the planting date. Lima beans require a really warm soil for good germination: a minimum soil temperature of 65° F (18° C). Do not sow limas until mid-June. The pole limas are of better quality than the bush, but in areas with a short frost-free season, it is better to grow the bush. Bush limas take 60 to 75 days to mature; pole limas 85 days.

Shelling or Navy Beans: *Phaseolus vulgaris*

These are grown for winter use as dried beans. Unless there is plenty of space available, the shelling bean is not an economical home-garden crop. Culture is the same as for bush beans.

Shelled beans provided the early settlers with a highly nutritious winter food. However, I find that the labour expended in producing and drying this crop is not economical. (It should be noted that the beans already discussed also are suitable for drying.)

If there are still plenty of pods on the main crop of pole or snap beans, these can be left to mature, harvested and dried.

Broad or Fava Bean: *Vicia faba*

Broad beans were introduced into England by the Romans. They became part of the staple diet of the working man, being particularly rich in protein and salts, and sustaining for a hard day's work.

The broad bean is not a reliable crop in our garden. We plant a row each year because we enjoy the unusual flavour. Some seasons the results are excellent, and we have plenty for the freezer; other times we only harvest a few basketsful.

Unlike snap beans, the broad bean thrives only in cool conditions. The seed must be planted as soon in spring as the ground can be worked. Space the seed 8 inches apart and 3 inches deep, allowing 3 feet between rows. If untreated seed is used, double the quantity of beans in the row, then thin the seedlings to 8 inches apart.

Broad beans are upright 3-foot plants. The thick pods are 6 to 8 inches long and contain up to eight large beans. Most people eat the mature beans, but when young and tender, the entire pod can be cooked and eaten. Broad beans are only recommended for gardens where space is plentiful. Some support may be necessary in windy locations.

The worst enemies of the broad beans are small black flies, or black aphids. These can be readily controlled by regular dustings with rotenone. When the pods are formed and the plants about 3 feet high, pinch out the growing points. This allows all the strength to go into the beans, and also removes the part of the plant most desirable to the insects. Broad beans take 80 to 90 days to mature. Late spinach or lettuce can be planted as a second crop after the beans are harvested.

Soybeans: *Glycine max*

Soybeans have been a most important food in the Orient since at least 3000 BC. They are one of the most nutritious of all vegetables, containing approximately 40% protein, 20% fat and are rich in vitamins A, B, G, calcium and iron. They are also starch-free. The soybean deserves a place in the garden plot. Whether eaten green or dried, they retain their food value to a greater extent than all the other varieties of legumes.

Soybeans are a comparatively new addition to Canadian home vegetable gardens. A great deal of research has been done to develop short season varieties not only at the Central Experimental Farm in Ottawa, but also at agricultural centres from the Maritimes to British Columbia. Home gardeners can now avail themselves of these new varieties and satisfactorily grow their own crop.

The culture of soybeans is similar to that of lima beans. Do not sow seed until June 15 or when the soil temperature is 65°F (18°C). Grow varieties developed in Canada such as Friskeby or Blackeye, that mature more rapidly in our short season. Soybean bushes will grow to about 3 feet in height. They require full sun, a rich well-drained soil, and plenty of moisture at the growing stage. Towards maturity, they are drought-resistant. If it is cold and rainy when the flowers are in bloom, the insect pollinators may stay at home, thereby reducing the size of the crop. Soybeans are not recommended for small gardens — the space required is not justified by the return.

Soybeans do not have many pest problems; rabbits are often the most annoying one.

Peas: *Pisum sativum*

Pease porridge hot
Pease porridge cold
Pease porridge in the pot
Nine days old.

Some like it hot
Some like it cold
I like it in the pot
Nine days old

Anonymous

Throughout history peas have been highly valued as part of the staple diet of man. The findings of a recent expedition at "Spirit Cave" near the Burmese border of Thailand have carbon dated the seeds of peas and beans at roughly 9750 BC.

Peas were also found in Egyptian tombs and are known to have been grown by the early Greeks and Romans. It was the pea that Mendel used for his experiments in hybridization, and there are many recorded illustrations of the popularity of peas in both continental Europe and the British Isles.

Peas were used in dried form until the seventeenth century, when they were made into soup or peasmeal pudding. Later, they became fashionable as a fresh vegetable, and still retain their immense popularity today.

Vast strides in plant breeding have made available to us the many varieties offered through the seed catalogues. Peas are very high in food value and rich in vitamin A and the B group, as well as vitamin C. They are always more tasty when freshly picked, and well worth a place in the home garden. Study the different varieties offered in your catalogue and note the following variations:

Height: dwarf or tall (staking)
Maturity: early, medium or late
Number and size of peas in pod
Treated or untreated seed
Edible pods

My preference is for a tall variety, which occupy less room in the garden than the dwarf types to produce the equivalent crop. Staked peas are much easier to pick — there is no bending down. I grow an early and a late variety, both of which are planted at the same time but mature ten days apart.

Since peas are a cool-weather crop, it is essential to plant the seed as early as possible in the spring, that is, as soon as the ground can be worked. Later plantings only succeed during a cool spring season. Frost does not damage pea seedlings.

Over the years we have tested a number of the different varieties of peas listed in seed catalogues. Some had small, very tasty peas, which I found most tedious to shell; others were large, but rather dry and uninteresting. The differing qualities are innumerable and quite distinct. As a result of our tests we prefer "Three Kings — new" for our main crop. This is a triple-podded pea, meaning that each flowering stem produces three blossoms and, subsequently, three pods. These pods are easy to pick and shell, and the peas are of superb quality and flavour for both table and freezer. The catalogue describes them as growing 2½ feet tall, but we have found they always attain a height of at least 4 feet.

Most seed offered in catalogues has been treated with a fungicide. This treatment helps combat damping-off and other destructive organisms which attack both seed and seedling,

The shelling peas planted in trenches have germinated. I am driving in metal posts; then I attach poultry netting upon which the vines will climb.

In the foreground poultry netting will support the vines of "Three Kings" peas. Behind them is the trellis for taller growing sugar peas.

especially those planted before the ground has had time to warm up.

I always plant treated seed, but organic gardeners may prefer their seed untreated. In doing so, however, they run the risk of poor germination or damage to the emerging seedling, a chance I am not prepared to take in our limited growing season.

Peas grow best in a good loam that has been enriched in the fall with well-rotted manure or compost. When working the ground in the spring, incorporate a few handfuls of 5:10:10 to each row.

My method of planting is to dig a trench about 4 inches deep and the width of the spade. I then broadcast the seed in the trench, cover it with one or 2 inches of soil and tamp. As the plants grow, I add more soil. For the tall varieties allow 4 feet between rows and for

Shelling peas (Three Kings) will soon be ready to harvest.

Two rows of peas (Three Kings) in foreground climb poultry netting. In background, snow peas (Mammoth melting sugar) in flower have reached the top of the 6-foot trellis. Both varieties were planted on the same day in late April.

dwarf, 2 feet. Some gardeners sow their peas in single lines.

The tall varieties should be staked right away. Use whatever staking materials are available to you: prunings from trees or shrubs, chicken wire, nylon netting, string stretched between rails, old snow-fence or trellis. Even dwarf peas do better if they have some support.

Edible-podded or Snow Peas:
Pisum sativum macrocarpon

Snow peas are available in both dwarf and tall varieties. Their cultivation is the same as for ordinary peas, but daily harvesting becomes essential. The pods must be picked before the peas form and while they are still flat and stringless. The more regular the harvesting, the longer the plants will continue to produce.

Snow peas are very popular in Chinese dishes. They may be eaten raw in salads, or steamed until tender but still "crisp." They freeze well too!

Picking sugar peas which have grown well above the height of the trellis.

Sugar Snap Peas

The sugar snap pea is a new cultivar (variety) which combines the best qualities of both snow peas and shelling peas. They are delicious, tender and crisp, especially when eaten raw.

Sugar snap peas develop vigorous 6- to 10-foot vines which must be supported, and the pods must be harvested regularly to promote continuing development of seed pods. Cultural requirements are the same as for ordinary peas. Because you eat both the pea and the pod, sugar snaps provide twice as much food as shelling peas and give you half the work in preparing them for the table. They are a vegetable well worth growing.

There are seldom many problems with peas, adverse weather conditions being the most likely one. For any insect infestations I apply rotenone powder. As mildew has attacked only the sugar peas late in the season after many weeks of harvest, I pull up the plants and burn them. This is the best way to prevent the fungus from spreading.

Peanuts: *Arachis hypogaea*

Although peanuts are listed in Canadian seed catalogues, they are only grown as a novelty plant in Canada. Our hot growing season is not nearly long enough for peanuts to ripen. I have several friends who have grown them with moderate success, but for gardeners whose space is limited, there is no economic value from growing this plant. The greatest value will be as an experiment for children.

The peanut is a member of the pea family, but its growing habits are very different to ordinary garden peas. The nuts should be planted outdoors in May. The plants will grow 12 to 18 inches tall and, after the flowers have been pollinated, the stalks will become elongated, bend down and root themselves in the soil. The peanuts develop in clusters under the ground. Peanuts prefer the poor, slightly acid, sandy soil that sweet potatoes like.

Harvest before the first frost by digging up the entire vine and hanging it in the garage or open shed to cure. Peanuts are relatively trouble-free.

Problems and Controls

Mexican bean beetles can easily be mistaken for lady bugs. However, they are slightly larger and have sixteen spots rather than twelve. These pests overwinter in piles of leaves and emerge in the spring at about the same time as the beans are germinating. After a week or two the females lay eggs on the undersides of leaves which hatch within fifteen days. The larvae and adults then feed on the undersides of leaves, chewing holes right through and giving the leaves a lacy appearance. They will also attack the stems and pods when a plot is badly infested. It is important when spraying or dusting to cover the undersides of leaves.

Mexican bean beetle.

Leafhoppers and aphids, by feeding on infected weeds and plants, spread disease when they move on to attack healthy beans. To prevent disease, these pests must be controlled. Treatment is the same as for Mexican bean beetle.

Bean weevils are small, white grubs that may infest dry beans in storage. To prevent this happening, bake the beans for thirty minutes on a cooking sheet with the oven temperature set at 130°F (54°C).

Anthracnose is a fungal disease that attacks stems, leaves and pods of beans, causing reddish-brown, elongated sunken areas to appear. It is a seed-borne disease and prevention is by planting Western-grown seed. Never work among the plants when the foliage is wet.

Bacterial blight in beans is recognized by brown blotches encircled by a reddish-yellow ring. Control is the same as with anthracnose.

Virus diseases such as mosaics can be controlled by spraying or dusting for insects, or by planting resistant varieties.

Rust appears as reddish pustules on leaves and causes them to die and fall off. There is no control, but disease-resistant varieties are available.

Pea aphids are large, green plant lice that suck the juices from the plant tips, eventually causing the plant to die. Control is by dusting or spraying as soon as aphids are noticed.

Enlarged photograph of adult lady bug stalking pea aphids.

Pea weevil larvae are brownish grubs with black, white and grey markings that burrow into the pods of the peas. If peas are being dried for storage or seed, weevils could be a problem. Control is by spraying or dusting with a recommended insecticide and also by burning pea vines after harvest.

The vine on left is an example of peas yellows disease.

Yellow vines are caused by a virus that is spread by aphids, producing yellow stunted plants and curled or misshapen pods. Control of aphids is essential. Immediately diseased plants are seen, they should be removed from the garden and burned.

Fusarium wilt is a soil-borne fungal disease that causes stunting with a downward curling of leaves. The most effective preventative measures are planting treated seed, practising crop rotation and locating peas in well-drained soil.

Root rot is caused by several soil-borne fungi that may live in the soil for many years. It causes the vines to turn yellow, then brown at the roots and to eventually die. Control is the same as for Fusarium wilt.

Burgundy crimson Swiss Chard makes a colourful addition to flowerbeds. Both leaves and stalks are delicious.

Brushwood is used in this garden for pea vines to climb upon — an excellent free support when available.

Garden huckleberry produce large, tart, black berries, ripening late in the season. Excellent for pies and jam.

Broad or fava beans do best in a cool season. They have a unique flavour, popular in Europe.

Crabapple blossom brings colour to our young orchard in early spring. The fruit makes delicious jelly.

Red currants are too acid to eat fresh, but make excellent desserts, jams and jellies.

(Below.) Strawberries are the most popular of all the soft fruits. They are at their most succulent when sun-ripened and freshly picked. A few plants are a worthwhile addition to any garden.

LILIACEAE:
The Lily Family

Asparagus: *Asparagus officinalis*

The tender spring shoots (or spears) of this delectable perennial vegetable were known and cultivated by the Romans at least as early as 200 BC. Cato's cultural directions would still serve us well today.

Early settlers brought plants to America, where they thrived in our cold climate. No garden with space available is complete without asparagus.

Asparagus can be grown from seed, but for the small quantity required for a home garden, I would recommend good-quality one-year-old

crowns. These should have at least ten vigorous roots, each not less than 6 inches in length. Early spring is the time to start an asparagus bed.

The location of the asparagus bed must be chosen with care, as the plants will produce for about twenty years. The ground should be well-drained and sunny, and warm up early in the spring. The proximity of large trees, or of young trees likely to grow rapidly over the next few years, should be avoided as the roots will deprive the asparagus of essential nourishment. When allocating an area, the number of crowns required depends on the size of the

An asparagus bed takes several years to establish. However, once it begins to flourish it is very rewarding. Here you see "tips" emerging from the cold ground in early spring. These tips can be cut (or broken off) when about 6 to 8 inches high. On a warm spring day they grow almost that much, so a daily harvesting is possible.

The asparagus season ends after six to eight weeks and, except for weeding, the bed can be left virtually unattended for the season, although it will appreciate a good top dressing of manure. This picture shows a plant in mid-summer and gives an idea of the area and size it grows to.

The asparagus trench should be about 16 inches wide, and 10 inches deep. The crowns are placed 16 inches apart, with the roots of each crown spread out around a small mound so that the roots slope downwards.

When the asparagus plants are three years old and well-established, spears can be harvested by either cutting or snapping off.

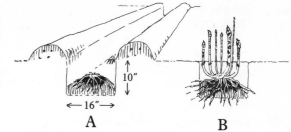

A   B

family. Fifteen plants for each member should be sufficient, but if a freezer supply is needed, add ten more plants per person.

Allow 3 feet between the rows, and set the crowns 12 to 24 inches apart. Where space is limited, prepare a bed 4½-feet-wide, with 18 inches separating two rows. Plants should be 16 inches apart in the rows.

Asparagus grows best in a neutral or slightly alkaline soil. A soil test will determine whether lime is needed and, if so, this is best applied in the fall. Digging and manuring must be thorough, and should be done well in advance of planting time, preferably in the fall. When re-working the ground in the spring, add bone meal as well as commercial fertilizer (20 pounds of 5:10:10 per 1,000 square feet).

The roots should be planted immediately they arrive in late April or early May. Mark each row with a garden line to make sure the trench is straight when dug out with a spade. The trench should be wide enough to take the outspread roots, and deep enough to cover the crowns with 4 inches of soil in a clay loam, or 6 inches in a sandy loam. Do not completely fill the trench at planting time; gradually do so as the plants start to grow.

Take care not to damage the fleshy, strip-like roots. These break very easily when being handled. After planting give the bed a thorough soaking.

It is most important to keep the asparagus bed free from weeds; regular attention is essential. Quack grass will become a serious problem if allowed to get out of control.

At my home in Ireland we applied a light sprinkling of agricultural salt during the summer, unless seaweed was available. Salt is now not generally recommended by the experts, and I am told its sole value is as a weed killer. Seaweed is not available in our area, so we now apply a mulch of well-rotted compost which helps control weeds and conserve nourishment. Hay is another common form of mulch, but it often harbours weed seeds.

Do not cut any spears until the plants are three years old. Then take only a limited quantity. Once the bed is well-established, six to eight weeks of harvest is sufficient, depending on the season. After harvesting is finished, the tops must be allowed to grow. These can be cut down during the fall garden clean-up, or may be left until spring to catch snow which insulates the ground.

Early each spring apply a complete fertilizer, 5:10:10 at the rate of 5 pounds to each 25 feet of row. Work this into the ground, taking care not to damage the tender young shoots. After harvesting, give a light application of 10:10:10 fertilizer, or spread well-rotted manure around the plants. The latter is likely to encourage weed growth, but it is the practice I prefer.

When harvesting with a knife, care must be taken not to damage the tips of adjacent spears still below the soil. Many people maintain they increase the yield of crops by snapping the spears off, rather than cutting. Grasp the spears in the hand, bend it downwards, and the entire spear that snaps off will be tender enough to be eaten.

Note: You will find that some plants produce large, fat spears, while others a far greater number of spindly ones. The former are female plants which, when mature, will produce seeds in the fall. The latter are the male plants. Both are equally good to eat and each plant will produce approximately the same weight of crop.

Problems and Controls

Asparagus does not suffer many ailments. The asparagus beetle is the most common problem and causes the spears to have a grub-chewed appearance; growth may be distorted or stunted. Adult beetles overwinter in debris or old boards, emerging in spring as soon as the asparagus plants send up new growth. The females lay their eggs on the tips of shoots, and both the adults and the emerging larvae feed on the foliage and stems. About two weeks later the larvae burrow into the ground to

Asparagus beetle.

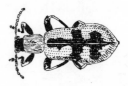

pupate. These, in turn, hatch and the cycle repeats itself. Several generations occur each season.

Asparagus beetles can be controlled by either dusting repeatedly with rotenone, or by spraying with the recommended insecticide.

Asparagus rust is unlikely to occur when rust-resistant varieties are grown. If spears show signs of orange, rust-coloured blemishes on the stem or foliage, immediately cut the infected shoots and burn or send to the garbage. Diseased material should not be put in the compost. Cut the plants close to the ground in the fall and destroy the refuse.

MALVACEAE:
The Hibiscus Family

Okra: *Hibiscus esculentus*

Okra, which is often referred to as gumbo, is a tropical plant native to Africa. It is not a popular vegetable for the Canadian home garden because it is very frost-tender. Although it *can* be grown, it is not reliable; the crop results depend on the season.

We have grown okra in our garden only as an experiment. We did not find that the harvested crop gave us a good return for the space it occupied or the labour involved. However, in locations where the growing season is longer than in the Ottawa Valley, growing okra might

be more rewarding. Okra occupies about the same amount of space as bush beans and can attain a height of approximately 3 feet, depending on the variety. The cultural requirements are similar to those of bush beans. The immature pods are used as a vegetable or to thicken soups or stews. The pods must be harvested at least every other day, otherwise they become tough and woody, and the plant will stop producing.

I do not recommend okra for gardens where space is limited.

Okra is not, however, bothered by any major pests and diseases in our colder climate.

POLYGONACEAE:
Buckwheat or Knotweed Family

Rhubarb: *Rheum rhaponticum*

A native to many parts of eastern Asia, rhubarb is believed to have derived its name from the Russian "Rhu" (now the Volga) River upon whose banks it grew, and from "Barbarum," from the barbarian districts beyond the confines of the Roman Empire. Rhubarb was first noticed in England in 1773, but was not in use as a culinary plant until the 1820s. In Victorian times rhubarb was known as "pie-plant."

Most early records make reference to the strong purgative properties of the plant, but this has been largely bred out of the varieties we grow in our gardens nowadays.

Rhubarb is a very hardy perennial and deserves a sunny, permanent place in every home garden. When well-cultivated it will produce a crop for many years, often twenty or more.

The preparation of the soil is approximately the same as for asparagus. Dig a deep hole at least 2 feet square and 15 inches deep. Fill the bottom of the hole with well-rotted manure or compost. Add some topsoil and a handful of bone meal, mix well, and replace an inch or two of topsoil before planting the roots.

There are several varieties of rhubarb: the

A healthy bed of rhubarb. They do best in a separate bed or at one side of the garden where they will not be disturbed by annual cultivation.

tart, green one for relishes, and the pink stemmed "strawberry" or "ruby" for desserts. The roots may be purchased from a nursery garden or obtained from friends who are dividing their clumps. Most rhubarb clumps need only be divided every five or ten years, but may be divided more often for propagation purposes. Each root planted must contain at least one strong bud — preferably two or three — which when planted should be just barely covered with soil. After planting, water thoroughly, then mulch. Under favourable conditions, each root will develop strong plants in one year.

Thereafter, top dress the plants each spring and fall with well-rotted manure. If manure is not available, apply one pound of complete fertilizer to each plant in the spring. I mulch the plants to control weeds and conserve moisture. This makes it necessary to pull the mulch back before spreading the manure.

Rhubarb is a gross feeder and is not easily overfertilized. No stalks should be harvested until the second year, and then only a small quantity. From the third year on, the stalks may be pulled, never cut, on attaining the proper size. Harvest for approximately eight weeks.

When pulling the stalk, grasp it firmly near the base and give it a sideways jerk. It will come away cleanly from the crown.

Two or three strong plants are usually enough for the average family, but double this quantity if you want to freeze a year's supply.

Note that only the stalks, or petioles, are edible. The leaves have been known to cause severe poisoning when eaten by humans or livestock.

Rhubarb is not generally injured by insects or diseases. Spindly stalks are the result of insufficient fertilizing or a lack of sun and moisture. Always remove flower stalks by cutting close to the ground. Allowing flowers to set seed drains strength from the plant.

To prepare for the freezer, simply wash and dry young stalks, and cut into one-inch lengths. Fill plastic bags, seal and freeze.

Rhubarb roots need dividing every five to ten years. These knarled orange-coloured roots can be dug out and simply divided by cutting with a sharp spade. This can be done either in early spring or late fall.

A May 24 weekend work party prepares rhubarb for the freezer.

SOLANACEAE:
The Nightshade Family

Soil Requirements for Eggplant, Peppers and Tomatoes

All these plants require the same soil preparation. They will grow in a wide range of soils as long as the soil is warm, has a high water-holding capacity and is fertile. The pH should be 5.5 to 6.5.

Whenever possible, add well-rotted manure or compost to the soil. Most soils also need additional fertilizer: 30 to 40 pounds of 5:10:10 per 1,000 square feet.

Work the ground deeply to ensure good friable conditions in which the plants can develop strong root systems. When setting transplants out in the garden, an application of transplant starter solution is beneficial. One cupful to each plant is recommended, using 2 tablespoons of 5:10:5 to one gallon of water or a commercial transplant equivalent.

After the soil is really warm, and the moisture level is deep, we apply a mulch. This is not essential, but it saves both weeding and watering. All three plants need full sun and protection from wind.

Eggplant: *Solanum melongena*

The eggplant, or aubergine, is not as easy to grow successfully as the tomato or pepper. It is native to India and the Far East. Because it is very frost-tender, it requires a long, warm growing season. Eggplant seed must be started indoors eight to ten weeks ahead of planting-out time. It requires warmer conditions than the pepper, if possible 70° to 80°F (21° to 26°C) at night, 80° to 90°F (27° to 32°C) during the day. Be careful not to place the flats too close to the source of heat; this might cause damage to the roots. Reduce the temperature slightly after the seedlings have developed. Keep the soil moist, but not soggy.

Harden the plants slowly — they are very temperamental. I always allow them about three weeks in the cold-frame, gradually increasing the length of time that the lid is open. They must be given shade from intense sun shining through the glass, and extra protection at night if the temperature drops. Their exposure to the elements is gradual but, with luck, they will have spent their last week in the frame with the lid open day and night. They should now be sufficiently hardened to be set out in the garden. If you only need a few plants, it is much simpler to purchase them from a reputable grower. Make sure that you know which variety you are buying, as the ultimate size of the plant depends on the variety. Many hybrids are smaller and can be

Close-up of young eggplant showing strong root growth emerging through nylon mesh.

A high gloss on the eggplant fruit is an indication of ripeness.

planted more closely in the rows. In general, the cultivation and planting of eggplant is the same as for peppers.

Eggplants are heavy feeders and benefit from additional fertilizing. I apply a balanced liquid fertilizer high in phosphorous and potash, giving each plant a good soaking every two or three weeks. If the plant has been mulched, pull back the mulch before fertilizing, then replace it.

Crop rotation is extremely important. Never plant eggplant where any member of the nightshade family was grown the previous year. Harvest the fruit by cutting with clippers or a sharp knife. Select young fruit while the skin is still very shiny purple. If eggplants are over-ripe, the skin will be dull with brown streaks, seeds will have formed and the flesh will be pithy and bitter. We prefer to eat eggplant fresh from the garden rather than frozen. Five or six plants give an ample supply to most families.

Sweet Peppers: *Capsicum annuum*

Hot Peppers: *Capsicum frutescens*

The garden pepper is now a very popular plant for the home garden. If you can grow tomatoes, you can grow peppers. A native to Central and South America, peppers are known to have been cultivated by the Aztecs. Early explorers introduced them to Spain and Portugal, and they are now grown in all parts of the world where the growing season is sufficiently warm and long. Climatic conditions at the time of flower development have a strong effect on fruit set. Periods of high temperature and low humidity, temperatures below 55° F (13° C), or strong winds will cause blossoms to abort and fall off.

In Canada, we must grow peppers as transplants, starting the seed indoors in March. By mid-May, the plants should be about 8 inches tall and have sturdy, strong stems. They are then ready for hardening, prior to being set-out in the garden.

If you plan to grow only three or four plants, purchase them from a dependable grower, and look for sturdy plants. Spindly, tall plants will not grow into productive

Peppers grown from seed in Jiffy-7's, ready to be planted out.

bushes. Do not set the plants in the garden until the soil has warmed up and the night temperature is above 60°F (15°C). In our area this is usually the first week in June. If necessary, give the plants some protection for the first few days. As the plants will become strong bushes about 2½ feet high, allow 3 feet between the rows and 2½ feet between the plants in the rows. Usually, it is not necessary to stake peppers, but if the branches should become heavy with fruit, support may be necessary.

Never work around the plants when the leaves are wet, and never smoke tobacco near them. If you do smoke, wash your hands before handling pepper plants. This helps prevent the spread of a viral disease, tobacco mosaic.

Sweet red peppers are the green pepper when it has ripened. I always leave some early fruit on the bushes, allowing them to ripen. Red peppers have a far higher vitamin C content than green peppers; they are sweeter too. We grow ten sweet pepper plants, which provide ample fruit for both fresh summer dishes and the winter supply in the freezer. Peppers are vulnerable to many of the same ailments as potatoes, tomatoes and eggplant.

The cultivation of hot peppers is identical to that of sweet peppers. Hot peppers can be eaten fresh or dried for winter use.

Peppers ready to harvest.

Tomatoes: *Lycopersicon esculentum*

The tomato, like its cousin the pepper, is native to the tropical Americas and was introduced to Europe at about the same time. In Elizabethan England tomatoes were called "love apples" and were grown in the flower garden. For many years the tomato was believed to be poisonous. George Washington Carver (c. 1864-1943), the famous American botanist and son of Negro slaves, is reputed to have eaten tomatoes publicly before a horrified crowd. This act helped dispell the poison myth, and today the vitamin-rich fruit is one of our main sources of vitamin C. In the United States it ranks second to potatoes in economic value. Tomatoes are now the most widely grown of all vegetables in the home garden. People who have only a balcony or verandah grow tomatoes in tubs, pots or hanging baskets.

There are well over a hundred so-called varieties offered through the seed catalogues. These may vary in days of maturity, habit of growth, size of plant, colour, size, shape of fruit and resistance to disease. A small type of plant does not necessarily produce cherry tomatoes, any more than a large plant produces large fruit. When selecting seed, it is advisable to know the ultimate size of the bush and what type of fruit it will produce.

Tomatoes are divided into two main groups: determinate and indeterminate. The determinate, or bush, tomato stops growing when the end buds set fruit, usually at about 3 feet in height. These are the early crops. The indeterminate tomato grows almost indefinitely because the end buds do not set fruit. In our area their growth is arrested by frost. Indeterminate tomatoes are grown in cages or are trained on stakes.

There are some varieties now being offered in Canada whose seed can be planted directly in the garden after all danger of frost is past. However, it is more usual to grow tomatoes as transplants — the choice of varieties is far greater. Tomato seeds germinate in six to four-

Flat of tomato seedlings.

Close-up of tomato plant in Jiffy-7 showing root system.

When planting out sturdy plants, set ²/₃ of the stem in the soil (with leggy plants, ³/₄ of the stem). Lay the plant at an angle. Within a few days it will straighten out. Remove any leaves that would be below the soil. Wrap a paper collar around the stem.

teen days and should be started indoors six to eight weeks prior to planting-out time. The days to maturity given in seed catalogues are from the time the plants are set-out in the garden. Tomatoes can be set-out a little earlier than eggplant and pepper. They also are very frost-tender, and the slightest frost will damage the young plants. It is better to wait until the soil is warm than to take any risks. If you must set them out early, give them some protection until they become established.

Tomatoes prefer full sun and fertile, well-drained soil. They tend to ripen earlier in sandy soil, but will produce a larger crop in clay. When setting out transplants, plant at a 45° angle with half to two-thirds of the stem under the ground. The plants will straighten up in a day or two. This allows roots to grow along the stem, giving added support and a greater root system for nutrient up-take. Watering with a transplant solution gets tomatoes off to a good start.

Tomatoes are heavy feeders and benefit from regular applications of either liquid manure or a complete fertilizer during the early stage of growth; then, after fruit has set, with a high phosphorous and potash compound. Never permit the soil to dry out. Smokers should be warned that they could transmit tobacco mosaic to the plants and should always wash their hands before entering the garden.

Tomatoes are vulnerable to a number of pests and diseases, especially "wilts" transmitted by insects. Grow varieties that have been bred for their resistance to disease. In seed catalogues the letters "V" (Verticillium), "F" (Fusarium) and "N" (nematode) denote such varieties. The letter "H" indicates that it is a hybrid.

Whether growing your own or purchasing transplants, look for stocky, strong-stemmed plants. If you are a newcomer to the area, inquire as to which varieties have been proven satisfactory there. Avoid purchasing leggy plants that are already in bloom or have set fruit. You may get an early ripe tomato, but the ultimate crop will be poor.

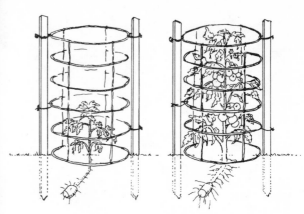

Tomato cages using page-wire fencing.

Tomato plants in wire cages. Straw mulch covers the ground.

Close-up of cherry tomatoes, commonly used in salads.

Tomato Supports

Many varieties of tomatoes grow very tall and need support to prevent the stems from breaking and to keep the fruit off the ground. For many years it has been customary to prune tomato plants, leaving one main stem. With this technique a stout stake is needed and must be driven into the ground prior to planting the transplant. As the plant grows, it is tied to the stake and the shoots that grow in the axils of the leaves pinched out.

We have found this technique to be time-consuming and now grow all our tomatoes in homemade page-wire rings. This method eliminates pruning. As the plant grows, it supports itself inside the ring. We secure the rings firmly to the ground by stakes. Harvesting through the open mesh is simple. Garden centres now sell tomato rings ready to assemble.

Old Car Tires It was through information passed on at a Horticultural Society meeting that I first learned how useful old car tires can be in the garden. I have since heard that in windy areas along the Prince Edward Island coast tomato plants are frequently seen growing inside old car tires. The tires not only protect the plants from the wind, but also retain heat, hastening the maturity of the fruit. Several tires can be stacked around the plant as it grows.

Potatoes: *Solanum tuberosum*

The potato is native to South America, probably Peru, and was brought to Europe by the Spaniards early in the sixteenth century. Sir Walter Raleigh is generally credited with its introduction to the British Isles in 1586. There is little doubt that it was he who brought the potato to Ireland after he was granted large estates there. It is surprising to find another two centuries were to elapse before the potato gained further attention. Today, it is among the world's leading crops.

Potatoes are one of the cheapest sources of carbohydrates and contain appreciable amounts of vitamins and minerals, especially when eaten skin and all. There are few vegetables more delicious than early potatoes freshly dug from the garden. I rate freshly picked corn and newly dug potatoes in the same class. Only those who have tasted them will understand what I mean. So-called "new" potatoes in the supermarkets bear no comparison. I dig only as many as we need for each meal — even 24 hours seems to alter the flavour.

A few early potato plants deserve a place in the garden. The main crop for winter storage is easy and inexpensive to purchase in the fall. I do not recommend growing a main crop of potatoes unless ample space is available.

Most garden soils are suitable for potatoes, but the best results are obtained from a slightly acid, well-drained soil rich in humus. The texture and colour of the tubers will vary according to the type of soil in which they are grown. Always rotate the potato patch, remembering that potatoes, tomatoes, peppers and eggplant belong to the same family and are grouped together for rotation purposes.

Always plant certified seed unless you are quite certain that your own crop was absolutely healthy. I prefer seed potato to be small 1½- to 2-ounce tubers from a good, clean crop. If these are not available, larger potatoes can be cut into chunky pieces, leaving two eyes on each. After cutting, these should be dusted with a fungicide and then left for several days in a warm, dry place to heal the wound.

Seed potatoes sprouting in trays in the basement.

I find I get the best results from small seed potatoes which are sprouted before planting. This is done by placing the tubers, with the "rose," the end with most eyes, facing up in a flat (preferably of peat moss). The tubers should not be crowded. Opinion varies as to how much light should be given, but I prefer to leave them in the dark where they will sprout

Egg-sized seed potatoes show at least one eye that has already sprouted.

anyway. The temperature should not be above 40°F (4°C). The length of time for sprouting depends on the temperature, anywhere from three to six weeks. Great care must be taken when planting-out not to damage the sprouts. By exposing the seed tubers to the sun for

is to dig holes and plant tubers 4 inches deep. Another is to dig a trench 12 inches deep; work in well-rotted manure or compost; replace a little soil; plant the potato and cover with an inch or two of soil, adding more soil as the plants grow. However, some authorities warn

Sprouted tubers being planted out.

Potatoes being grown under hay mulch. The ridges are made by the growth pushing up from below.

about one hour, the sprouts will wilt and be less brittle. The extra time taken is well spent, for there should be a significant increase in the yield of crop. It is often recommended that the seed tuber should have only two eyes sprouting, the rest should be rubbed off. I find that this is not important because the weight of crop from each plant will be the same, the ones with only two sprouts left having fewer, larger tubers. Plant out as soon as the ground dries up sufficiently to work, and there is little danger of a killing frost.

There are many different methods of planting, but the rows are always 3 feet apart and the tubers 12 inches apart in the row. One way

that the use of fresh manure in the ground the year before potatoes are sown is conducive to scab.

Ruth Stout, in her book *A Green Thumb Without an Aching Back*, has a completely different method. She just spreads the potatoes on the ground and covers them with old hay! We have tried this method and it really works. Our only problem was in not spreading the hay deeply enough. We had a number of green potatoes, the result of exposure to light. Green potatoes are poisonous, as are the fruits or seed pods of the potato.

When potatoes are planted in the ground

without a mulch, regular cultivation will be necessary to keep the weeds under control. As the plants grow and the tubers develop, hill up the earth around the tubers. This is usually done twice during the season. After flowers have formed on early potato plants, it is time to

After digging, the potatoes dry in the sun before being brought into storage.

start harvesting. I do not dig the entire plant. Instead, I scratch away some soil and look for tubers large enough to eat, leaving the rest undisturbed to continue growing. Main crop potatoes should be left in the ground until the tops die down and the skin becomes firm. A light frost will not damage the tubers. We dig our main crop early in October.

Dig the crop with a fork on a warm, dry day when the soil is not wet. Leave the potatoes on the surface for an hour or so to dry, then bring them indoors and store in a cool place where they will not freeze. The ideal temperature is 36° to 40°F (2° to 4°C), seldom possible in modern houses.

Garden Huckleberry: *Solanum nigrum*

The garden huckleberry, an annual, produces quantities of large, blue berries all along the branches. It is only used cooked and sweetened because the raw berries are extremely tart. Four plants should be ample for a family. The seeds should be started indoors or in the hot-frame six weeks prior to planting out. A distance of 4 feet between plants is necessary for they will become large spreading bushes. Although the fruit may turn blue in August, it is seldom ripe until September, and anyone picking it too early will be disappointed with the results.

This is an easy fruit to grow and, although not susceptible to many pests and diseases, is sometimes attacked by the flea beetles or succumbs to mildew. A combination spray or dusting does the trick.

The fresh fruit can be put directly into the freezer and used when needed during the winter. Our family is particularly fond of Huckleberry Crumble served hot with whipped or sour cream.

A healthy garden huckleberry transplant grown from seed. I plant two of these approximately 3 feet apart. They will provide all the fruit we need.

Ripe huckleberry.

Ground Cherry: *Physalis pruinosa*

The ground cherry — or husk or strawberry tomato, as it is sometimes called — is a close relative of the ornamental Chinese lantern. The fruits of this annual are produced inside a paper-like husk. They are golden in colour and about the size of cherry tomatoes, but are much sweeter than tomatoes.

Some of our neighbours have had successful crops from direct outdoor seeding. Not so in our garden; we have to grow them as transplants.

Cultural requirements are similar to tomatoes. The ground cherry plants will attain a height of about 3 feet. They will not require staking.

Problems and Controls

The Colorado potato beetle overwinters in the soil emerging in the spring to lay her eggs on the undersides of leaves. In about a week red, hump-backed larvae hatch to spend the next three weeks voraciously eating the foliage of the plants. They then burrow into the soil, pupate and re-appear as yellow, hemispherical beetles that have black spots on their heads and five black stripes on each wing sheath.

Adult Colorado beetle.

In a small garden the egg clusters and beetles may be hand-picked and crushed. In larger gardens regular dusting or spraying with an insecticide may be necessary. Another control is to sprinkle bran over the plants when the dew is still wet on the leaves. The beetle will gorge itself on the bran, fall to the ground and become dehydrated.

Flea beetles, leafhoppers and aphids may spread bacterial diseases, viruses and spindle tuber. All these insects can be controlled with spraying or dusting.

Cutworms can destroy newly set-out transplants. Some species even attack young potato plants.

When necessary, apply paper collars at ground level to protect tender stems. When

Cutworm.

Hornworm.

you find stems that a cutworm has severed, dig down around the plant to find the culprit and destroy it.

Wireworms often attack potato tubers by tunnelling into them and rendering them inedible and unfit for storage.

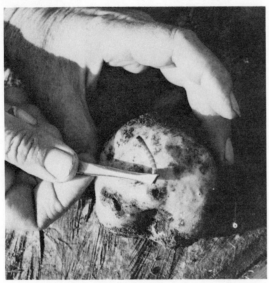

Wireworm being extracted from potato with tweezers.

Pepper maggots are sometimes found in the fruit. They are half-inch white grubs that are the larvae of a yellowish striped fly. Dusting or spraying with an insecticide at weekly intervals after the fruit has set will keep these under control.

Tomato fruitworm is the same insect as the corn earworm. They are not a common problem, but if you notice holes in the fruit, spray or dust with insecticide.

Tomato hornworms are bright green with eight yellow stripes and a "horn" that protrudes from its hind end. They are large, ugly worms

that usually measure from 3 to 4 inches in length. This pest pupates over winter in the soil and emerges in early summer as a large hawk or hummingbird moth with a wingspan of up to 5 inches. The females lay single, spherical yellow-green eggs under the leaves. In about a week the caterpillars hatch and begin feeding.

They are ravenous feeders and can defoliate a plant very rapidly. As they are seldom numerous, the simplest control is to pick off any that are found by hand. You can spot them in the area where defoliation has occurred and by a pile of mouse-sized feces.

The natural predator of the hornworm is a parasitic wasp which lays her eggs on the insect's back. When you see a hornworm carrying these eggs, you should not destroy it. The young wasps will kill this hornworm and mature to fly off and attack others.

Whiteflies are sucking insects found on the leaves and stems of plants. They are usually noticed when a plant is disturbed, when they fly out in a cloud. To control, spray at four to five day intervals with rotenone or insecticidal soap.

Slugs can be a perfect menace in the garden. They feed from early spring until late fall. These pests have never been a serious problem in our garden, but I know from my viewers that they can cause severe damage.

There are commercial slug-baits available, but the simplest control is to place shallow dishes of beer around the garden in which the slugs will drown. A simple trap can be made by inverting half grapefruit rinds on the soil surface.

Virus diseases such as mosaics and leaf roll are transmitted by insects, which, after feeding on infected plants or weeds, move on to healthy stock, taking the disease with them. In general, these diseases can be identified by mottling, yellowing, curling and crinkling of the leaves. To prevent spread of viruses, it is essential to control weeds and insects: there is no cure for infected plants.

Early blight   is a fungal disease that overwinters in discarded potato debris and is spread the following spring by wind, rain and insects. The symptoms include small, circular or oval brown-black spots on the leaves which gradually increase in size, forming concentric rings which readily identify this disease. Early blight is not often a serious problem and can usually be controlled by burning old plants after harvest, or by treating plants with a fungicide at ten-day intervals during the growing season, especially when the weather is hot and humid.

Late blight   on potatoes is an extremely serious fungal disease. It usually occurs when the weather in late summer and late fall is wet and cool. It can attack the crop very suddenly, and the unwary home gardener might mistake the symptoms for an early frost.

A very clear description of "The Blight" is given in Desmond Guinness's and William Ryan's book *Irish Houses and Castles*. It includes an extract from the diary of Miss Frances Cobbe of Newbridge Co. Dublin in which she states,

> *"I happen to be able to recall precisely the day, almost the hour, when the blight fell on the potatoes and caused the great calamity. A party of us were driving to a seven o'clock dinner at the house of our neighbour, Mrs Evans, of Portrane. As we passed a remarkably fine field of potatoes in blossom, the scent came through the open windows of the carriage and we remarked to each other how splendid was the crop. Three or four hours later, as we returned home in the dark, a dreadful smell came from the same field, and we exclaimed, 'Something has happened to those potatoes; they do not smell at all as they did when we passed them on our way out.' Next morning there was a wail from one end of Ireland to the other."*

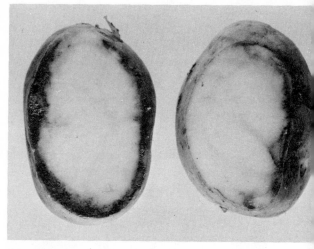

Late blight on potatoes — internal symptoms.

Late blight can be controlled by burning old plants after harvest and spraying or dusting with a recommended fungicide. It is most important to repeat this treatment every seven to ten days until September.

Kenebecs and Sebagos are moderately resistant to late blight.

Potato scab   is a soil-borne bacterial disease that favours alkaline or neutral soils, but seldom occurs in acid soils with a reading of pH 5.6 or less. Potatoes attacked by scab are unattractive to look at, but the eating quality is not affected. To prevent scab, do not apply fresh manure to the soil where potatoes are to be grown and, if necessary, apply sulphur to reduce the pH level.

Black leg   in potatoes is caused by a bacteria that overwinters in plant debris and stored tubers. It causes a black ring to girdle the stalk at ground level, and the plant gradually wilts and dies. The tubers develop a soft rot near the stem. Control is by planting certified seed.

Rhizoctonia,   or black scurf, is a fungal disease that is common to potatoes everywhere. The home gardener can identify it by the black lumps that look like dirt on his mature potatoes which do not wash off. In severe cases the plant produces clusters of small, misshapen pota-

Rhizoctonia: The "soil" that does not wash off.

Fusarium wilt of tomato.

toes, and the crop is of little value. The fungus lives indefinitely in the soil, making crop rotation of little value in controlling rhizoctonia. The scurf will be less prevalent if the seed potatoes are planted only about 2 inches deep after the soil has warmed up. Harvest the crop as soon as the potatoes are mature.

Bacterial ring rot in potatoes is identified by a wilting and slight rolling of lower leaves during the day. The tubers develop a yellowish ring about ¼ inch below the skin surface. These tubers will not keep in storage. Control is by planting certified seed.

Anthracnose causes small, dark sunken spots on ripe fruit that often increase in size to cover a large portion of the fruit.

Verticillium wilt is recognized when the older leaves turn yellow and wilt. The plants seldom die, but growth will be poor because the older leaves are constantly dying and dropping off.

Fusarium wilt has similar symptoms to Verticillium wilt, but can be diagnosed by the black-brown interior of a cut stem.

The latter three fungi mentioned live in the soil. To protect your crop from infection, plant disease-resistant types. Always observe crop rotation practices and good garden hygiene.

Blossom end rot in tomatoes may be caused by environmental conditions. The blossom end of the fruit exhibits a dry, firm rot which provides an opening for secondary infection. A deficiency of calcium in the soil and hot, dry weather combine to produce this condition.

Sun scald on tomatoes will occur when the fruit is subject to excessive sun. Overpruning of staked plants is the most common cause.

Blossom drop in peppers occurs during periods of low humidity and high winds. If enough of the growing season remains, the plants will re-blossom and set fruit.

The Parsley or Carrot Family

Carrot: *Daucus carota*

The carrot is one of the most popular and widely grown of vegetables, mainly thanks to the work of a French plant breeder, Vilmorin-Andrieux, whose efforts in the late 1800s led to the development of today's varieties.

Although carrots can be grown in a wide range of soils, they do best in either a deep, loose, sandy loam or loam or muck high in fertility and moisture-retaining capacity. The ground should be worked to a depth of 9 to 12 inches and be free from stones and clods; these could cause misshapen roots. Not everyone has ideal conditions. If carrots must be grown in a clay soil, add and work in as much humus as possible prior to planting. Avoid strawy manure and raw compost because these tend to cause misshapen roots covered with fibrous side rootlets. The selection of seed will depend to a certain extent on the type and depth of soil in the garden.

Carrot varieties are available in a wide range of sizes and shapes. If your soil conditions are perfect, you can grow long, tapering carrots. If hard clay conditions prevail, stumpy, short or round carrots would be preferable.

Carrot seed is slow to germinate, usually taking two to three weeks. Some radish seed planted with the carrot will germinate rapidly, marking the row and breaking the soil surface, thereby assisting the more delicate young carrot plants to emerge. The radishes can be harvested before the carrots require the space.

Sow the seed half an inch deep in rows 12 to 15 inches apart in a sunny spot in the garden. A method I use when planting carrots alone is to place a board over the row after seeding, and remove it at the first sign of germination. As soon as the plants are 2 to 3 inches high, I start thinning them out. Eventually, I thin to a

Two varieties of carrots and a row of beets planted on the same day. Note how they all produce different growth.

The same rows as shown above a month later.

spacing of 1½ to 2 inches. If large storage carrots are desired, thin again. Experience will teach the gardener how and when to thin.

As carrots are at their prime when young, make successive plantings every two to three weeks. The first seeding is done as soon as the ground can be worked, the last in early August. The main crop, or June seeding, is the best one to plan for winter-storage carrots.

Many gardeners place a board between the rows to step on while working. This prevents the soil from becoming too compacted. As I have seen many other equally satisfactory methods used in my friends' gardens, I feel all practices should be used as guidelines, and the one found best suited to the individual gardener adopted.

Carrots are not often subject to pest and disease problems. If you notice anything amiss, it is more than likely either the carrot rust fly or yellows.

Celery: *Apium graveolens dulce*

Celery is a superb crop for eating raw or cooked, and when well-grown few other vegetables equal it in crispness and flavour. It is not easy to grow in the average home garden, but for gardeners prepared to devote a little extra time in preparing the ground, the results are well worth the effort.

Celery, in its wild state, grows in the marshy areas of northern Europe. We must, therefore, try to simulate these conditions. It requires moist, rich soil — not waterlogged. Light or clay soil must be adapted by a generous application of well-rotted manure, compost, leaves or other organic material. Rich living conditions and continual thirst-quenchings are of prime importance. The most satisfactory plan is to dig a trench 10 to 12 inches deep and 15 to 18 inches wide, running north and south. The soil taken out is placed on either side of the

Thinning carrots for the table. The remaining main crop is left to mature for winter storage.

A row of well-established celery seedlings growing in a trench.

trench in such a way that it does not fall back in when it rains. In areas where the topsoil is shallow, dig out only to the depth of the topsoil. If this leaves a very shallow trench, dig out several inches of subsoil and remove it from the garden. The bottom of the trench is then broken up deeply, using a fork or spade and plenty of organic matter or manure incorporated. A couple of inches of topsoil is then returned, and a sprinkling of bone meal applied. These are then worked in lightly. The bone meal should be applied as long as possible in advance of planting.

We had difficulty in growing celery until a soil test revealed a shortage of boron. This was remedied by an application of borax (solubor) worked into the trench prior to planting-out.

For the home gardener who only grows 10 or 12 plants, it is easiest to purchase a small flat of seedlings from a nursery. For those gardeners needing larger quantities, celery must be started indoors as a transplant, starting ten to twelve weeks ahead of planting-out time. In our area we plant-out in late May or early June. The young plants are set out 9 inches apart in the centre of the trench in a single line, planted at the same depth as they were growing in the flats. Leave them very firm in the soil, and give them a thorough soaking. Celery must never be allowed to dry out and, when watering, always soak the trench thoroughly so that the moisture gets down below the roots.

Celery is a very heavy feeder and benefits from an application of liquid fertilizer every two or three weeks. I use liquid manure when available, or a fish-based fertilizer. The plants will grow rapidly. Side shoots which will arise from the roots must be watched for and removed by breaking away. If this is neglected, much of the strength of the plant will be wasted.

There are new varieties of celery on the market which do not require blanching; however, we still find all celery more tasty when blanched. Store-bought celery is usually unblanched and therefore green. It has a stronger flavour than blanched celery, and the fibre or strings in the stalks are tougher.

Black heart of celery, usually the result of a boron deficiency.

The entire blanched celery plant is like the heart of an unblanched plant. Blanching celery is a common practice in Europe and I would recommend that home gardeners in North America try it. The method we have now adopted is extremely quick and simple. Place a board on either side of the row when the plants are large and well-established, leaving only the tops of the plants sticking out. Before doing this I bunch the stalks of each plant together, firmly held with a couple of strong rubber bands. We have found this method vastly superior to earthing up with soil or wrapping in strong paper.

Harvesting a few outer stems during the growing season will not damage the plants in any way. As celery takes 90 to 100 days to mature from planting-out time, the main crop will be ready from September to freeze-up. Remove a board and dig a plant as required. Mature celery can withstand a limited degree of frost. Plants can be dug in the fall, keeping the root system intact, and replanted in a box. Store in the cool room or root cellar for about a month.

We have not found this method satisfactory, and so we grow only sufficient to eat fresh.

To blanch, place boards on either side of row when plants are well established, exposing only plant tops.

Harvesting a celery root. First remove the blanching board and dig deeply with a spade.

Blanched celery showing the strong root system. Note the rubber band which held the petioles (stems) together.

Celeriac: *Apium graveolens rapaceum*

Celeriac is a turnip-rooted celery very popular in Italian cooking. The cultural requirements are the same as for celery but it need not be planted in a trench. No blanching is necessary. The edible part is the root, which is used for soup and stew flavouring, grated raw in salads or cooked in the same manner as other root vegetables. The leaves may also be used to flavour soups. Celeriac roots are very easy to store and will keep for several months under the same conditions as beets, carrots and turnips.

The seedlings should be planted in the ground at the same depth as they were growing in the seed-bed. As the turnip-like roots develop, trim or pull off the outer petioles.

Celeriac is a cool-weather crop and, like celery, responds to an ample supply of water and fertilizer.

Parsley: *Petroselinum crispum*

Parsley is one of the most popular garden herbs and is very high in iron and vitamin content.

Parsley grows well in any good garden soil; however, because the seed is slow to germinate, sow as early as possible in the spring.

A few radishes sown with the parsley seed will mark the row. As the parsley germinates, the radishes will mature and can be pulled. Another method which I have adopted and find most satisfactory is to place a board over the row after seeding. After about two weeks, when germination could be starting, I keep looking under the board to check whether there are any signs of life. As soon as there are, I lift the board immediately. Germination using this technique is very high.

Thin the parsley to approximately 6 inches between plants. Harvest by picking stalks as required. A few plants left in the ground over winter usually provides an early spring crop. Also, a few plants dug up, potted and kept in a sunny window will give the house fresh parsley all winter. Parsley is relatively trouble-free; yellow leaves are usually due to dry soil.

A row of young parsley plants.

A row of parsnips in the fall showing the lush foliage. Note the grass clippings mulch laid over newspaper.

Parsnip-Rooted Parsley:
Petroselinum crispum tuberosum

"Hamburg-thick rooted parsley" is grown for its root rather than leaf. Culture is the same as for carrots and parsnips, as is the cooking and serving. Excellent for soups and stews.

Parsnip: *Pastinaca sativa*

This highly nutritious plant is a native of Europe and Asia. It was introduced to North America by early colonists at the turn of the seventeenth century. A most useful crop in the home garden, it can be left in the ground all winter to provide a fresh root vegetable as soon as digging is possible in the spring. The old wive's tale that parsnips become poisonous if allowed to sprout in the spring is completely erroneous. Sprouting only causes a decline in flavour, making it advisable to harvest the whole crop before sprouting begins.

The general cultivation of parsnips is much the same as for beets and carrots, but because

Freshly dug parsnips which have wintered outdoors.

the tapering root of the parsnip will grow to a depth of around 3 feet, much deeper cultivation is required. For this reason, if the parsnips can be grown in the area previously occupied by leeks, the ground will already have been loosened to a reasonable depth.

The soil should contain some lime, should be rich in humus or well-rotted manure; best worked in the previous fall; and free of stones which would prevent the straight growth of the root.

Although the seed is usually viable for two years, it is best to purchase fresh seed each year to assure good germination. The seed is extremely slow to germinate, so mark the row by also planting some radish seed in the drill or by placing a board over the row and removing it at the first sign of germination, anywhere from 15 to 25 days.

Plant as early as possible in the spring in a furrow half an inch deep, leaving 2 feet between rows; cover the seed very lightly with a little soil, sand or vermiculite and tamp it down. The seedlings often have difficulty pushing through dry soil, so try to keep them well-watered.

After the seedlings are about 2 inches tall, thin to 4 to 6 inches apart. The roots will not be mature until September. The flavour is greatly improved after several frosts and when eaten freshly dug.

The roots will keep in plastic bags in the refrigerator or cool room for several months. Check occasionally for excess humidity. They can also be cooked and frozen.

Parsnips are relatively disease-resistant, but can be subject to the same problems as other members of the carrot family.

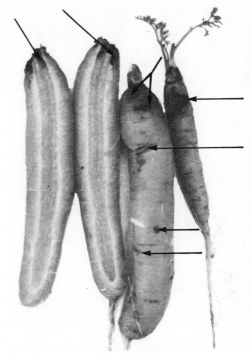

Carrot rust-fly damage.

Problems and Controls

The carrot rust fly attacks all members of this family. This fly is shiny green with black eyes, a yellow head and is one-fifth of an inch long. In late spring the female fly lays her eggs near the crowns of plants. Carrots, parsnips and celery are the most susceptible. The larvae are yellowish-white worms, about one-third of an inch long, which tunnel into the outer layer of the roots.

The carrot caterpillar is about 2 inches long and is green with black and yellow markings. They are striking in appearance and, when noticed, can usually be picked off by hand. Carrot caterpillars are seldom a serious problem.

Wireworms are about an inch in length. They are wiry, hard-skinned, copper-coloured worms that burrow into the roots. They can be discouraged by working diazinon crystals into the soil before planting or, if you notice just a few, place a sliced potato on the soil surface. The potato will attract the wireworms, and they can be destroyed along with the potato.

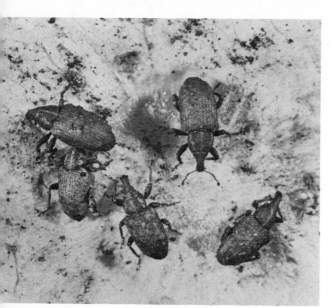

Carrot weevils.

Carrot weevil damage.

The carrot weevil is a snouted, beetle-like insect that attacks the fleshy roots of the carrots, leaving great gouges, rendering a carrot unattractive and inedible quite quickly. When good garden hygiene and crop rotation are practised, carrot weevils are not a serious problem.

Black slug These pests are far worse some seasons that others. When control becomes necessary, use slug-bait or set out shallow dishes of stale beer in which the slugs drown.

Leafhoppers cause the spread of carrot yellows. Weeds in or near the garden plot may harbour these insects. When they move from plant to plant, they carry the disease with them and infect the other plants they touch. To prevent contamination, control the weeds in and around the garden and dust or spray as required.

Carrot yellows is a virus disease that causes the development of hairy roots on carrots or parsnips and the purpling and twisting of the tops. Prevention consists of controlling the leafhoppers and removing and destroying infected plants.

Black slug attacking a celery petiole.

The Herb Garden

Chefs delight in adding herbs to enhance the flavour of many of their dishes. Some have even gone as far as to grow the fresh produce under fluorescent lights in their kitchens. We home gardeners can all enjoy these delicious extra flavours, and with very little trouble or expense after the initial plans have been made. To make the best use of herbs, grow as many as possible within easy reach of the kitchen door. In having them so near at hand, you will find you use them constantly. It's the little snips here and there that make for easy use and experimenting while cooking. The list of culinary herbs included in this chapter is only a few of the many in general use. I hope this list will prove to be of encouragement to novice herb growers who, after tasting the results of their labours, will add yearly to their list of species.

Chives: *Allium schoenoprasum*

This hardy perennial is a member of the onion family and well worth a place in every garden. It takes up very little space and both the top and bottom can be used: the tops in salads and soups and the bulbs as mild-flavoured onions. Chives thrive in a wide variety of soils and can be used as a decorative edging to flower beds — decorative because the small mauve flowers are produced freely.

The simplest method to establish chives is by planting bulbs. A few bulbs planted in the spring will become a good-sized clump within one season. Bulbs can be purchased, or perhaps a neighbour will present you with some when he is dividing his clumps. Dividing can be done any time during the season, but always cut back the tops when replanting. If bulbs are

not available, seed can be sown in April or early May and the seedlings thinned to 6 inches apart. In the fall, pot up some bulbs and grow indoors for winter use.

Garlic Chives

Garlic chives have a wide, flat leaf and a tall, white flower. The leaves have a mild garlic flavour and are a delicious addition to salads and soups. The cultural needs are the same as for the common chive.

Dill: *Anethum graveolens*

Dill is native to Europe, but has been naturalized in North America. Both the Romans and Greeks are known to have enjoyed it. Its properties have been considered both aphrodisiacal and soporific, and in the Dark Ages it was associated with black magic. Today we use dill as a culinary herb — the young green leaves in

Harvesting dill. In our garden it seeds itself and has no special place allotted for growing.

the spring in salads and sauces and, later on, the seeds to give flavour to our dill cucumber pickles and many other preserves and winter dishes.

Dill is an annual and should be planted as soon as the garden can be worked. Thin the seedlings to about 6 inches apart. It does best in a well-drained, sunny location and will attain a height of about 3 feet.

In our garden we find that so many seeds scatter each season and emerge the next spring among the rows of vegetables that it is never necessary to plant a row of dill. The seedlings are very easy to identify with their feathery leaves, and enough can be left undisturbed to supply the household. Dill does not transplant well.

Horseradish: *Amoracia lapathifolia*

Where space is not a problem, a 3 by 3 foot horseradish bed will provide an ample supply for the family. Once established it is hard to eradicate, for every small piece of root left in the ground will grow the next season. Horseradish is a member of the mustard family; the plants grow to about 3 feet in height; and are a vigorous moisture-loving plant. The large dock-like leaves are not edible. All the value lies in the roots, which are ready for lifting in September or October. We prepare our year's supply by grating the cleaned pieces of root in the blender with vinegar, then bottling it. Horseradish, if grated on an open grater, will make the eyes weep in the same manner as a strong onion does.

To establish a bed, plant pieces of root of any length, as short as 3 inches or as thin as a pencil. If these are broken, the top should be cut squarely, and a bud will form after planting. They should be planted upright in holes one foot apart. Make the holes with a stick or crowbar about 10 inches deep. Drop the roots in so that they go right to the bottom. The better quality the soil is, the larger the roots will become. Try to prevent the bed from drying out in a hot season.

Preparing to dig a horseradish root. Note the size of the leaves and upper growth.

Horseradish root. This specimen has branched out more than usual. Ordinarily we only get one main root on each plant.

Lovage: *Levisticum officinale*

Lovage is a perennial member of the carrot family. It is a native of the Mediterranean countries and was brought to America by the early settlers, who grew it in their herb gardens for both medicinal and culinary uses.

One clump of lovage is ample for a household. The plant grows to a height of about 4 feet, with leaves that have a celery-like appearance as well as flavour. Stems and leaves are used in soups and stews, either chopped or in a bouquet garni. Freshly chopped young leaves add a celery flavour to salads.

The leaves may be dried for winter use, but more flavour is retained when they are chopped and frozen.

Propagation is by seed sown in spring or by root division.

Lovage thrives in a wide range of soils, provided there is good drainage as well as moisture retention during summer months. It is extremely easy to grow, seldom has any problems, and is an excellent herb for the home garden.

Marjoram: *Majorana hortensis*

> *Indeed, sir, she was the sweet*
> *Marjoram of the salad, or rather*
> *the Herb-of-Grace.*
>
> *All's Well That Ends Well*
> Shakespeare

Marjoram, or sweet marjoram, is a popular herb that is easily grown from seed. Although it is a perennial, due to our severe winters it is treated as an annual in northern climes. I grow a small row in the vegetable garden alongside the summer savory and the sweet basil.

The leaves must be harvested before there is any risk of frost and hung to dry in a dark, airy place. Fresh marjoram can be obtained all winter by potting up a plant and bringing it indoors before the first frost; it will require a sunny window or fluorescent light. Marjoram will grow in any good garden loam that is well-drained. It needs full sun, and plenty of moisture, but allow the soil to dry out between waterings.

Mints: *Mentha species*

Mints are native to Europe and the British Isles. There are three main groups: culinary, medicinal and aromatic. The species usually grown in our gardens is the field mint, the leaves of which are used for sauces and to spice drinks.

Mint prefers a moist soil and partial shade. It increases by underground stems or runners and, given ideal conditions, can rapidly become a pest in the garden. Whenever possible, allot it a small area on its own.

To start a mint bed, either purchase roots or get some from a generous neighbour — once a mint bed is established, there is always plenty to give away.

Oregano, or Wild Marjoram: *Origanum vulgare*

Oregano is the trade name given to various herbs of European origin used in cooking, but in North America usually refers to wild marjoram (*Origanum vulgare*). It is a frost-tender perennial, grown from a root division, and must be brought indoors before the first frost. I find it desirable to start new plants every two or three years.

The small, oval leaves of this medium-height plant may be used fresh or dried. The flavour of oregano and marjoram is rather similar.

Rosemary: *Rosmarinus officinalis*

There's Rosemary, that's for remembrance; pray you love, remember.

Hamlet, Shakespeare

Rosemary is a frost-tender perennial herb or sub-shrub, which must be kept indoors during the winter. It is believed to have been introduced into England by Queen Philippa, wife of Edward III, the lady who pleaded with her husband to save the lives of the six burghers of Calais. Throughout history rosemary has been

considered a herb of great importance, possessing medicinal, aromatic and culinary qualities.

The history of rosemary is a long and interesting one. It is a native of the Mediterranean and, as its botanical name denotes, grows near the sea coast; it delights in sea spray. The best we "land-lubbers" can do is to give it a sandy soil containing lime and plenty of sunshine.

Propogation can be from seed, but the easiest way is from cuttings, taken in July, of half-ripened wood pulled away from the main stems and rooted in a sandy soil. In good conditions the plants will grow to about 3 feet in height.

Some culinary uses are in stuffings, bouquet garni, and rubbing on lamb before roasting.

Sage: *Salvia officinalis*

One of the most popular herbs used for cooking, sage is very easy to grow, and one plant in the herb garden will keep the family amply supplied. Although sage will grow in partial shade, to achieve optimum flavour and aroma it should be grown in full sun.

Sage can be started from seed sown as soon as the ground can be worked, or can be propagated from cuttings. These may be taken in summer and rooted in sand or in the location where the plant is intended to remain. Although sage is a hardy perennial, it has a shallow root system and benefits from a fall mulch of well-rotted compost or manure. To keep the plants tidy and obtain sufficient leaves to dry for winter use, cut the plants back in July and again before freeze-up.

Summer Savory: *Satureja hortensis*

Although there are both perennial and annual savories, the one generally grown for culinary use is an annual. By buying fresh seed each year, you avoid the risk of poor or slow germination. Sow the seed after all risk of frost is past and thin the seedlings 6 to 9 inches apart. Summer savory enjoys rich soil and full sunshine. Feed with a complete fertilizer a couple

of times during the season at intervals of about one month. The plants will grow to 12 to 18 inches in height, and when the flowers begin to form, the plants should be cut to the ground, tied in bunches and hung up to dry.

We grow a 6-foot row in the vegetable garden, which provides the family with both fresh and dried leaves throughout the year.

Summer savory is our main herb for use in poultry stuffings. I use double the quantity recommended in most recipes, and always find this stuffing very popular. I also add a sprig to the stock pot for added flavour.

Sweet Basil: *Ocimum basilicum*

Sweet basil is an annual herb best grown in the main vegetable garden in the same manner as savory. There are several varieties, including one with purple leaves. Three to four feet of row is ample for the average family. Mature basil plants are about 2 feet tall and, being very

SUMMER SAVORY

frost-tender, should be cut for drying before there is any danger of frost.

The leaves and flowers are used fresh in salads, and as a garnish for tomatoes, eggs, etc. The dried leaves are stored for winter use.

Tarragon: *Artemisia dracunculus*

Tarragon is a popular perennial herb, which is propagated from cuttings or root divisions taken in the spring. The plants prefer a slightly acid, not too rich soil, and will thrive in either sun or partial shade. They must not be crowded, so allow plenty of room for the roots to spread. The best variety for culinary use is the French tarragon. This is not grown from seed, hence the necessity to acquire cuttings or plants. The variety offered through most seed companies is Russian tarragon, which is not as flavoursome for culinary purposes. The plants will usually survive our winters, but a covering of mulch applied after freeze-up is beneficial. Tarragon can be used fresh in salads, the leaves dried for winter use, or sprigs steeped in vinegar for salad dressings and sauces.

Thyme: *Thymus vulgaris*

A member of the mint family, thyme is a low-growing creeper or bush plant mostly evergreen, or nearly so. There are a number of different varieties, all native to the islands of the Mediterranean, southern Europe and western Asia. The early settlers brought plants to America, where they have retained their great popularity both for culinary and aromatic purposes.

Thyme is a hardy perennial and enjoys our cold climate. A rock garden with a soil high in lime is the ideal, but I have found it grows perfectly in any well-drained sunny location.

Propagation may be from seed, but the best results are from cuttings or plant divisions. The common thyme (*vulgaris*) is the usual one grown, but if space is available, it is worth growing several varieties in the rock garden.

BASIL SWEET-

FRENCH TARRAGON

LEMON THYME

Fruit

Planning the Orchard

When we purchased Evergreen Farm, there was one big, old, lonely, neglected apple tree, the sole remaining member of what had once been an orchard. In the spring the blossoms were a joy to behold, and the hum of bees filled the air. But alas, as the fruit developed, it fell to the ground — small, runted, and riddled with worms. This is a common example of what happens nowadays to unsprayed fruit trees. Not so long ago you could grow fruit with very little spraying, but this is not the case now. To produce pest and blemish-free fruit, a spray program must be maintained.

I am happy to report that our old tree, which appears in a number of photographs in this book, has taken a new lease on life. Having been pruned and sprayed regularly each year, it now gives an excellent crop of early eating apples with enough left over for a winter supply of juice and sauce. It is an old-fashioned, self-pollinating tree of a variety long since forgotten.

We have not only nursed the old tree back to health; we have also planted a small orchard, which contains apples, crabapples, plums and cherries. So far, the pear trees which we also tried to establish have not been a success, but we intend to re-plant. The old saying, "They that plant pears, plant for their

Our orchard.

A: Tree with roots spread out in planting hole. Short stick placed at ground level to test planting depth.

B: Roots incorrectly planted; too deep.

C: Roots incorrectly planted; too shallow.

D: Drive in a supporting stake and begin easing soil around the roots. Shake the tree gently to settle the soil evenly.

E: Compact the soil around the roots by firmly treading on the loose soil. Leave compacted soil slightly below surrounding area. Water thoroughly.

F: Shape tree by cutting back approximately half the length of limbs. Leave six or so of the strongest and best branches. Tie tree to supporting stake. Protect against rodents and garden equipment.

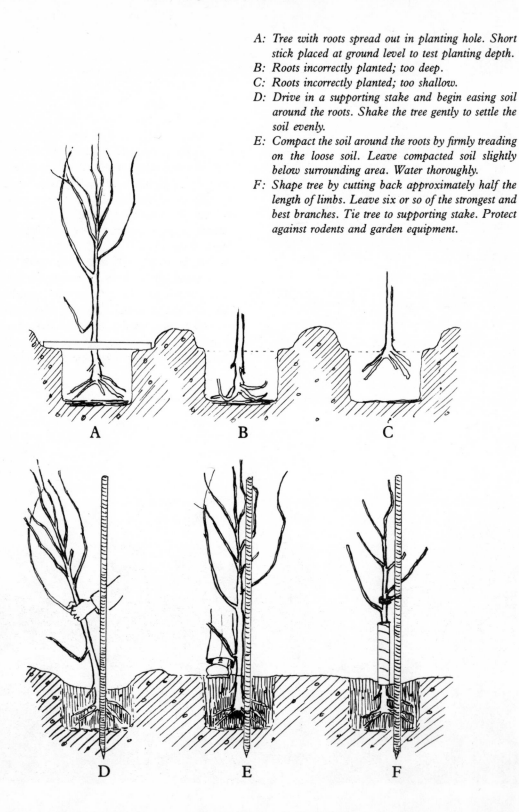

heirs," tells us it is unlikely that we will reap a harvest from this planting.

The new orchard had plenty of blossoms but little fruit during the first years, in spite of the number of bees during pollination time. We were afraid that we had not selected the right varieties. However, the recent heavy crop has shown us that in previous years the trees were not mature enough to bear fruit heavily. Varieties vary in their fruit-bearing age and our trees were still too young. Some apples and pears bear fruit annually, others every other year.

The correct start for perennial fruits, whether they be trees, canes or strawberries, means not only good crops later on, but also less work for the gardener. What is done incorrectly at planting time is hard to rectify later.

The preparation of the ground, the depth of planting, the space for the roots, the drainage, the staking and tying are all simple items, but of great importance. When siting a tree, anticipate its size twenty or thirty years ahead. One often sees a garden which must have been charming when first established, but now is an overgrown jungle.

Planting Fruit Trees

All trees and bushes should be transplanted during their dormant period. Deciduous plants can be moved in the fall, but it is preferable to transplant them in the spring. This gives them time to re-establish themselves and develop a new root system before the winter sets in.

Fruit trees grow well on a wide range of soil types, as long as there is good drainage. If the ground has been under cultivation and is fertile, all that is required is the preparation of the planting holes. These should be wide enough to allow the roots to be spread out, and deep enough to allow the tree to be planted at the same depth at which it stood in the nursery garden. That point is usually indicated by the soil mark on the stem. The bottom of the hole should be broken up with a fork.

When the subsoil is very poor and the topsoil thin, it is often better to excavate a much larger hole than required. Remove the poor soil and replace it with a good loam. Chopped turves (the sod), upside down, will do fine for putting in the bottom of the hole. If the subsoil is a heavy clay, make it porous by adding sand, rubble, or ashes from the bonfire, or anything that will allow better drainage. Good drainage is of great importance. No manure should be added unless the ground is extremely poor. If manure is added, it must be well-rotted and placed so as never to come in contact with the roots of the plant when it is put in position because of its tendency to burn.

A soil test is helpful to ensure that the fertility and pH level of the soil is correct for the plants you are about to establish.

When planting a tree, it should be placed in the middle of the prepared hole. The handle of a rake or a stick then can be laid across the hole to make sure that the soil-level mark on the stem coincides with the ground level after the hole has been filled in. Planting too deep is definitely wrong. The small, thin fibrous roots at the top should be covered with 4 to 5 inches of soil in light ground and not more than 3 inches if the ground is heavy. The roots must be spread out around the stem, and any damaged or broken ends cut back cleanly with a sharp knife or clippers. Great care must be taken not to damage the fibrous roots when the soil is replaced. Use as fine a soil as possible, shaking the tree gently as the soil is added. When the roots are well covered, the soil should be made firm around and above them by treading. The top inch of soil which completes the fill can be left loose. Water thoroughly after planting. In dry seasons, make certain newly planted stock never lacks moisture.

Dwarf trees should be planted so that the union between the scion and the rootstock is just above ground. If the scion variety develops roots above the graft union, the dwarfing affect may be lost. Dwarf trees are not recommended for all areas. I strongly rec-

In early spring I spray all fruit trees with a dormant spray, and at the same time, if necessary, I do some pruning. The wound is painted with tree dressing.

The same tree a few weeks later is covered with blossom. Regrettably, the spray program must continue all season. The mulch is old hay which is not, in fact, touching the trunk.

ommend that prospective fruit growers consult a local authority before purchasing trees.

When a tree is planted, it will require a stake to prevent the roots from moving. This stake will hold the tree upright, replacing the taproot which was severed when the tree was lifted from the nursery. The stake should be put in place before the roots are covered. If it is driven in after planting, it is liable to damage the roots. No part of the tree should rub against the stake. To prevent any such injury, both stake and stem should be protected. Any padded tying material will do. We find the most convenient method is to pass a length of soft wire through an old piece of garden hose and form a "figure of eight" between the stake and stem. In very windy areas two stakes may be required.

After planting, I like to apply an organic mulch around the tree, but not against the trunk. It should be deep enough to suppress weeds and to conserve moisture. The mulch can be well-rotted compost, old hay or straw, sawdust, shavings or any other organic waste available. If the ground is in good tilth, there is no need to fertilize the tree at planting time. In the following years fruit trees will usually benefit from a light application of fertilizer early each spring. I prefer to use a complete fertilizer, which I sprinkle in a circle around the tree. The amount applied depends on the age of the tree. A small tree will get one or two handfuls, whereas a large tree will get a light sprinkling, reaching out underneath all the branches.

If well-rotted manure or compost has been used as a mulch, very little fertilizer will be required. If the trees are thriving, it may be unnecessary to fertilize them at all until they start bearing fruit.

It is essential for the future well-being of the tree that it be pruned after planting. In general, fruit trees are pruned to a single whip (shoot or stem) and headed (cut off) at about a 4-foot height. However, if the tree has a number of well-developed branches, some of these can be left as three-bud stubs, that is, they should be pruned after the third bud.

It comes as a great shock to gardeners who have just planted their first fruit tree to be told that half to two-thirds of the growth must be removed. This drastic pruning allows the root system to re-establish itself and balances the aboveground growth with the underground growth.

In subsequent years young fruit trees should be lightly pruned while they are still dormant each spring. Dead or broken branches, as well as lateral branches pointing into the centre of the tree, should be removed. The cuts should be flush with the parent limb. Do not overprune young trees, for this will delay fruiting. Remove any suckers that appear, especially those growing from the rootstock.

Older fruiting trees should be pruned each spring to remove dead or weak limbs and to prevent overcrowding of branches in the interior and top of the tree. Apple trees can be pruned in such a way that the growth pattern of the tree will enable the gardener to pick the fruit more easily and, when spraying, the branches can be reached with a home-garden sprayer.

Overpruning causes suckers, or "water-sprouts," to develop. All those coming from the base must be removed, but in older trees the odd water-sprout can be left to replace worn out or dead fruiting branches.

Apples and Pears

Many varieties of apples are grown throughout the temperate zones of North America. Some are better suited to specific climatic conditions than others.

We have been advised professionally against growing dwarf apples because they are not considered fully hardy in our zone. Evidently some people have had success, but it is quite common for a dwarf apple tree to thrive for a

Melba apples ready for harvest.

number of years and then suddenly die, for no apparent reason. In our area it would be wiser, therefore, to plant standard apples.

People living in southern Ontario, around the Great Lakes, on the eastern seaboard, in coastal British Columbia and in many areas of the United States can certainly grow dwarf trees as well as espalier (see Glossary). The latter are ideal for small gardens, are easy to harvest and can be an attractive addition to landscaping.

Pears will grow in most areas where apples and peaches thrive. California is the main pear-producing area in North America, but I have come across many home gardens in the Ottawa Valley where pears are grown successfully. Most pears are self-sterile, making it necessary to plant two compatible varieties for cross-pollination.

Plums and Crabapples

These fruits require the same general growing conditions as apples. Both are easy to grow and provide eye-catching blossom in the spring and plenty of fruit later on. When purchasing, check to see whether the variety of crabapple you select will produce edible fruit; some are solely ornamental. Most plums need a tree of another variety nearby for pollination. Plums take six or seven years after planting-out before they start bearing fruit. Plums and crabapples require a regular spray program, as do apples and pears.

Peaches, Apricots and Cherries

These stone fruits require very stringent climatic conditions, and as a result, they can only be grown satisfactorily in a few select areas. They need a temperate climate with freezing weather during dormancy to assure fruit set. However, the lows should not exceed 0°F (−18°C). The humidity in winter should be high. The summers should be hot and sunny, although excessive heat might damage the fruit.

Apricots bloom about a week earlier than peaches, rendering them even more vulnerable to late frosts. It is very important that, whenever possible, these fruit trees are located in a northern exposure, thereby delaying blossoming and the possibility of damage by late frost.

Both apricots and peaches will do well in a wide range of soils as long as the drainage is good. The land should be deeply cultivated, and the young trees set out in the spring. Wherever it is possible to grow these trees, you might consider their ornamental value, and regard the fruit as a bonus. As they are self-pollinating, isolated, single trees are capable of producing fruit.

Southern Ontario, coastal British Columbia and the interior of California are the best peach and apricot growing areas of North America. The immediate area surrounding the Great Lakes is particularly suitable also. Regrettably, I have been unable to grow peaches and apricots successfully in the Ottawa Valley, and I am not aware of anyone who does.

Problems and Controls of Fruit Trees

Insects cause serious problems in the orchard. There are a great number of different pests that attack fruit trees throughout the growing season. To have insect-free fruit, it is essential to maintain a regular spray program with a recommended insecticide.

Curculio

    larva   *adult*

The curculio is a small weevil that lays eggs in the developing fruit of apples, pears, plums and most stone-fruit trees. After laying the eggs, the female makes a crescent-shaped cut around them, and a scar develops that provides protection. In about a week grey grubs hatch and feed inside the fruit. Damaged fruit falls early, and unless removed and destroyed the grubs move out to pupate in the soil. To control this pest it is essential to establish a spray program. Your local agricultural representative can provide guidance.

Bacterial and fungal diseases are another major problem, but they can be controlled by spraying with fungicides. All home gardeners who grow fruit should obtain the most recent government publication *Insect and Disease Control in the Home Garden*, which will recommend the most suitable combinations of insecticides and fungicides. It also gives the correct timing, which is of the utmost importance. Start the spray program in spring while the trees are still dormant and continue throughout most of the summer. I usually spray my trees about six times, but I know commercial growers sometimes spray as many as sixteen times, expecially during rainy seasons.

Virus and mycoplasma diseases cannot be cured. All infected trees should be removed and burned. Infected trees, when left in an orchard, will cause the diseases to be spread by insects to the healthy trees. Good garden hygiene and a regular spray program should prevent an outbreak.

Rodents Rabbits and mice find the stems of young fruit trees especially tasty. It takes a number of years for the bark to mature sufficiently to be immune to rodents. The stems of young trees should be protected from ground level to about 18 inches up with either a fine wire mesh, a plastic tree guard (which will also protect the trees from lawn mower damage) or by painting the bark of the stem with a bitter-tasting rodent repellant. The time to apply protective measures is before any damage is done. The protection of the stems of young trees should be part of the fall work program. I recommend goggles be worn to protect the eyes when painting with rodent repellant. We learned our lesson the hard way!

It is not my intention here to discuss fruit trees in any detail, only to give a few general recommendations. I would suggest that before embarking on this quite costly capital outlay, the would-be fruit grower seek advice from a local export, who will know which varieties to suggest.

Blueberries

In our present garden we do not attempt to grow blueberries because the soil pH is 6.5 to 7.0. However, when we lived in the Laurentian Mountains north of Montreal, blueberries grew wild. They require a very acid soil, and unless a home gardener has a naturally acid soil, the labour involved in preparing a bed for blueberries is not worth the effort.

If you wish to grow blueberries, select a sunny spot where you can maintain a pH of 5.00 or below. Early in the spring plant two-year-old certified bushes about 4 feet apart. Prune the bushes back to about 3 inches at planting time and remove all the blossoms that appear during the first two years of growth. This procedure prolongs the life of the bushes and improves the subsequent crop. Watering,

Blueberry bush at the Central Experimental Farm.

fertilizing and mulching all help to develop strong healthy bushes. At least two varieties should be planted to ensure cross-pollination.

Mature blueberries require little pruning, but any dead or damaged branches should be removed.

There are very few disease and insect problems with blueberries. However, if birds are attracted to your garden, be prepared to spend time and energy protecting your blueberry crop with netting or screening.

Currants and Gooseberries

I am very fond of both currant and gooseberry jam and feel my garden is incomplete without a bush or two of each. However, as they are self-pollinating, a single plant can bear fruit. They are generally very easy to grow, require little attention and they will grow in places with partial sun.

Things can go wrong, however, as we found out last year in our garden. The bushes developed anthracnose (leaf spot), and after much discussion we decided it would be prudent to

Currant bush in early spring showing pruning to allow sun to enter and air to circulate.

Close-up of flowers on red currant.

dig up the entire planting and burn it. Disease is not common with currants and gooseberries, and most bushes remain healthy for many years.

In a year or two we hope to plant new stock in a different part of the garden, as far away as possible from the old planting.

Currants and gooseberries are the alternate hosts of the white pine blister rust fungus, a disease that spends part of its life cycle on the canes of these bushes. It does not harm the canes but is often fatal to white pine. In areas where white pine grow, currants and gooseberries should not be cultivated, except the black currant variety, "Consort," which is resistant to rust.

There are three types of currants: black, red and white. The black and red are the most popular. All the gooseberries that are hardy in our area are of the cooking variety. They are too tart to eat fresh, unlike some European strains, but are excellent for pies and jams.

Both fruits freeze well without processing, and can be used during the winter as needed. They are also a very rich source of vitamin C, especially black currants.

Purchase strong, well-rooted, one-year-old plants. These will go into production just as soon as two-year-old stock and be less expensive. Be sure the plants are disease-free. Reputable growers will guarantee their stock. However, if you have a friend who grows healthy currant or gooseberry bushes, they can be propagated very simply by "layering" (see Glossary) a branch or taking cuttings. After a season's growth these propagated plants are ready to move to a permanent site.

As bushes will remain productive for eight to ten years, the ground should be thoroughly prepared before planting. The soil should be rich in organic matter and the stock planted immediately it arrives in the spring. The plants should be set slightly deeper in the ground than they were when growing in the nursery. Dig the hole large enough to accommodate the outspread roots, then cover them with soil.

Currant bush ready to be harvested.

Branch of gooseberry bush showing fruit forming behind the flower petals.

Tamp the ground firmly around each plant and water it if the soil is dry. Prune back the branches to a length of about 6 inches to stimulate new growth. Allow about 5 feet between the bushes, as they are all vigorous growers.

Planting can be done in either spring or fall. I prefer the spring, but if fall planting is done, wait until spring to cut back the bushes. After planting, I like to apply a heavy mulch to control weeds and conserve moisture. Hay, straw or sawdust are all equally suitable.

Pruning should be done in the fall or early spring when the bushes are still dormant. Black currants produce the best fruit on one- and two-year-old shoots. Keep ten to twelve canes per mature bush.

We have found that both currants and gooseberries grow profusely. But unless we are rather drastic with pruning, the branches become overcrowded, restricting the circulation of air, causing many of the branches to come into contact with the ground, with subsequent rooting. Overgrown bushes make it much harder to control diseases and insects. All sickly, damaged or late leafing-out branches should be removed.

Red currants and gooseberries produce most of their fruit on two- to three-year-old wood. Remove all older shoots.

Problems and Controls of Currants and Gooseberries

Currants and gooseberries can be seriously damaged by a number of insects.

The currant borer is the larvae of a moth, rather like a small housefly, which lays her eggs in the axils of leaves. The larvae bore into the pith of the young shoot and feed there. The following spring when sickly shoots are cut, a dark hole can be seen where the larvae have burrowed into the pith. Prune and burn all sickly shoots.

Aphids feed on the undersides of leaves and

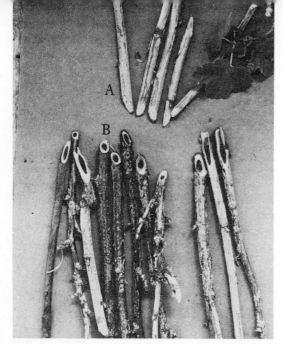

Currant canes
A: *the clean centres are healthy.*
B: *the blackened pith shows that they have been attacked by borers.*

Leaf convolutions on currant caused by aphids on lower leaf surface.

on young shoots. They are more often seen on red currants than gooseberries or black currants, and can be controlled by insecticides.

The currant fruitfly is a common pest and familiar to most currant and gooseberry growers. The adult flies emerge at about the same time as the bushes are in bloom. The females lay their eggs in the developing berries. Most affected fruit falls to the ground prematurely and, if inspected, a white maggot will be found in each. These insects leave the berry and spend the winter in the soil. The currant fruitfly can be controlled by insecticides.

The currant sawfly lays her eggs in early summer. The larvae are greenish worms with black spots, and about three-quarters of an inch long when fully grown. They are voracious eaters and can defoliate a bush quite rapidly. If only a few worms are noticed, they can be picked by hand, otherwise an insecticide spray is the easiest control.

Scale insects can be seen on dormant wood. They suck the juices from young branches, but are not often a serious problem. An insecticide spray will control them.

Powdery mildew is a common problem with gooseberries and occasionally with currants. It is more likely to occur during warm, humid conditions. This white, powdery fungus appears in early summer on the tips of new shoots and young leaves. It is spread by spores and may affect the entire bush. Later in the season the white powdery growth turns brown and forms a covering over the affected parts of the plant. The growth of the entire bush will be stunted, and the tips of the shoots killed. Cut off and destroy all diseased branches and make sure the bush has good air circulation. Fungicide applications are an effective control.

Anthracnose (leaf spot) is brown spots that appear on the leaves in mid-summer. These spots gradually turn yellowish-brown and the leaves fall, defoliating the bushes. Early defoliation retards the growth of the bushes and reduces the next year's crop. The fungus lives over the winter in the fallen leaves, so damaged leaves should be raked up and burned.

Fungicides should provide adequate control. Our problem, referred to earlier in this section, may have been in not recognizing the symptoms early enough.

Raspberries

An altogether delightful fruit, the raspberry is always in demand for dessert, jam and the freezer. Growing your own seems the only way to obtain fresh raspberries; they are both expensive and scarce in stores.

There are three kinds of raspberries: red, purple and black. Red raspberries are the most popular. Everbearing varieties give a fall crop in addition to the normal summer crop. This fall crop is produced on the tips of strong new shoots.

A new raspberry patch can be planted in either the spring or the fall. Always plant "certified stock," identified by the label which certifies that the stock has been inspected by government officials and shown to be virus-free. The site for the new canes should be prepared by cultivating a 3-foot-wide strip for each row and incorporating well-rotted manure or compost to a depth of 9 inches. In heavy clay ground also add sand, charred woody material from the bonfire, or strawy manure when available.

To ensure that both sides of each row receive maximum sun, the rows should run north and south when possible.

The quickest method of planting is to dig out a trench the width of the spade and about 6 inches deep. Space the roots about 1½ feet apart and cover with the excavated soil. Firm the plants in by treading. Rows should be at least 5 feet apart.

Raspberries need some support. This can be provided by erecting a series of posts, either metal or wood, at 20 to 30 foot intervals along the row. Wires are then pulled tautly between the posts, the lower wire 2 feet from the ground, the upper wire about 4 feet high. The canes can be spaced out evenly and tied securely to the wires.

The size and quality of the crop depends largely on an adequate water supply. In dry weather soak the bed thoroughly once a week from spring onwards. A mulch of well-rotted manure, compost, lawn clippings or sawdust over the root area will help retain moisture.

Our raspberries emerging from the snow in the spring. The canes stood up to the winds and weather by being well-secured to supporting wires.

Manure will also give extra nourishment to the plants. Food can be given through the mulch in the form of liquid manure or a complete fertilizer. This feeding should start as soon as the berries begin to swell.

Keep weeds under control. This is best done by hand, loosening the roots of the weeds with a fork. Mulching also helps control weeds.

All newly planted canes should be cut down to a good bud about 6 inches above ground level. There will be no fruit the year of planting. However, the roots will send up new growth, which will bear fruit the following year. As soon as possible after the harvest is over, the fruited canes should be cut down close to the ground. Weak, new canes are also cut back. The strong, new growths remaining are tied to the wires, replacing the old canes that have just been removed. These new canes will produce the following season's fruit. Cane removal after the harvest helps control disease and improves the circulation of air around the plants. No further pruning is done at this time.

In early spring prune the weak and dead tips off the canes. Shorten tall canes to a convenient height for picking. Thin out all the weak growth, leaving only the strong canes, spaced 4 to 6 inches apart in the rows.

Propagation of raspberries is by suckers which appear in profusion on either side of the rows. These can be dug up with a spade, complete with their own roots, in either the fall or spring, and transplanted. This is a particularly simple and economical method of establishing a new raspberry bed. Suckers should only be taken from thoroughly healthy plants. To propagate from unhealthy stock is to propagate trouble.

Problems and Controls of Raspberries

Aphids attack the leaves of raspberries at any time of the season, but are most prevalent when the bushes are in their most rapid growth. This is usually early in the season and again in August or early September when new growth is emerging. Although the aphids themselves do not necessarily cause serious harm, they spread viruses which cause leaf curl and mosaic leaf. Both these viruses are serious problems, and controlling the aphids minimizes the risk of contracting disease. The first spraying should be done early in the season and a further spraying after harvesting is completed.

Leafhoppers are frequently seen on raspberry leaves, jumping and flying about when the canes are disturbed. They are small, wedge-shaped, yellow-green insects which produce several generations each season. They are not often a serious problem and can be controlled by spraying.

The raspberry sawfly lays her eggs early in the season, and the resulting larvae are green caterpillars which devour the leaves. Sawflies can easily be controlled by spraying or dusting with insecticide.

Raspberries pruned to allow light in and air to circulate. This is the best protection against disease. Note the plastic-covered TV wire used for support.

Raspberries showing an old cane that was not cut out, an invitation to disease.

The raspberry cane borer can cause considerable damage in the raspberry patch. The first sign of damage is the shoot tips wilting. On closer examination the gardener will see that two rings about a half inch apart have been cut around the stem, and the growth above these has wilted.

This damage has been caused by a long-horned beetle with a black body and a yellow neck about half an inch long. She lays her egg between the rings. This egg hatches into a grub that burrows a short distance down the stem and remains there for the winter. The following spring it burrows on down the cane into the root and usually kills the cane. Later, it emerges as a beetle and repeats the cycle. Some years the cane borers are far worse than others.

The best control is to cut off and burn the tops of damaged canes immediately wilting is noticed. Make the cut about 6 inches below the two rings.

Eastern raspberry fruitworm is often found in home gardens. They are small worms that are found in the central cavity of the berry at harvest time. These worms are the larvae of a small, brown beetle that feeds on the flower-bud clusters in early spring. The larvae feed on the developing berries and remain in the berry when it is picked. Although they are harmless, they make a dish of raspberries rather unappetizing.

These beetles can be controlled by dusting or spraying with rotenone.

The tarnished plant bug can be a great nuisance in the raspberry patch. They are shiny, brown bugs that feed early in the spring on blossom buds, causing crumbly, misshapen berries. Good garden hygiene and weed control usually prevent the spread of these pests, but if they should become numerous, spraying with the recommended insecticide will control them.

Nematodes are sometimes found in the soil of raspberry plantings. They are minute, worm-

After the harvest old fruited canes and weak new growth are removed from the patch and burned.

Raspberry anthracnose. Elongated grey spots on canes. Spur blight on cane at right.

like creatures that can cause damage to the roots of plants and stunt the growth of the canes.

Nematodes are hard to identify without a magnifying glass. If you notice continued poor growth for no apparent reason, consider nematodes as a possible cause. Control of nematodes is not easy, and it would be advisable to consult the nearest government agency.

Mosaic leaf   is a virus disease that is transmitted by aphids. These aphids feed on diseased plants, become contaminated and then move on to healthy plants, spreading the virus.

Mosaic leaf can be identified by a mottled, crumpled look of the leaves. Pale-green or yellow blotches appear, and the growth of the plant is stunted. Once a plant is infected, it never recovers.

To avoid mosaic leaf, purchase certified disease-free plants. Make new plantings at least five hundred feet from old plantings. Control weeds and aphids and destroy any plants that show signs of disease.

In the fall I put out mouse poison in glass jars. These are laid on their sides along the row and in positions where birds cannot get at the treated seed.

Leaf curl   is another virus disease in which the leaves curl tightly downwards and inward. It is not common. The control is the same as for mosaic leaf.

Anthracnose, spur blight, cane blight and Verticillium wilt   are all diseases that are caused by fungi. Damage will occur on canes, leaves and fruit. These diseases are described more fully at the beginning of this chapter. They can be controlled by spraying with fungicides.

Mice   have been a problem some years, eating the bark of young canes during the winter.

Strawberries

When the first colonists landed in America, they were amazed to find magnificent wild strawberry plants. The species they found is now known as *Fragaria virginiana*. Later, another excellent wild species, *F. chiloensis*, was found growing along the Pacific coast from Chile to Alaska. All the popular strawberry varieties which are now grown in our gardens in North America are descended from these two species. Strawberries are very hardy, and can be grown in all the cultivated areas of Canada and the United States.

Strawberries do best in a well-drained soil that is rich in organic material. When possible, prepare the bed in the fall prior to planting by incorporating well-rotted manure or compost. A warm, sunny location is essential for good results.

Do not plant strawberries in ground previously occupied by potatoes, tomatoes, peppers or eggplant. There is a risk that the soil might harbour the fungus disease, Verticillium wilt, which would damage the strawberry plants.

Select the variety best suited to your area. There may be several which would provide you with successive crops. Always purchase certified plants and thereby minimize the risk of bringing diseased stock into your garden. Strawberries are considered a perennial. Vig-

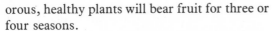

Establishing runners around a first-year "mother" strawberry plant.

Second-year plants matted and showing a strong flowering in late spring.

orous, healthy plants will bear fruit for three or four seasons.

The time to start a new bed is in the spring as soon as the ground can be worked. This allows the plants time to establish themselves and produce runners. Remove all the flowers formed on the "mother-plants" during their first season, permitting the strength to go into forming runner plants. Early formed runners are the best fruit bearers the following season. These young plants form flower buds within the crown during the latter part of the summer and in the fall. The flower buds emerge early the following spring and bear fruit. Newly purchased plants should have well-developed crowns and plenty of strong roots. Twenty-five plants are ample for the average family and should produce 60 to 80 pounds of fruit. In Europe strawberries are often grown as single plants, all runners being cut off. However, in

North America strawberries are usually grown in the "matted-row" system.

To follow this method allow at least 4 feet between rows, and set the plants 2 feet apart within the row. Each plant will send out runners which will establish themselves around the mother plant and form a thick "matt." I am still undecided as to whether the rows of single plants or the matted system is the best.

The number of plants to be set out will depend on the space available. Twelve plants will make a strawberry bed 25 by 4 feet. When setting out the plants, dig a hole with a trowel large enough to take the spread-out roots. Water thoroughly and firm into the ground. Make sure the plants are set with the mid-point of the crown at ground level.

Many home gardeners like to start a small, new bed every year and maintain a three-year-cycle, discarding the oldest bed after it has

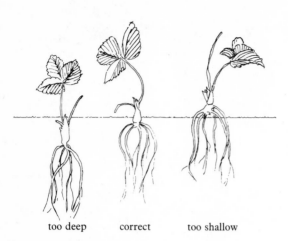

too deep   correct   too shallow

Setting out strawberry plants.

In early summer fruit begins to form while some plants are still in flower.

fruited. If you observe this program, ten to twelve new plants each spring would be sufficient. You can use your own stock if you are certain that it is strong and healthy.

It is most important that the plants do not lack moisture from blossoming time until the end of the harvest. Lack of moisture causes hard, runted berries. After the harvest is over, apply a complete (10:10:10) fertilizer to the bed when the foliage is dry. Mow the plants with a rotary lawn mower, set high, or cut with garden shears. Take care not to injure the crowns of the plants. In northern areas where the season is short, it is best not to mow.

Winter protection is recommended. Freezing and thawing of the soil causes the plants to heave, breaking the roots, and low temperatures injure the roots, crowns and flower buds. Straw is the best mulch as it is usually free of weeds. One bale is often sufficient for the home strawberry patch. The straw should be applied after there have been several light frosts, and the ground has started to become frozen. The plants will then be dormant. If applied too early, the crowns are liable to rot.

Hay is not recommended for winter protection because it also brings in grass seeds. Leaves, grass clippings and garden waste can smother and kill the plants. If no straw is available cover the bed with "brush" cuttings,

the old Christmas tree, etc. This will collect a deep snow mulch.

In the spring remove the straw from the plants as soon as new leaf growth appears. Lay the straw to the side of the patch or between the rows. It can be replaced on the plants if there is a risk of frost during blossoming or left to control weeds and conserve moisture.

Everbearing strawberries produce several crops during the season. The berries are often much smaller than regular varieties. Follow general rules for culture.

Strawberries are quite prone to root infections and to several viruses. Collectively, these contribute to the usual "decline" of the berry patch — another reason for replanting with certified stock.

Problems and Controls of Strawberries

White grubs   are the larvae of the June bug and damage the roots of young strawberry plants. They are only likely to occur in soil that was recently in sod. So to avoid this problem do not plant strawberries in newly broken land.

Strawberry root weevils can be a serious problem throughout most of North America. The larvae feed on the roots of plants and the beetles damage the foliage. The plants will be stunted and unproductive. Control the beetles by dusting or spraying the plants with an insecticide before bloom and after harvesting. If root weevils remain a problem, remove and burn the old plants and make a new bed as far away from the old as possible.

Strawberry clipper weevils are very small beetles that cut the blossom stems. The gardener will be aware of their presence if he sees any clipped blossom stems on his plants. Control by spraying with a recommended insecticide. If the blossoms are open, spray in the evening to avoid killing bees. By then the bees will have returned to their hives.

Plant bugs are a common strawberry pest and can be a great nuisance. They are generally the cause of runted, small, deformed berries. These insects pierce the developing fruit and suck the sap. Control by spraying or dusting before the blossoms open and again ten days later. These pests are hard to observe, and the gardener is usually aware of their presence only after he finds his berries are deformed and hard. The following season preventative action should be taken.

Spittle bugs can do a great deal of damage in a short time. Their presence is indicated by frothy blobs on stems. Control by spraying before the first blossoms open.

Aphids and whiteflies must be controlled because they are the agents that spread diseases from weeds and other infected plants.

Root rot refers to several soil-borne fungi that attack strawberry roots. Gardeners will notice a decline in the healthy growth of the plants, and the berries from diseased plants will be small, but not deformed. The roots start to blacken and decay, and gradually the entire root rots. The best prevention is to practise crop rotation and to avoid planting strawberries in heavy or poorly drained soils.

Small, runted berries due to an attack of plant bugs. Compare the large, juicy healthy berries.

Fruit rot or grey mold (Botrytis) is a fungal disease particularly prevalent in wet weather between blossoming and harvest. Infected berries usually rot just before ripening, but green fruit may also suffer. Prevention is important, because once this disease is established it is very hard to eradicate. Control is by spraying with a recommended fungicide at the first sign of blossom.

Red stele is a fungal disease that thrives in cold, wet soils and can remain viable in soil for up to seventeen years. Spores swim through soil water to spread infection. The gardener can identify red stele by noting a temporary wilt of plant during the day followed by a recovery in the cool evenings, and by a loss of the shiny green appearance of the leaves. The plant stops growing, and by harvest time the leaves are small and the fruits are dried up. The roots become rat-tailed, and the central core or stele become brick-red. To avoid bringing this disease into your garden, examine new plant roots carefully for symptoms. Always purchase disease-resistant varieties.

Verticillium wilt is a disease caused by a soil-borne fungus that can live in the ground indefinitely. It is spread by cultivation, wind and soil erosion and penetrates the roots of susceptible plants. It does not need a wound to enter the plant. The symptoms may occur during the planting year. The outer leaves wilt and turn brown, while the new leaves curl and loose colour. Brownish-black streaks may appear along the grooved surface of the leaf stem. Eventually, more leaves collapse and the plant dies.

In fruiting years the outer leaves turn yellow or red soon after bloom. The plants wilt and die just as the fruit begins to ripen. Verticillium wilt strikes plants sporadically rather than in large patches in the plot, as does red stele. Any infected plants must be removed and burned. Once plants are infected, there is no cure, but good garden hygiene and growing resistant varieties can help prevent an occurence. This fungus also infects all solanaceous plants such as tomatoes, peppers and eggplant; therefore, strawberries should be included with these in the crop rotation plan.

Grapes

Wild grapes are found all over the North American continent, and it is from these native vines that a few of the varieties we grow today are descended. Some are cultivated, some hybrids, and some used as rootstock on which European varieties are grafted. The early settlers found that the European vines they brought with them were unable to survive our winters when grown on their own roots. Great strides have been made in developing suitable varieties for different North American zones. In some climatic regions of Canada and the United States, grapes are an important commercial fruit crop. Gardeners in these areas will have no problems. However, for most of us easy grape growing is not the norm. People interested in growing grapes should first inquire from the nearest Research Station as to which varieties are recommended for their area.

Grapevines are drastically pruned in early spring. We grow Concord (blue) grapevines on the south and west sides of a shed. Only new growth carries leaves and fruit.

Grape vines can form an interesting part of a garden landscape. They can be trained to grow over an arbour or trellis and provide a delightfully shaded nook for summer living.

Many people have found it necessary to surround their property, or perhaps the swimming pool, with a chain-link fence. Grape vines grow well on these fences. They are ornamental, grow rapidly during the season, give privacy to the enclosed area and, with any luck, provide a good crop of fruit.

Grapes require a temperate climate and,

A close-up of three clusters of grapes on new shoots.

Grapes ready for harvesting.

although the vines may survive the winter, they may not produce fruit. Frost in late spring can cause severe damage to the young shoots and flowers. It is essential to grow a variety suited to the micro-climate of your garden, and the length of frost-free period in your garden.

Grapes will grow in a wide range of soils as long as it is well-drained; they cannot tolerate wet feet. They also require sun and heat to mature.

We have several grape vines which bear fruit every year. One of our vines is located against a wooden shed wall facing southwest.

This is a Concord variety and is shown here in the spring. Earlier we had cut it back quite severly to a trunk and four canes. Each cane carried two buds, and these gave rise to new shoots from which the leaves and young fruit are seen emerging. As the season progressed, the shoots were encouraged to grow along ties of bindertwine which support them across the face of the shed. The results vary annually with the seasons, and on the whole the fruit is sweet but rather small.

Growing grapes is a study in itself, and I recommend one of the excellent government pamphlets which are available at no cost.

Nutrition and the Vegetable Garden

One of the great advantages of growing your own vegetables is being able to harvest, prepare and serve them within the shortest possible time. The vitamin content and food value of vegetables depreciates rapidly after harvesting.

Vitamin A

An indication of vitamin A content in fruit and vegetables is the colour. It is usually present in the yellow-orange colour of a mature vegetable or the creamy colour of an unripe fruit. Examples are carrots, tomatoes, apricots, potatoes, spinach and peas. When these vegetables become dehydrated, most of the vitamin content is lost. Any shrivelled vegetables are lacking in vitamin A.

The B Vitamins

Thiamine. Unless vegetables and fruit are used immediately after harvesting, they must be stored in cool conditions. Heat in storage will destroy thiamine very rapidly. Cook in the minimum amount of liquid for the shortest period of time because 50 per cent of thiamine is lost by boiling. Steam whenever possible and use cooking liquid when making soups, sauces and gravies. Examples are potatoes, peas and turnip greens.

Riboflavin. This vitamin is easily destroyed by overexposure to light. Unless eaten immediately, these vegetables should be stored in the dark to prevent this loss. Examples are potatoes and peas.

Vitamin C or ascorbic acid

Vitamin C is one of the better known vitamins, easily obtained through fruit and vegetables. But if these are not treated properly, it is easily destroyed. With all fruit and vegetables that contain vitamin C, the motto should be: the fresher, the better.

Although some of these vegetables listed below will be cooked, the loss will not occur during cooking but because of incorrect preparation. For optimum vitamin retention, salads should be "made" immediately prior to serving; vegetables prepared immediately before cooking; and juices squeezed as needed. When these foods are not used right away, they should be refrigerated or put directly into cold storage. Examples are green vegetables such as asparagus, spinach, broccoli, Brussels sprouts, cabbage, peas, lettuce, cauliflower, tomatoes, potatoes, carrots and water cress, as well as many others. If a vegetable is a growing shoot such as broccoli or Brussels sprouts, it usually contains large amounts of vitamin C.

Protein

In a vegetarian diet it is necessary to have an adequate supply of protein-producing vegetables to substitute for the lack of animal protein. All legumes are an important source of protein. Some examples are peas, beans, soybeans and sunflower seeds.

Carbohydrates

In the vegetable family the chief source of carbohydrates are potatoes and the seeds of leguminous plants such as peas, beans and lentils. Bulbs, roots and tubers store sugars and starches in roots and underground stems and are therefore an important consideration in diet planning.

Iron

As a general rule the greener the leaf, the more iron it contains.

"Putting By" Vegetables and Fruit

Many home gardeners grow far more produce than their family can possibly eat fresh during the growing season. With the exception of salad, none of these vegetables need be wasted but should be "put by," (or as some prefer, "put up" or "put down") for winter use.

When planning a garden, consideration should be given to using all such surplus produce and, indeed, expanding the garden to meet as much as possible the year round needs of the family. The facilities for storage will also dictate the size and type of crops you plan to grow.

Methods for putting by include freezing, canning, drying, preserve-making, salting or storing in a cool room, root cellar or a cool, dry location. There are so many ways of putting by fruit and vegetables that it is impossible to cover the subject fully here. Free government pamphlets are available on request, and many books have been written giving both old and modern methods.

The Home Freezer

The home freezer represents a considerable capital outlay, but freezing is a far quicker and safer method of putting by fruit and vegetables than any other with the possible exception of the root cellar for root crops. A freezer reduces the risk of spoilage or dangerous toxicity that can be encountered with home canned foods held in storage. Vegetables surplus to your immediate needs should be harvested while still in their "prime," processed, bagged and put straight into the freezer. Prime means while they are young, tender and with a delicate flavour. The shorter the time between harvesting and freezing, the better the quality and nutritive value of the produce. The commercial grower is unable to compete with the home gardener for these qualities. His crops must be able to withstand mechanical harvesting and shipping.

You can start filling the freezer around May 24 with rhubarb, then continue all summer as crops mature. Leeks and Brussels sprouts harvested in November are the last crops to go in the freezer.

I have found the best bags to use for the freezer are the clear, plastic ones that milk comes in. They are very strong and can be re-used several times if thoroughly washed and disinfected. A dash of disinfectant in the rinse water is a simple precaution against infection. I also prefer to package vegetables in small quantities and to use two or more packages if needed.

Canning

Not so long ago in North America, canning was the most popular home method of putting by food. Today, the freezer has replaced it. Very few households now have the equipment required to safely can low-acid foods at home.

Low-acid vegetables include peppers, squash, carrots, cabbage, beets, beans, asparagus, spinach and cauliflower. Unless these vegetables are being pickled (a large amount of acid added in the form of vinegar), they must be processed in a pressure cooker. This involves a considerable expenditure.

However, high-acid vegetables and fruit such as tomatoes, apples, rhubarb and gooseberries can safely be processed in a "boiling water bath." I prefer to freeze rhubarb and gooseberries because they require no cooking, just dicing and freezing. But I find tomatoes and tomato juice far nicer put by in glass sealers. I recently acquired a hand press which has taken the tedious work out of the job of extracting juice. Visiting friends also enjoy cranking the handle, and this way we prepare bucketfuls of juice in no time. It is also excellent for processing apple sauce, which may be frozen or bottled.

Drying

Drying is one of the oldest-known methods of preserving food, dating back to pre-Biblical times. Early settlers in North America were taught the art by the Indians, and many of us use the same techniques today. Our microwave ovens and dehydrators are a far cry from the primitive methods, but are not essential for the home gardener.

Herbs are the simplest produce to dry. This is done by harvesting, washing and air drying them in a warm, dark, dry airy place. We have an attic that is ideal for this. If you don't have such a place, put the bunch of herbs in a brown paper bag and hang them up. When the drying process is complete and you have the time, the herb leaves can be crushed and stored in dark jars in a dark cupboard. Parsley can be dried this way. However, I have found the best results are achieved when I dry it in a very low oven. It keeps its colour much better.

Practically all vegetables and fruit can be dried successfully if they are exposed to low heat and good ventilation to remove moisture. Most of us have a romantic picture in our minds of pioneer kitchens festooned with strings of fruit and vegetables hanging to dry. Nowadays, we have more efficient and convenient methods. Dehydrators range from the simple, solar-powered food dryers to sophisticated electrically operated models. Home convection ovens are excellent for drying.

Vegetables must be blanched and drained before being set on the racks in the dryer. Fruit does not require blanching. Fruit leather is a chewy, candy-type food, made from fruit pulp. This pulp is spread on cookie sheets and dehydrated until it is dry enough to handle. It will be rather leather-like in appearance and consis-

tency and can be stored in jars or bags. It has a delicious flavour and can be given to children as a substitute for candy.

As I have a freezer, I freeze vegetables rather than dry them, but for those who are not so fortunate, a homemade solar unit would make it possible to preserve surplus vegetables and fruit at very low cost. Information is readily available through libraries.

Preserves

A great variety of fruits and vegetables can go into the making of jams, jellies, relishes, chutneys and pickles. With the increased concern over additives in processed food, many families are now making their own preserves at home. I rather enjoy this job. The sight of shelves lined with jars and bottles of homemade produce is very satisfying. I am delighted to hear that men as well as women are finding it a relaxing occupation and are making preserves just for the fun of it.

When all the bulk ingredients are grown in the garden and only sugar, vinegar and spices have to be purchased, the cost of the jams and relishes is considerably lower than that of their store-bought counterparts. Also, with home preserves you know exactly what goes into each jar.

Preserves are best stored in a cool, dark, dry cupboard. As we don't have this ideal situation in our house, we keep ours in the next best place, the cool room. Spoilage of preserves is readily detected.

Salting Vegetables

The salting of vegetables is an ancient method of preserving, but with modern storage facilities, it is seldom used nowadays.

In Ireland the only salting we ever did was of green beans. These were frenched (sliced) and put in a large earthenware crock with dry salt sprinkled between the layers. They added to the variety of vegetables during the winter. However, I find frozen beans are far superior to salted ones.

PRESERVING GARDEN PRODUCE

Name of produce	Freezing Raw	Blanched*	Canning	Root Cellar 32°-39°F (0°-4°C) No. of Months	Dry Warm Cellar No. of Months	Preserves and Pickles	Drying	Salting
Artichoke — globe						X		
Artichoke — Jerusalem	leave in ground			4-6				
Apples	X	X	X	4		X	X	
Asparagus		X	X					
Beans — fresh		X	X			X		X
Beans — ripe shelled					more than one year			
Beets		X	X	6		X		
Blueberries	X		X			X		
Broccoli		X						
Brussels sprouts		X		1 on stalk				
Cabbage		X		2 on stalk				X
Cabbage — Chinese				2				
Cantaloupe	X							
Carrots		X	X	6		X		
Cauliflower		X				X		
Celeriac		X		6				
Celery				1½-2				
Corn		X	X			X		
Cucumber						X		
Currants	X	X				X		
Eggplant		X						
Garden huckleberry	X					X		
Ground cherry	X		X			X		
Herbs	X (some)						X	
Horseradish				6		X	X	
Kale		X						
Kohl-rabi		X						
Leeks	X			1-2				
Melons	X							
Onions					6-8	X	X	
Parsnips	leave in ground	X		6				
Peas		X	X				X	
Peppers	X						X	
Pumpkins		X			2-4			
Raspberries	X		X			X		
Rhubarb	X		X			X		
Rutabaga		X		3-4				
Spinach		X						
Squash		X			4-6			
Strawberries	X		X			X		
Swiss chard		X						
Tomato		X	X	until ripe		X		
Turnip		X		4-6				

* Blanched: To prepare produce for freezer by plunging first into boiling water for a required length of time, then into cold water.

Brine-Cured Pickles and Sauerkraut

Brine-curing cucumbers and cabbage is very popular in Europe, and an excellent way of preserving cucumbers and cabbage for the winter if you have the know-how. I would suggest to those brining for the first time that they get some lessons from a knowledgeable friend or neighbour before starting. It is easy to lose a whole batch through inexperience. This happened to me, and I had to throw out an unpleasant, mushy mess.

Dill pickles After the disastrous results with the only batch of cucumber pickles I ever tried making in a crock, I returned to my old method of making "dill" pickles in quart sealers.

Sterilize four quart sealers. Place in each sealer, one clove of garlic (optional), six peppercorns, one clove and a flower of dill. Scrub and dry sufficient small (halved or quartered lengthways) cucumbers and pack tightly into the sealers. Bring to the boil one quart of water, two quarts of vinegar, and one cup of coarse pickling salt. Fill the sealers with this solution and seal immediately. Allow the pickles to cure for a week or longer before serving them.

Sauerkraut. Sauerkraut is cabbage cured in brine and fermented. It is an excellent way of preserving surplus cabbage. I have never made sauerkraut myself, so I asked my neighbour to give me her recipe. In the fall she always has large earthenware crocks of cabbage fermenting in her kitchen.

Here is the recipe: To each 5 pounds of finely shredded cabbage add 3½ tablespoons of coarse salt. Sprinkle the salt over the cabbage and mix together in a large open pan. Allow to stand while you shred the next batch. It is important that the measurements are accurate, because the cabbage will not ferment properly if there is too much salt.

Pack the salted cabbage and liquid it has produced into a large earthenware crock and continue adding batches until the crock is filled to within 6 inches of the top. This allows sufficient "head" room for fermentation. The cabbage should be completely covered by brine, but if more is needed add a weak solution of 1½ teaspoons of salt to one quart of water.

To make a cover, partially fill a large plastic bag or three smaller bags with water and seal or tie the tops tightly. Place the bag or bags of water on top of the cabbage. The water-filled bags will spread out to completely fill the top of the crock, excluding all air and preventing a white film or mold from forming. Check the kraut daily and, if necessary, remove any film that may have formed.

Fermentation will take two or three weeks in warm weather, four weeks when cool. When bubbling stops, tap the crock gently, and if no bubbles rise, fermentation will have ended. At this point, the kraut can either be canned or left for up to two weeks, depending on the cook's schedule. Next, pack the kraut into sterilized sealers to within one inch of the top. Cover with juice. Set the sealers in a cold water bath; the water should reach the shoulder of the jars. Bring the water slowly to the boil. Remove the jars, wipe the rims, put on the lids and process in a boiling water bath. Quart jars take thirty minutes. Remove from the canner and complete the seals unless the lids are self-sealing.

Sauerkraut can be frozen, but my neighbour tells me the flavour of canned sauerkraut is far superior.

The Cool Room

Not so long ago the "root cellar" and "cold pantry" were considered essential in all well-managed households. With technological advances, cool, damp basements gave way to dry, cozy recreation rooms, and the cold pantry off the kitchen was converted into a powder or utility room.

Many people are once again considering the advantages of having a cold room in their basement where they can store fresh produce. This room can be very small but should be insulated against heat. There should be a window or air vent so that the temperature can be controlled at between 32° to 40°F (0° to 4°C). Freezing would damage most vegetables.

There are excellent government pamphlets on this subject. Anyone planning to store fresh produce such as potatoes, carrots, beets, parsnips, turnips, cabbages and celeriac should make sure they have a suitable cool room before either growing or bringing the produce indoors. Rotting vegetables, especially cabbages and turnips, have a most unpleasant odour that permeates the whole house.

Our cool room measures 4 feet by 8 feet and is in the northwest corner of the basement where there is a small window. Since a stone basement in a stone house is never warm, even in the heat of summer, we have not insulated the cool room walls. However, modern houses usually have warm basements, particularly in winter when the furnace is running. In this case, insulation would be essential.

Our walls are lined with shelves, some narrow for bottles and jars, others wide and deep to house containers of vegetables. The potatoes are in sacks on the floor.

In addition to storing fresh produce, the cool room is suitable for keeping home-canned goods and preserves from spoiling. One of the great features of root-cellaring is that there are no "hidden dangers" lurking, undetected in the produce, as is the case with canning or bottled goods. When fruit and vegetables are spoiled, we know from looking, smelling and touching. However, there is no possible danger of food poisoning.

In our household we put by enough fresh vegetables in the cold room to last until February; after that we eat frozen produce. Potatoes are the only exception. They carry us through until the ground outdoors has thawed sufficiently for us to dig Jerusalem artichokes.

Approximate length of time vegetables will remain in good condition in the cool room.

Celery: several weeks
Cabbages: until Christmas
Carrots: early May
Celeriac: early May
Beets: early May
Turnips: early May
Parsnips: until the ground is thawed sufficiently to dig those remaining in the garden
Potatoes: until the next season's early crop is ready to harvest

A Cool, Dry Location

Certain vegetables such as squash and onions keep better in a slightly warmer, drier atmosphere than the average root cellar provides. However, they need cooler temperatures than in the average house. A cupboard on an outside wall is often suitable. These vegetables will then keep well until the following spring.

Glossary

Annual: A plant that grows from a seed to maturity, blooms and dies within one growing season.

Axil: The v-shaped angle between a branch or leaf and the main stem.

Balanced or complete fertilizer: A fertilizer that contains nitrogen, phosphorus, potash and trace elements.

Biennial: A plant grown from seed that flowers and fruits the second season; then it dies.

Blanch: To whiten plants by excluding light, thereby making the edible portions more tasty. Also, to plunge into boiling water for a required length of time, then into cold water.

Bolt: To send up a flower stalk and go to seed. Lettuce and spinach bolt rapidly in hot weather and become useless for eating.

Broadcast sowing: Seed scattered evenly over a planned area or bed. Not grown in rows or hills.

Bulblet: A small bulb.

Bulbs (true): A modified bud with fleshy scales. Usually underground. Examples are daffodil, lily, onion.

Carbon-nitrogen ratio (C/N ratio): the relationship between the amount of carbon and the amount of nitrogen in organic matter. The ratios vary according to the different organic materials involved in composting. In general, home-garden waste will result in a mixture whose C/N ratio will be adequate for decomposition.

Clay: Minute particles of soil that pack together tightly, thereby deterring the drainage of water.

Cold-frame: A wooden or insulated box-type structure with a glass or plastic lid used to grow certain seedlings and to harden plants.

Collard: A type of nonheading cabbage popular in the southern United States because of its ability to withstand intense summer heat.

Companion cropping: Planting two or more crops together, each requiring a different length of time to mature.

Compost: Decomposing organic matter.

Cool crop: Crops that prefer cool weather conditions. Some examples are the cabbage family, lettuce and peas.

Corm: The enlarged fleshy base of a stem; bulb-like but solid. See gladiolus, crocus.

Crop rotation: To rotate crops grown in a given area. Controls pests and diseases. Enhances soil fertility. Increases crop yields.

Crown: The heart of the plant from which several leaves branch or roots grow.

Damping-off: Term applied to condition of seedlings which topple over with a dark, rotted area at the surface of the soil. This is caused by a fungi and should be treated immediately to prevent rapid spreading.

Dormant: The inactive or resting condition trees, shrubs and plants assume during the winter.

Drill: A straight trench or row in which seeds are planted.

Espalier: A fruit tree or ornamental shrub which is trained to grow in a flat plane against a wall or trellis.

Fertilizer: Organic or inorganic materials usually added to the soil to provide correct usable amounts of nitrogen, phosphorus, potash, and trace elements.

Flat: A shallow rectangular or square container used for starting seeds and cuttings.

Fruit: The ripened result of a fertilized ovary in any seed-bearing plant. May be edible and even referred to as a vegetable.

Fungicide: A material to control fungal disorders of plants.

Genus: Botannical name for a group of closely related species of plants.

Germination: The development of the plantlet from the seed.

Grafting: To graft is to successfully unite a scion with a compatible root stock, plant or tree.

Growing season: The period between the last spring frost and the first fall killing frost.

Half-hardy plants: Plants unreliably resistant to cold.

Hardening: To gradually introduce plants raised in a controlled indoor environment to outdoor conditions.

Hardy plants: Plants resistant to cold.

Hill: Several seeds planted in a circle. The weak ones are thinned as the growing season progresses, leaving three or four of the strongest. Squash are usually planted in hills.

Hill-up or earth-up: Draw soil up against the growing stalks of a plant.

Hot-cap: A protective cover, usually for a transplant. Helps plant re-establish its root system without injury from sun, wind or cold.

Hot-frame or hot bed: A frame heated by electric cables or fresh horse manure, used as a miniature greenhouse to start seedlings early in spring.

Humus: Decaying animal and vegetable matter that should be present in all good soils.

Hybrid: A plant resulting from a cross between two or more dissimilar parents of the same kind in an attempt to obtain the best characteristics of each kind.

Inorganic or chemical fertilizer: A fertilizer derived from chemical sources. Not of plant or animal origin. Often water soluble.

Insecticide or pesticide: The general terms used to describe materials, liquid or powder, which control pests causing damage to plants. These can be herbal or chemical.

Intensive gardening: The use of raised beds, double digging, non-linear, intensive planting, and companion planting to increase crop yields and improve quality. This is accomplished in a limited space with no machinery necessary.

Intercropping: A method of planting more than one crop simultaneously in a piece of ground to increase productivity.

Jiffy-7: A compressed pellet specially designed for starting plants and seeds. Expands in water to form a small pot.

Larva: The second stage of a complete metamorphosis undergone by such insects as the butterfly. Larvae are variously referred to as caterpillars, maggots and grubs.

Layering: A method of propagation in which an attached stem of a plant is put into the ground, covered with soil, weighted down and allowed to root.

Leaching: The action of water to dissolve and wash away valuable nutrients in the soil to a depth where plant roots cannot reach them.

Leader: The main shoot of a plant or tree. If the leader is damaged, the nearest sideshoot can be trained or will naturally take over as the new leader.

Leaf mold: Composted leaves used as plant food and/or mulch.

Leggy: A seedling that has grown tall and weak — a result of overcrowded flats, lack of sun or too much nitrogen.

Legume inoculation: Seeds of legumes that are inoculated with nitrogen-fixing bacteria allow the plant to make greater use of the nitrogen in the air to increase yields and quality. Especially valuable in green manuring. (See nodules.)

Legumes: Pod-bearing plants such as peas or beans.

Loam: A good soil consisting of sand, clay, silt and humus.

Mother plant: A plant, usually brought in from the garden towards the late summer, from which cuttings are taken during winter and spring. Examples are rosemary and oregano.

Muck soil: Poorly drained areas that are, in fact, natural compost heaps. Properly managed, they will support most crops.

Mulch: A layer or layers of organic material placed on top of soil to conserve moisture, to insulate, and to control weeds. Black plastic is another form of mulch.

Necrosis: Dead plant tissue indicating disease.

Nematode: Microscopic worm-like creatures that, when present in the soil, may cause damage to the root systems of plants.

Nitrogen: An element which promotes strong vegetative growth; good dark-green colour.

Node: The points on a stem from which buds, branches and leaves originate.

Nodule: Tiny, round swellings on roots of inoculated leguminous plants that contain bacteria, capable of changing atmospheric nitrogen into forms available to plants.

Off-shoot, or off-set: A lateral shoot growing from the main stem of a plant; or a shoot growing from the base of a plant or shrub — usually to one side. These frequently develop their own root systems and can easily be severed from the mother to start a new plant.

Organic fertilizer: Of plant or animal origin, usually insoluble in water. Must be broken down by micro-organisms before nutrients are available to plants. Some soluble products are now available.

Osmosis: The process of diffusion whereby plant roots absorb food from the soil's nutrient solution.

Parasite: A plant or animal that lives on or in another living creature and derives its sustanance from it. The host may be killed as a result of this relationship.

Pathogen: A living organism that causes disease.

Peat moss: The partially decomposed remains of sphagnum moss. May be added to growing mediums or as a mulch or soil conditioner.

Perennial: A plant that continues its life cycle for many years.

Perlite: A sterile, lightweight material used in growing and planting mediums to increase soil porosity. Usually used instead of sand.

pH: The symbol for potential of hydrogen used to express the acidity (sourness) or alkalinity (sweetness) of soil.

Phosphorus: An element which helps promote maximum fruit formation. Aids seedlings to re-establish after transplanting.

Pinch back or pinch out: To remove growing points in order to promote bushy growth.

Pollination: The process by which pollen is transferred from the male to the female part of the flower, or from the male flower to the female flower. The result is fertilization and ultimately fruit.

Potash: An element which promotes stronger stems and roots. Deepens flower colour. Helps produce starch and sugar.

Propagation: To reproduce. To have offspring either from seed or by asexual means (grafting, cutting, budding, layering, root division, etc.). The resulting plants always "come true" if asexual techniques are adopted.

Resistant varieties: Varieties of plants that are naturally able to ward off certain diseases and insects.

Rhizome: An underground stem often enlarged by food storage, for example: the iris.

Rotenone: An organic insecticide.

Sand: Large irregularly shaped particles of soil which do not pack tightly, thus permitting water to drain through freely.

Scallion: Young onions grown from seed and pulled before the bulb has formed.

Scion: A scion (or cion) is a bud or shoot detached from the mother plant ready for grafting.

Set: Immature bulbs, such as onions, stored over winter to be replanted the following year.

Setting of fruit: The term used to describe the successful fertilization of blossoms. It is indicated by the swelling of the ovary, or the beginning of fruit formation.

Shallot: Small, multiplier onions grown from sets or small cloves.

Silt: Particles of soil between sand and clay in size.

Soil: The top layer of the earth's surface containing minerals and organic materials — that will support plant life.

Species: Botannical word describing a group of closely related plants. Species will breed true from seed.

Subsoil: The layer of soil beneath the topsoil (or loam). If the topsoil is shallow, small amounts of subsoil and humus can be incorporated occasionally with the topsoil in order to obtain a better depth of workable garden. A packed subsoil may also be the cause of poor drainage.

Succession planting: Also known as catch-cropping, this term refers to the practice of planting a second crop on the same area of ground either before or right after the first crop has been harvested.

Tender: Plants not resistant to cold or extreme heat.

Thinning: The process of removing some plants in a row to leave room for the rest to grow.

Till: To work or prepare soil for growing crops.

Tilth: The quality of the soil tilled.

Trace elements: Those mineral elements essential to plant growth that are needed in minute quantities.

Transplant: May be a seedling or tree. In the vegetable and flower garden it usually applies to annual plants that must be started indoors early in the season and planted out when the weather is suitable.

Tuber: A thickened portion of a subterranean stem or branch provided with eyes (or buds) on the sides. Examples: dahlia, Jerusalem artichoke, potato.

Tuberous: Bearing or producing tubers.

Vermiculite: A sterile, lightweight mica product which absorbs water and is used in planting and rooting mixtures.

Viable or viability of seed: The length of time a seed retains its ability to germinate. May be days or hundreds of years.

Variety: A subdivision of species which may or may not breed true.

Whip: A shoot or stem of a woody plant, usually without branches.

Zone: Maps are available showing hardiness zones based on the average annual minimum temperature.

Further Reading

While researching the technical aspects of this book, I found that there was an abundance of publications that discussed the many facets of home vegetable gardening. A number of these were most helpful; others were not. It would be impossible to list all the pamphlets and books consulted, so I have named only those that I feel would be helpful to the novice gardener for further reading.

My primary source of information has always been the government pamphlets that are put out by the federal, provincial, and state departments of agriculture. Readers may obtain a list of publications from the Department of Agriculture and Food, and then send away for those titles that they desire. There are also numerous periodicals and magazines concerned with the home vegetable garden that are readily available on magazine racks or in local libraries.

For general information about gardening see:

The Encyclopedia of Organic Gardening, Steven Symser, ed., Rodale Press, Emmaus, Pennsylvania, 1978. This encyclopedia is simple to understand and deals with methods of gardening without chemicals.

Wyman's Gardening Encyclopedia, by Donald Wyman, Macmillan, New York, 1971. This publication is a more comprehensive collection of information concerning plants, cultivation, fertilization and pesticides. It tends to be rather technical but is good for reference, and I find myself frequently reaching for it.

For readers interested in an excellent introduction to botany try:

The Plant World, (5th ed.) by Harry J. Fuller *et. al,* Holt, Rinehart and Winston, New York, 1970.

If you wish more information on insect friends and foes, the Petersen Field Guide Series has a fascinating collection in *A Field Guide to the Insects of America North of Mexico,* by Donald J. Borror and Richard E. White, Houghton Mifflin, Boston, 1970. The coloured and line drawings used in conjunction with the rather technical descriptions make insect identification fun.

A natural companion to the above is the *Field Guide to the Butterflies of North America, East of the Great Plains,* by Alexander B. Klots, Houghton Mifflin, Boston, 1951. Those caterpillar pests and butterflies that are not found in one of these books is sure to be in the other.

Many books have been written about soil. So many of these make the study of soil such a complicated science that the average home gardener is "turned off." Gene Logsdon's book, *The Gardener's Guide to Better Soil,* Rodale Press, Emmaus, Pennsylvania, 1975, presents a discussion of soil in a manner which is both common sense and pleasurable.

> *"Food problems are becoming more and more acute as the demand for food increasingly overshadows the supply. Primitive peoples depended upon food resources which are now neglected. Other sources of possible human nutrition have doubtless remained untouched, and the time may come when a comprehensive utilization of food plants will be essential to human sustenance. It is believed, therefore, that the information so ably brought together by Dr. Sturtevant cannot fail to become increasingly useful."*

This extract from a letter of June 1, 1919, written by W. H. Jordan, then director of the New York Agricultural Experiment Station at Geneva, New York, is ample introduction to an extremely interesting book, *Sturtevant's*

Edible Plants of the World, U. P. Hedrick, ed., Dover Publications, New York, 1972. Although quite technical in many aspects, this book is very descriptive and easy to read.

The title of Reay Tannahill's book, *Food in History,* Stein and Day, New York, 1974, describes it fully. It is an interest-only book.

Seed Houses in North America

Canada

Alberta Nurseries and Seeds Limited, Bowden, Alberta	Seeds
Bishop Farm Seeds, Box 338, Belleville, Ontario, K8N 5A5	Seeds
Dominion Seed House, Georgetown, Ontario, L7G 4A5	Seeds
Gaze's Farm and Garden Supplies, Box 640, St. John's Newfoundland, A1C 5K8	Seeds
J. Labonte et Fils, 560 Chemin Chambly, Longueil, Quebec, J4H 3L8	Catalogue $1.00 Seeds
Lowden's Better Plants and Seeds, Box 10, Ancaster, Ont., L9G 3L3	Organic
Lindenberg Seeds Limited, 803 Princess Avenue, Brandon, Manitoba, R7A 0P5	Seeds
McFayden Seed Co. Ltd., Box 1600, 30-9th Street, Brandon, Manitoba, R7A 6A6	Seeds only
Otto Rictter and Sons, Box 26, Goodwood, Ont., L0C 1A0	Herbs
W.H. Perron Co. Ltd., 515 Labelle Blvd., City of Laval, Quebec, H7V 2T3	Seed and Nursery stock. Catalogue $1.00
Pike and Co. Ltd., 10552-114 St., Edmonton, Alberta, T5H 3J7	Seeds. Specialize in short season varieties.
Stokes Seeds Ltd., Box 10, St. Catherines, Ont., L2R 6R6	Seeds

T. and T. Seeds Ltd., Box 1710, Winnipeg, Manitoba, R3C 3P6	Seeds and some nursery stock.	Harris Seeds, Moreton Farm, Rochester, New York, 14624	Seeds
Thompson and Morgan, 132 James Avenue East, Winnipeg, Manitoba, R3B 0N8	Seeds	Herbst Brothers Seedsmen Inc., 1000 North Main Street, Brewster, N.Y., 10509	Seeds
Vesey's Seeds Ltd., York, P.E.I.	Seeds only	Johnny's Selected Seeds, Albion, Maine, 04910	Seeds. Specializes in fast maturing varieties.
William Dam Seeds, West Flamboro, Ont. L0R 2K0	Seeds. Some plants.		
		Stokes Seeds Ltd., Box 548, Buffalo, N.Y., 14240	Seeds
United States			
Burpee Seed Co., Warminster, Pennsylvania, 18991	Seeds	Thompson and Morgan Inc., Box 24, Somerdale, New Jersey, 08083	Seeds
George W. Park Seeds Co., Box 31, Greenwood, South Carolina, 29647	Seeds	Vermont Bean Seeds Co., Garden Lane, Bomosean, Vermont, 05732	Specializes in legumes.
Grace's Gardens Autumn Lane, Hakettstown, New Jersey, 07840	Seeds		

Index

Note: Italic page numbers indicate illustration